# EMBODIED MASCULINITIES
## IN
# GLOBAL SPORT

**Titles in the Sport & Global Cultures Series**

*Case Studies in Sport Development: Contemporary Stories Promoting Health, Peace, and Social Justice*

*Long Run to Freedom: Sport, Cultures and Identities in South Africa*

*Reading Baseball: Books, Biographies, and the Business of the Game*

*Rethinking the Olympics: Cultural Histories of the Modern Games*

*Sport for Development, Peace, and Social Justice*

*Sport, Race, and Ethnicity: Narratives*

*For an updated list of Sport & Global Culture Series titles, please visit www.fitpublishing.com*

# EMBODIED MASCULINITIES IN GLOBAL SPORT

JORGE KNIJNIK • DARYL ADAIR

EDITORS

**FiT Publishing**
*A Division of the International Center for Performance Excellence*
375 Birch Street, WVU-CPASS • P O Box 6116
Morgantown, WV 26506-6116

Copyright © 2015, West Virginia University
All rights reserved.

Reproduction or use of any portion of this publication by any mechanical, electronic, or other means is prohibited without written permission of the publisher.

Library of Congress Card Catalog Number: 2014947621

ISBN: 978-1-935412-16-8

Cover Design: 40 West Studios
Cover Photos: Figure Skater courtesy DAVID W CARMICHAEL: davesk8@bellaliant.net; Swimmer © muzsy courtesy of bigtockphoto.com
Production Editor: Nita Shippy
Copyeditor: Rachael Kelley
Typesetter: 40 West Studios
Proofreader: Geoffrey Fuller
Indexer: Geoffrey Fuller
Printed by: Publishers' Graphics

10 9 8 7 6 5 4 3 2 1

FiT Publishing
A Division of the International Center for Performance Excellence
West Virginia University
375 Birch Street, WVU-CPASS
PO Box 6116
Morgantown, WV 26506-6116
800.477.4348 (toll free)
304.293.6888 (phone)
304.293.6658 (fax)
Email: fitcustomerservice@mail.wvu.edu
Website: www.fitpublishing.com

# Contents

Foreword
Eric Anderson . . . . . . . . . . . . . . . . . . . . . . . . . . . VII

Acknowledgments. . . . . . . . . . . . . . . . . . . . . . . . . IX

| CHAPTER 1 | Conceptualizing Embodied Masculinities in Global Sport<br>Jorge Knijnik and Daryl Adair | 1 |
| --- | --- | --- |
| CHAPTER 2 | "Cock Up": Emasculating American Athletes Through Sick Humor<br>Rob Baum | 15 |
| CHAPTER 3 | On Being a Warrior: Race, Gender, and American Indian Imagery in Sport<br>C. Richard King | 35 |
| CHAPTER 4 | "Other" Masculinities: Equestrianism in Uruguay<br>Luiz Rojo | 53 |
| CHAPTER 5 | Football, Cinema, and New Sensibilities in the Masculine Territory: An Analysis of *Asa Branca, a Brazilian Dream* (1981) and *New Wave* (1983)<br>Jorge Knijink and Victor Andrade de Melo | 71 |
| CHAPTER 6 | I Am Dancing on the Courts: Masculinities in Brazilian Sports<br>Jorge Knijnik | 91 |
| CHAPTER 7 | Dance, Masculinity, and Physical Education: An International Perspective<br>Michael Gard | 111 |
| CHAPTER 8 | Sport, Masculinities, and Pain: An Australian Rules Football Perspective<br>Deborah Agnew and Murray Drummond | 129 |

CONTENTS

| | | |
|---|---|---|
| CHAPTER 9 | **Steroids, Male Body Image, and the Intimate Self**<br>Daryl Adair | 151 |
| CHAPTER 10 | **Manliness and Mountaineering: Sir Edmund Hillary as New Zealand Adventurer and Male Icon**<br>Toni Bruce and Richard Pringle | 171 |
| CHAPTER 11 | **Manner(s) Maketh the Man: Embodied Masculinities in a Japanese University Rowing Club**<br>Brent McDonald | 197 |

Index . . . . . . . . . . . . . . . . . . . . . . . . 217

About the Editors . . . . . . . . . . . . . . . . . . 221

About the Authors . . . . . . . . . . . . . . . . . . 223

# Foreword

It is a pleasure to write a foreword for *Embodied Masculinities in Global Sport*. The idea for this book came in 2011, when Jorge Knijnik and Daryl Adair decided the field of sport and masculinities studies maintained too narrow a focus, both in terms of which sports and physical cultural practices were analyzed and the geographical loci of those analyses. Knijnik and Adair recognized the need to expand the scope of masculinity and sport studies, providing both academics and those outside of the academy new perspectives from which to view sport and new locations to do so. Thus the aim and purpose of this volume was to trace the development and complexities of the gendered and sexualized dynamics of sport and physical practices, outside standard tropes of investigation.

There has been a great deal of focus on masculinity within the sport sociological literature, a discipline of sport sociology that has grown substantially since its infancy in the early 1990s. However, the field remains limited. This is mostly because empirical, cultural, and theoretical work comes from the examination of mainstream sports among men competing in dominant Western cultures. Thus, the majority of research has focused on soccer or American football, or other highly masculinized sports, mostly in the United States and United Kingdom. Sport scholars have examined how men stratify themselves within these sports alongside the importance of race and class. Yet, we have consequently neglected other types of sports from other parts of the world. We have overlooked the importance of sport to the production of masculinity in less mainstream places, in parts of the globe infrequently recognized.

From examining how humor is used as a status-leveling device against elite athletes to how Native American usurpation reifies hegemonic notions of masculinity; from exploring the ways men establish their gender in sex-integrated sporting spaces to nonhegemonically masculine sports like handball and dancing; and from studying hegemonic masculinity in exalted sporting figures to how pain and steroids affect gender in contemporary sport, this edited volume offers something new. The editors have carefully selected original essays and evidenced-based chapters, written both

# FOREWORD

by well-established sport researchers who have made important contributions to the discourse around sport, gender, and sexuality, as well as by those who examine the field with fresh eyes. The authors of the volume's chapters have keenly balanced academic sophistication with accessibility and engaging writing.

This volume examines structural and cultural forms of gender segregation, homophobia, and domination in men's sport. Its chapters uncover ideological struggles and changes leading to contemporary complexities and nuanced ways of thinking about the sport, gender, and sexuality nexus. These complexities break out of their normal geographical terrains (a few dominant countries in the West), allowing the authors to examine these relationships across the globe. Collectively, these wide-ranging chapters include narratives of the personal and political, spanning a variety of different sports and physical activities. They draw from both the historical and contemporary examples, from local and global. This edited volume, therefore, makes an important resource for academics, as well as providing an informative and interesting read for sport practitioners and undergraduates.

Professor Eric Anderson is an American sociologist at the University of Winchester, England and an academician of the British Academy of Social Sciences. He is known for his research on sexualities and masculinities studies, particularly concerning sport and relationships. He has authored 11 books, including *Inclusive Masculinity: The Changing Nature of Masculinities; In the Game: Gay Athletes and the Cult of Masculinity; Sport, Masculinities and Sexualities;* and *Sport, Theory and Social Problems: A Critical Introduction*

# Acknowledgments

This book, as a cooperative enterprise of creating and disseminating experience and knowledge, is in debt to several people who have at some stage traded ideas with us and helped our work from behind the scenes. Therefore, while knowing that we might leave someone out as there would never be enough room to recognize everyone who has inspired our work, we would like to convey our appreciation and thankfulness to the many people who were a terrific source of motivation to us.

First of all, thank you to all the chapter authors and contributors in this book. Their patience, confidence, and trust in our work were outstanding; without their commitment and high level of expertise this book would never see the daylight. We appreciate the entire staff at FiT Publishing for their conviction and generosity. We also want to recognize the School of Education at the University of Western Sydney and the Management Discipline Group at the University of Technology Sydney, institutions that provided us with different types of assistance that helped us to complete this book.

Jorge would also like to express gratitude to the following individuals:

Dr. Peter Horton for being such a supportive colleague and friend; Bob Petersen for showing to me the other side of the masculinities studies; Dr. Claudia Vianna, who first introduced me to masculinities issues many years ago; professors Michelle Simons, David Rowe, Brett Nielson, and Carol Reid (University of Western Sydney) for their support to my research; Paulo Falcão, who shares with me the will to support boys in their endeavor to be who they want to be; Thabata Ventura and Adelma Pimentel, for their permanent passion; Patricio Casco, Leo Lopes, and QK Barbosa—more than friends; São Paulo FC; and TC Ceroulas de Olinda.

Most importantly, I want to recognize my beloved parents Carlos and Olga in Brazil and to my adored family in Australia; beyond all to my partner Selma, who makes me a better person; my son Alezão, whose dance enlightens my life; and to my daughters Juju, who smiles her way on life; Marinoca, whose songs make me fly; and Luizinha, who has a golden heart. They make me the happiest man in this world!

## ACKNOWLEDGMENTS

Daryl would also like to express his gratitude to the following individuals:

Jorge for his patience and good cheer in bringing this book to fruition. Learning the Brazilian way of masculinities has been an intriguing experience. My colleagues at UTS, Tracy Taylor, Paul Jonson, Simon Darcy, Nico Schulenkorf, Steve Frawley, Johanna Adriaanse, and Ashlee Morgan were an encouragement to this book. My family in Sydney, Cheryl and Kane, understood my time away from them in preparing this book; I hope I made it up to them.

Finally, I would like to dedicate this book to my parents in Adelaide, Audrey and Garry Adair. You have always supported me, and I hope that this text is a small indication of your faith.

# Conceptualizing Embodied Masculinities in Global Sport

Jorge Knijnik and Daryl Adair

Toward all,
I raise high the perpendicular hand—
I make the signal,
To remain after me in sight forever,
For all the haunts and homes of men
(Walt Whitman)

## DYNAMIC GLOBAL MASCULINITIES

What does it mean to be a man? What does it mean to be "masculine"? Why do some males feel a need to prove their sense of "manliness"? Such questions have attracted a growing body of scholarship over recent decades. This is not merely about academics; issues of gender identity are part of the daily lives of people globally (Heasley, 2013). There is often a desire for a simple conception of what men (and women) either "are" or "should be" and how they ought to conduct themselves publicly and privately in accordance with "routine" gender norms.

There have been popular essentialist definitions of masculinity that attempt to reduce the male gender to rather narrow characteristics (Pollack, 1998; Sommers, 2000). The assumption here is that it is possible to see all boys and men as having

# CHAPTER 1

"natural" and "essential" male traits, even though they come from distinctive cultural-historical backgrounds and their life experiences are derived from very different social contexts. The lived reality of men around the world is indeed complex. Males are much more than the sum of their bodies and hormones; they vary fundamentally in respect to behaviors and beliefs drawn from diverse, even contrasting, sociocultural influences. As Demetriou (2001) has put it, men should not be reduced to a single "homogeneous, internally coherent bloc" (p. 340). By taking a global perspective of concepts of manliness, it is possible to appreciate that men express their gender identities in heterogeneous ways such as the hypermasculinity associated with bodybuilders and boxers (Hunt, Gonsalkorale, & Murray, 2013), less physical notions of manliness such as suave gentlemen attending the opera (Purvis, 2013). This reminds us of opposing ideas of what is thought to constitute "being a man": For those who value physical capital, a hypermasculine identity may be prized; for those who value cultural capital, an intellectual male identity is likely to be admired (Coles, 2009).

It is not possible, therefore, to approach the study of men and masculinity with essentialist ideas or by looking solely through a biological lens. Men are physically constructed in unique ways, which is a product of the male sex and genetics, but they are not programmed to behave in a particular manner as social beings. They are male by nature, but men by nurture (Edwards, 2006). Thus it is important to highlight, at the beginning of this book, the position we take as editors. We are interested in masculinity as a function of nurture; from this perspective, manliness is a social construct that is part of complex, multifaceted gender systems. These "ways of being" men or women are central to the structure and function of various societies and are embedded in power relationships in sociocultural, economic, and political contexts across the globe (Connell, 1995; Demetriou, 2001). As Connell (1995) has put it when discussing men: "Masculinities are configurations of practice structured by gender relations. They are inherently historical; and their making and remaking is a political process affecting the balance of interests in society and the direction of social change" (p. 44).

As Connell has intimated, gender relations and the place of men and women therein are a consequence of history. In most societies, males have asserted dominance over females, doing so for a range of reasons, but mostly because of cultural norms and religious beliefs that privilege men over women. This fundamental gender inequity has, of course, been the subject of vast scholarship (Bennett, 2011; Scott, 1996). From the perspective of this edited book, there is nothing "natural" or "explicable" about the myriad ways in which females have been subordinated by patriarchal societies. Our focus is with men, but their sense of manliness can hardly be understood in isolation from a profound awareness of women's history, the influence of feminism, and dialectical relationships between masculinities and femininities. Indeed, as Coad (2008) has deftly asserted, masculinity is a process, not "a state of inner being. . . . A 'man' is a becoming, not an achieved end result" (p. 29–30). Therefore, because men's lives are multiple and diverse, as well as embedded in various societal contexts, the process of "becoming" manly is inherently plural. In this book we are therefore dealing with *masculinities,* the gender characteristics and behaviors that males create or experience through their social interactions as *men* (Butler, 2006; Hollander, 2002). Hence, in this book, discussion of masculinities involves investigating men's social lives; that means males interacting and relating to other men and women in a social environment. This approach is consistent with Connell's (1995) observation that "masculinity as an object of knowledge is always masculinity-in-relation" (p. 44). Interpersonal relations are thus essential to the social process of "doing" masculinities. These manifold relational forms provide a basis for the production of gendered identities, their modification, and the creation of new forms of masculinity (Connell & Messerschmidt, 2005; Hollander, 2002). As Deutsch (2007) has put it, "men and women create gender within social relationships throughout their lives. This formulation . . . is dynamic . . . [for] what is considered appropriate gendered behavior changes over time" (Deutsch, 2007, p. 107).

Given the centrality of social interactions for the enacting, reproduction, or even subversion of masculinities, it is important to bring to the fore two essential "actors" in this process. The first is *discourse*. There are no social interactions without the presence of discourses—some hegemonic, others subordinate; some orthodox, others heterodox; some trying to sustain the social order, others looking to subvert this order. Discourses articulate, via language, the rationale for and power of human actions. Hollander (2002) asserts that "as the dominant discourse on gender reflects and recreates hegemonic masculinity and dominant femininity, alternative discourses on gender resist these conventional constructions" (p. 477). Discourses therefore affirm, prioritize and assert, via words and ideas, the legitimacy, potency, and urgency of values and causes. However, discourses do not act independently to promote, resist, or even transform the gender social order. There are other actors and influences at play, and in the context of this book, *bodies* are the second most crucial of these drivers.

Bodies are the physical locus of gender identity, with maleness embodied in flesh, dress and appearance. The physical form of men, therefore, is a *sine qua non* of varying forms of masculinity, which are staged, performed, and (re)constructed in the social arena. Anderson (2009) reminds us of the importance of both discourse and embodiment in this process: Male identities are constructed by "talking the masculine talk and walking the masculine walk" (p. 10). By stating that bodies are crucial to norms of masculinity, we are not reducing the male body to a biological object that might imply an essentialist, singular type of manliness. Instead, our assertion is that bodies (while biological) are social and not static; the male physical form is used by men to construct, modify and perform their masculinities in an ever-changing environment. Men's bodies are, of course, wide-ranging in size and shape; they are diverse in form and appearance. This difference can, in and of itself, precipitate divergent ideas about the value of particular male body types and images. As Connell (1995) has pointed out, bodies are "inescapable in the construction of masculinity. But what is inescapable is not fixed" (p. 56). Connell affirms that social practice drives ideas about different types of human bodies, and thus gendered bodies are part of an ongoing process—both subject and agents of continuity and change.

Because bodies are central to the social construction of gender, and therefore to masculinities, an understanding of body cultures is critical. Our book, in focusing on sport and physical culture, examines one of the most important sites for the public articulation and negotiation of men's bodies and associated notions of masculine physicality. Sport and masculinity, as we will now argue, have had a longstanding symbiotic relationship. Messner (1990) has put it this way: It is the overt and public display of physical performance "which gives sport its salience in gender relations" (p. 204). And sport is principally a male domain.

## EMBODIED MASCULINITIES AND SPORTS

A major theme in sports history and sociology is how competitive sports in economically advanced, highly developed Western societies have been a critical element in the construction of hegemonic forms of masculinity (Kidd, 1987; Whitson, 1990; Messner & Sabo, 1994; Jansen & Sabo, 1994; Anderson, 2005b Coad, 2008; Horton, 2009). Put crudely, modern sport has been invented by men, for men, and in the interests of men.

Sport, whether in ancient Greece or in the English public schools of the 19th century, has been thought to epitomize various values and virtues that embody "being a man." Whether the rugged individualism of the boxer or the team-oriented collectivism of the footballer, sport has long been assumed to be character building for *men* (Mangan & Walvin, 1987). The position of women in this story is by contrast problematic; if sport has been about "making" men and displaying masculinities through physical contests, then females have been presented with cultural obstacles in respect of their gender identities—particularly when sport participation has been labeled as inimical to femininity, a point we return to presently (Hargreaves, 1994). In terms of sport and masculinity, the focus of this book, ideals of manliness through the physicality of the athletic contest, have typically reinforced narrow, rather stereotypical ideas of what it is to be a man. Critics have contended that modern sports have become a special arena, a public stage if you will, for the production and reproduction of hegemonic forms of masculinity (Connell, 1995; Terret, 2004; Knijnik & Falcao-Defino, 2010). Via the playing field, sports have been assumed to "build the character" of young males, helping them to learn to be "real men" via a shared sense of physical struggle and the social capital that derives from male bonding in athletic environments (Drummond, 2002).

The North American sports historian Joan Hult (1994) recounts that during the late 19th century, Theodore Roosevelt (who was to become US president in 1901-09) contended that the American male was becoming too soft and even "effeminate" (p. 84). At that time there were no major wars to "test" men's bravery and self-assurance. Roosevelt declared that "only aggressive sports could create the brawn, the spirit, the self-confidence and the quickness of men." The football field, Roosevelt contended, "is the only place where masculine supremacy is incontestable" (Hult, 1994, p. 84). It is ironic, therefore, that in the early 20th century, when Roosevelt presided at the White House, he formed the view that American football, while still a sport for male bravado, was nonetheless overly dangerous. In 1905, for example, there were eighteen deaths nationwide, including three in college football. Roosevelt's son was a freshman at Harvard, which may have influenced what was now his view that the physical side of the game was excessive. He argued that "brutality in playing a game should awaken the heartiest and most plainly shown contempt for the player guilty of it" (Morrison, 2010). Thereafter he supported efforts to reform American football and to endeavor to reduce the volume of casualties associated with what was supposed to be a physical, but not fatal, contest for young men.

In both Britain and America, the Christian churches were also important in the development of sport, and their principal focus was with young men. In the United States, the Young Men's Christian Association was the site for the invention of basketball and volleyball, and although they later evolved into games that involved females, they were principally established to address what was deemed to be excessively sedentary (and thus unmanly) behavior among male urban youth (Terret, 2004). Another key driver of masculinity was the 19th and 20th century nexus between battlefields and playing fields. In the British Empire, most notably, sport was deemed an ideal preparation for military service, with armed conflict thought to be the "ultimate proving ground" for a combination of patriotic duty and manliness. For soldiers, though, there was often a horrifying naivety about this; promised an "adventure" abroad they faced the harrowing reality of machine guns, grenades, and the trauma of witnessing human carnage on a mass scale (Adair, Nauright, & Phillips, 1998; Terret & Mangan, 2013).

Athletic bodies of today exude social power; the sports field itself is also a very public evocation of the dominant gender order (Connell, 1995). Indeed, the fact that men and women are almost always separated in sport, whether at elite or community levels, reaffirms the gendered "naturalness" of either observed or presumed differences in male-female athletic performance (Adair & Vamplew, 1997). Symbolic power within the context of sport has long been linked to the public prowess of the male body and associated assumptions about the field of sport and athletic habitus as male-centered (Bourdieu, 1978; 2001; Brown, 2006). As Brace-Govan (2010) has aptly put it, "Sport was defined through its antithesis to femininity" (p. 373). Pierre de Coubertin, the so-called father of the Olympics, was an opponent of female participation at the Games, as were many other sport administrators (Hargreaves, 2012). It was common for doctors in the 19th century to warn against exercise for women, assuming that it compromised their fertility (Vertinsky, 1990). Even though women now participate at the Olympics and the patriarchal nature of sport is less profound than it was, comparatively few women, relative to men, are able to make a career from their athletic attributes. Male professional sport is lionized by the media and broadcasters; female professional sport (other than at the Olympic Games and tennis, where men and women compete on the same stage, albeit in different events) is either ignored or demonized as inherently inferior (rather than different) to that offered by men (Leonard II & Reyman, 1988; Brace-Govan, 2010; Roberts & MacLean, 2012; Cooky, Messner, & Hextrum, 2013).

Sport and hegemonic masculinity has, of course, not only been about male dominance over women; it has also been a site for the affirmation of male heterosexuality and an associated reaffirmation of homophobia. The hegemonic position is that male athletes are not only assumed to be "straight," they also "provide constant [and] visible proof of heterosexuality" (Coad, 2008, p. 14). As public figures they are expected to be with female partners, or at least "available" for dates with women. Some of the biggest names in men's sport have been overtly sexualized; David Beckham, for example, has cultivated this by engaging in semi-nude photo shoots with his female partner Victoria (Homes, 2007). Sport, unlike other cultural domains such as theatre, dance, and music, has been an environment in which gay or bisexual men have typically hidden this aspect of their identity. The sports sexuality closet is still very full, with few male athletes coming out publicly. In a heterosexist sports world, the gay athlete faces numerous obstacles—whether in terms of public acceptance, attitudes of teammates, reactions by sponsors, or depictions by the media. However, as Anderson has observed in interviews with gay sportsmen, there are small cracks appearing in the monolithic realm of masculine orthodoxy; even athletes who choose to stay in the closet find ways to argue for change, this leading to a more inclusive environment for work and play (Anderson, 2005a, p. 42). Anderson (2008) has also interviewed heterosexual male athletes who are both liberal and fraternal, not only accepting gay athletes as colleagues but also developing friendships with them. Importantly, this type of male is also more likely to show respect towards women and people from other ethnic, racial, or religious backgrounds. Anderson (2008, p. 608) has described them as "stakeholders of an inclusive masculinity" within the world of sport.

How do male athletes manage their bodies in sport—particularly in physically demanding performance contexts? For male participants in collision sports, there are expectations of putting bodies "on the line"; men are "supposed" to be fearless and aggressive. Messner (1990) has observed that in such contexts the bodies of male athletes are "a weapon to be used against other bodies, resulting in pain, serious injury, and even death" (p. 203). In a similar vein, Connell (1995) has argued that "the [male] body is virtually assaulted in the name of masculinity and achievement" in contact sports (p. 58). But this embodied aggression has a price. As Connell has pointed out, "ex-athletes often live with damaged bodies and chronic pain, and die early" (p. 58). Hall (2011), who has conducted research on male athletes, pain, and resilience, found "almost a sense of pride about the types of injury received" (p. 75). The ability to absorb pain, play through injuries and "hang tough" under such pressures remains a badge of honor for many male athletes. Yet change is also evident. In American football, for example, new attitudes and policies are emerging in respect of the health and safety of players, particularly in respect of head knocks and long-term damage from concussion (McNamee & Partridge, 2013). Around the world, in various football codes, there are new protocols associated with concussion and mitigating against long-term damage. Whereas it used to be acceptable for players who were "knocked out" to return to play, this form of "courage" is now discouraged (Putukian, 2013). Relative to the previous two centuries, sport is now less likely to be seen as the route to manliness. Indeed, as participation rates in organized sport dwindle it is worthwhile asking how physical culture can be made more inclusive for males who hold varying ideas about masculinity. The simple notion of a symbiotic relationship between sport and manliness is therefore no longer a question of orthodoxy; it also involves an awareness of gender heterodoxy.

CHAPTER 1

## OUR BOOK

This book was inspired initially by the principal editor's interest in trying to understand masculinities in a Brazilian sports context. His relocation to Australia sparked a wider curiosity about such questions in a new environment and, indeed, beyond that. Both editors realized that in order to comprehend the complexities and nuances of masculinities and sport, discussions from different geographical and cultural contexts were needed. After approaching colleagues in various parts of the world, the editors quickly realized that there were important stories to be revealed about masculinities—their construction, persistence, and susceptibility to change. This book is the culmination of that global vision.

Some edited volumes claim that their chapter content embodies a discrete structure or thematic direction. This book, by contrast, is rhizomatic. It is, as Deleuze and Guattari (1987) have put it, an assemblage that intends to showcase multiplicities—in this case in terms of diverse masculinities. Readers can therefore begin with whatever chapter catches their eyes; narrative sequence—and thus textual experience—is in their hands. Starting with Chapter 11 could be as fulfilling as reading Chapter 2 last. All that said, this book contains particular chapter content. What can the reader expect? A brief linear summary of chapter characteristics now follows.

In Chapter 2, "'Cock up': Emasculating American Athletes Through Sick Humor," Rob Baum develops a focus that has rarely been addressed by researchers of gender or sport—satire and sarcasm. She notes that the sport field is actually a fertile place for comedic critique because it is a domain where competitors seek personal glory, put their bodies on the line, and experience victories and defeats, glories and humiliations, teetering from the sublime to the ridiculous. Baum is particularly interested in the genre of the "sick" joke, and how it has been manifested in the world of professional sport. The gender dimensions of humor in sport are an especially fascinating dimension to this study.

In Chapter 3, "On Being a Warrior: Race, Gender, and American Indian Imagery in Sport," C. Richard King rails against the longstanding practice of sport teams culturally appropriating Native American nomenclature, symbols, and mascots. He argues that although indigeneity and race are crucial to an understanding of this hegemonic process, so too are dynamics of gender—such as the conflation of mascots with a Native American "warrior" stereotype. King also looks at defenders of Native American imagery in sport, asserting that their sense of tradition is associated with a determination to cling to feelings of white, male dominance. A history of frontier conflict and aggressive masculinity are melded together, and sport symbolism is a reminder of European conquest over indigenous peoples.

## Conceptualizing Embodied Masculinities in Global Sport

In Chapter 4, "'Other' Masculinities: Equestrianism in Uruguay," Luiz Rojo explores a rare sport environment—one in which men and women compete together. Equestrianism has different disciplines, the best known of which are dressage and jumping, but all involve both genders, whether in individual or team events. Rojo interviews male and female riders to ascertain their attitudes about equestrianism and views about gender relations within the sport. His study reveals intriguing ambiguities and tensions about male-female participation and athletic performance in this equine context. In keeping with a book on masculinity, Rojo also examines notions of manliness within equestrianism. A sport involving Uruguay's social elite typically showcases men of wealth and status, but even "gentlemen" with resources and privileges are concerned about their position "as men." Equestrianism provides a context within which both genteel and athletic male bodies are on display.

In Chapter 5, "Football, Cinema, and New Sensibilities in the Masculine Territory: An Analysis of Asa Branca, a Brazilian Dream (1981) and New Wave (1983)," Jorge Knijnik and Victor Andrade de Melo provide insights into norms of manliness in Brazil via their discussion of two iconic films—*Asa Branca: A Brazilian Dream* (1981) and *New Wave* (1983). The first movie, *Asa Branca,* features the life story of an impoverished boy who eventually makes good as a footballer. His journey is very complex: He is an object of sexual desire for women, but eventually shares an intimate relationship with his male football mentor. He therefore crosses normative boundaries of sexuality. However, his public persona is heterosexual, as is expected of young, handsome, and successful footballers. He therefore accommodates his life to the dominant sexual order for males, even though he privately questions its relevance to his own sense of bisexual masculinity. In their discussion of *New Wave,* the authors consider the masculine hegemony of football; women "invade" this male space and challenge the "naturalness" of the male-centred space of the playing field. The involvement of two popular male Brazilian footballers of the time, Wladimir and Casagrande, gives the film cache among sports fans. The plot of the film, though, is subversive; an ironic response to the "problem" of women entering the field of play was for the men to dress as women. However, rather than mocking the female, this is a moment of reflection about what a new gender order might look like.

In Chapter 6, "I Am Dancing on the Courts: Masculinities in Brazilian Sports," Jorge Knijnik considers masculinities in Brazilian sport using a biographical methodology. The story of Lukas is a journey of self discovery; the sport of handball becomes a key field within which this boy becomes a man, yet in doing so he also clings defiantly to an aesthetic of movement and appearance that, by the standards of the day, was nonconformist. Lukas coveted and expressed an athletic form that was

CHAPTER 1

fit and graceful—a sensitive rather than power-laden body. As Knijnik shows, Lukas had the feeling of dancing on the handball court, moving to a rhythm that defied convention. Although attracting scorn and derision, Lukas eventually found admirers who appreciated a playing style that was creative rather than aggressive. In doing so, Lukas retained his individuality and, by his actions, displayed an innovative, even unique, sense of manliness.

In Chapter 7, "Dance, Masculinity, and Physical Education: An International Perspective," Michael Gard takes an international perspective to boys learning about their bodies through creative movement. His particular focus is with ballet and theatrical dance; Gard provides an historical sketch of these performance genres in international contexts. The vitality of classical male dance has, he argues, diminished in the West. One of the reasons for this, Gard asserts, is the failure of physical education to properly accommodate dance. He notes a decline in dance pedagogy, which has reduced opportunities for aesthetic physical experiences and space for creative body movements. The impact for boys has been especially profound: Given that "physical education" has aligned itself with the predominantly masculine world of games and sports, the male dancer has thus been excluded from this paradigm.

In Chapter 8, "Sport, Masculinities, and Pain: An Australian Rules Football Perspective," Deborah Agnew and Murray Drummond explore how Australian Rules footballers cope with the challenges of injury, recovery and the pressure to play while "hurt." There are two types of pain here: (1) the physical hurt of putting one's body on the line and the suffering this inflicts and (2) the mental struggle to absorb hurt to oneself and continue on—this being a commitment to the values of the team. In conducting interviews with players, Agnew and Drummond discovered that many of them thought of their health only in terms of their capacity to perform on the field; long-term health was scarcely a consideration. This meant that some of the athletes were prepared to take major risks with their bodies, submitting themselves to regimes designed to return them to play quickly, even if long-term recovery was compromised. In all of this an unspoken code of masculinity was manifest: pushing one's body to the limit, absorbing pain and injury without fuss, and a sacrificial commitment to the team before the needs of the self. Although the players saw this as a demonstration of manly valor, the personal cost of the physical extremes they were prepared to endure was too often not even considered.

In Chapter 9, "Steroids, Male Body Image, and the Intimate Self," Daryl Adair explores how men who use androgenic anabolic steroids (AASs) manage their bodies. His particular focus is three well-known side-effects of extensive AASs use (or abuse): testicular atrophy (shrinkage of testicles), gynecomastia (increase in the size of male breasts), and acne (a skin disease). The author's interest is with harm minimization: How do those who use AASs make sense of these risk factors or respond to them once observed? By searching through web-based steroid discussion groups, Adair has gained insights into how the AAS community tries to educate and inform users about how managing their bodies while using muscle-enhancing, steroid-based drugs. Given that AASs are used often, though not exclusively, by males to increase their muscular form in order to be more "masculine" and thus attractive, there is an assumption that steroid users are also interested in minimizing side-effects that might compromise those goals. Testicular atrophy, gynecomastia, and acne present three such challenges for either naive or hardcore AAS users.

In Chapter 10, "Manliness and Mountaineering: Sir Edmund Hillary as New Zealand Adventurer and Male Icon," Toni Bruce and Richard Pringle examine the role of New Zealander mountain climber Sir Edmund Hillary as both adventurer and male icon. The authors found a very complex individual. On the one hand, Hilary, who was one of the first to climb Mt Everest, was a physically courageous individual who epitomized the ideal of the rugged "Kiwi bloke." On the other hand, Hillary was later renowned and respected for his humanitarian work and care of others. As a male icon, he evolved over time into a rounder, perhaps softer, ideal of manliness: classically masculine in terms of his love of the outdoors, but also nurturing towards others, particularly those less fortunate than himself. He was able to straddle what might be regarded as both masculine and feminine discourses: rugged individualism and selfless compassion.

In Chapter 11, "Manner(s) Maketh the Man: Embodied Masculinities in a Japanese University Rowing Club," Brent McDonald examines gender relations and codes of manliness in Japanese university rowing. Having lived in Japan, the author was well-placed to observe the complex rituals and ceremonies associated with athletic sports in that culture, and in this case within elite rowing. Drawing on Bourdieu's conceptual tools of habitus, social field, and capital, McDonald evaluates the totalizing structural apparatus of the club, the boat, the river, the dorms, and the kitchen, together with bonding rituals such as drinking and partying that, altogether, provide a common existence for the dedicated rower. The athlete's identity is subsumed within the club; he suffers for the crew, he laughs with the crew, he exists for the crew. In this sense, a Japanese university rower is a man because of the company he keeps and their attitude towards him.

Please begin your rhizomatic journey into *Embodied Masculinities in Global Sport*.

CHAPTER 1

## REFERENCES

Adair, D., & Vamplew, W. (1997). *Sport in Australian history*. Melbourne, Austraila: Oxford University Press.

Adair, D., Nauright, J., & Phillips, M. (1998). Playing fields through to battle fields: The development of Australian sporting manhood in its imperial context, c. 1850–1918. *Journal of Australian Studies, 22*, 51–67.

Anderson, E. (2005a). *In the game: Gay athletes and the cult of masculinity*. Albany, NY: SUNY Press.

Anderson, E. (2005b). Orthodox and inclusive masculinity: Competing masculinities among heterosexual men in a feminized terrain. *Sociological Perspectives, 48*, 337–355.

Anderson, E. (2008). Inclusive masculinity in a fraternal setting. *Men and Masculinities, 10*, 604–620.

Anderson, E. D. (2009). The maintenance of masculinity among the stakeholders of sport. *Sport Management Review, 12*, 3–14.

Bennett, J. M. (2011). *History matters: Patriarchy and the challenge of feminism*. Philadelphia, PA: University of Pennsylvania Press.

Bourdieu, P. (1978). Sport and social class. *Social Science Information, 17*, 819–840.

Bourdieu, P (2001). *Masculine domination*. Stanford, CA: Stanford University Press.

Brace-Govan, J. (2010). Representations of women's active embodiment and men's ritualized visibility in sport. *Marketing Theory, 10*, 369–396.

Brown, D. (2006). Pierre Bourdieu's "masculine domination" thesis and the gendered body in sport and physical culture. *Sociology of Sport Journal, 23*, 162–188.

Butler, J. (2006). *Gender trouble. Feminism and the subversion of identity*. New York, NY: Routledge.

Coad, D. (2008). *The metrosexual: Gender, sexuality and sport*. Albany, NY: SUNY Press.

Coles, T. (2009). Negotiating the field of masculinity: The production and reproduction of multiple dominant masculinities. *Men and Masculinities, 12*, 30–44.

Connell, R. W. (1995). *Masculinities*. Berkeley, CA: University of California Press.

Connell, R. W., & Messerschmidt, J. W. (2005). Hegemonic masculinity: Rethinking the concept. *Gender & Society, 19*, 829–859.

Cooky, C., Messner, M. A., & Hextrum, R. H. (2013). Women play sport, but not on TV: A longitudinal study of televised news media. *Communication & Sport, 1*, 203–230.

Deleuze, G., & Guattari, P. F. (1987). *A thousand plateaus: Capitalism and schizophrenia. Vol. 2*. Minneapolis MI: University of Minnesota Press.

Demetriou, D. Z. (2001). Connell's concept of hegemonic masculinity: A critique. *Theory and Society, 30*, 337–361.

Drummond, M. J. (2002). Sport and images of masculinity: The meaning of relationships in the life course of "elite" male athletes. *The Journal of Men's Studies, 10*, 129–141.

Edwards, T. (2006). *Cultures of masculinity*. London, England: Routledge.

Hall, N. (2011). "Give it everything you got": Resilience for young males through sport. *International Journal of Men's Health, 10*, 65–81.

Hargreaves, J. (1994). *Sporting females: Critical issues in the history and sociology of women's sport*. London, England: Taylor & Francis.

Hargreaves, J. (2012). Chapter 9-Olympic women: A struggle for recognition. In J. Hargreaves (Series Ed.), Sporting females: Critical issues in the history and sociology of women's sport. *Routledge Online Studies on the Olympic and Paralympic Games, 1*, 209–234.

Heasley, R. (2013). Twenty years and counting: The relevance of men's studies in a gendered world. *The Journal of Men's Studies, 21*, 9–13.

Deutsch, F. M. (2007). Undoing gender. *Gender & Society, 21*, 106-127.

Hollander, J. A. (2002). Resisting vulnerability: The social reconstruction of gender in interaction. *Social Problems, 49*, 474–496.

Homes, A. M. (2007). David and Victoria Beckham: American idols. *W Magazine*. Retrieved from: http://www.wmagazine.com/people/celebrities/2007/08/beckhams_steven_klein_s/photos/

Horton, P. (2009). Rugby Union Football in the land of the wallabies, 1874–1949: Same game, different ethos. *The International Journal of the History of Sport, 26*, 1611–1629.

Hult, J. S. (1994). The story of women's athletics: Manipulating a dream. 1890-1985. In. M. Costa & S. Guthrie (Eds.), *Women and Sport: Interdisciplinary perspectives* (pp. 83–106). Champaign, IL: Human Kinetics.

Hunt, C. J., Gonsalkorale, K., & Murray, S. B. (2013). Threatened masculinity and muscularity: An experimental examination of multiple aspects of muscularity in men. *Body Image, 10*, 290–299.

Jansen, S. C., & Sabo, D. (1994). The sport/war metaphor: Hegemonic masculinity, the Persian Gulf War, and the new world order. *Sociology of Sport Journal, 11*, 1–17.

Kidd, B. (1987). Sports and masculinity. In M. Kaufman (Ed.), *Beyond patriarchy: Essays by men on pleasure, power and change* (pp. 250–265). New York, NY: Oxford University Press.

Knijnik, J. D., & Falcao-Defino, P. C. (2010). Esporte e masculinidades: uma longa historia de amor, ou melhor, de amizade. In Jorge Knijnik (Ed.), *Genero e Esporte: Masculinidades e feminilidades* (pp. 161–183). Rio de Janeiro: Apicuri.

Knijnik, J. D. (2010). Gender vertigo ou a la recherche d'une identite perdue. In Jorge Knijnik (Ed.), *Genero e Esporte: Masculinidades e feminilidades* (pp. 327–337). Rio de Janeiro, Brazil: Apicuri.

Leonard II, W. M., & Reyman, J. E. (1988). The odds of attaining professional athlete status: Refining the computations. *Sociology of Sport Journal, 5*, 162–169.

Loland, N. W. (1999). Some contradictions and tensions in elite sportsmen's attitudes towards their bodies. *International Review for the Sociology of Sport, 34*, 291–302.

McNamee, M., & Partridge, B. (2013). Concussion in sports medicine ethics: Policy, epistemic and ethical problems. *The American Journal of Bioethics, 13*, 15–17.

Mangan, J. A., & Walvin, J. (1987). *Manliness and morality: Middle-class masculinity in Britain and America, 1800–1940*. Manchester, IL: Manchester University Press.

Messner, M. A. (1990). When bodies are weapons: Masculinity and violence in sport. *International Review for the Sociology of Sport, 25*, 203–220.

Messner, M. & Sabo, D. (1994). *Sex, violence, and power in sports: Rethinking masculinity*. Freedom, CA: Crossing Press.

Morrison, J. (2010). The early history of football's forward pass. Smithsonian.com. Retrieved from: http://www.smithsonianmag.com/history/the-early-history-of-footballs-forward-pass 780152 37/

Pollack, W. S. (1999). *Real boys: Rescuing our sons from the myths of boyhood.* New York, NY: Henry Holt and Co.

Purvis, P. (2013). *Masculinity in opera.* London, England: Taylor & Francis.

Putukian, M., Raftery, M., Guskiewicz, K., Herring, S., Aubry, M., Cantu, R. C., & Molloy, M. (2013). Onfield assessment of concussion in the adult athlete. *British Journal of Sports Medicine, 47,* 285–288.

Roberts, L. J., & MacLean, M. (2012). Women in the weighing room: Gendered discourses of exclusion in English flat racing. *Sport in Society, 15,* 320–334.

Scott, J. W. (1996). *Feminism and history.* Oxford, UK: Oxford University Press.

Sommers, C. H. (2000). *The War against boys: How misguided feminism is harming our young men.* New York, NY: Simon & Schuster.

Terret, T. (2004). Sport et Masculinité: Une revue de questions. *Revue International des sciences du sport et de l'éducation physique* (Spécial Activités Physiques et Genre), *66,* 209–225.

Terret, T., & Mangan, J. A. (Eds.). (2013). *Sport, militarism and the Great War: Martial manliness and Armageddon.* London, England: Routledge.

Vertinsky, P. A. (1990). *The Eternally Wounded Woman: Women, doctors, and exercise in the late nineteenth century.* Manchester, IL: Manchester University Press.

Whitson, D. (1990). Sport in the social construction of masculinity. In M. Messner & D. Sabo (Eds.), *Sport, men, and the gender order: Critical feminist perspectives* (pp. 19–30). Champaign, IL: Human Kinetics.

# "Cock Up": Emasculating American Athletes Through Sick Humor

Rob Baum

## INTRODUCTION

Celebrities are prey to public favor and comment, and few aspects of their lives remain private. Celebrity athletes, whose bodies are expected to be not only beautiful but also perfectly conditioned, have become even easier game, their performances televised, reviewed, and intimately examined. The outcry over Australian swimming champion Grant Hackett's potbelly is a case in point, the result of a camera angle, tight lycra, a "full tank," and post-swim relaxation.[1] This chapter explores the culture and popularity of sick humor in sport, analyzing this genre of jokes by examining their intended target and the means by which jokes produce discomfort. The focus is on athletes and jokes pertaining to gender norms in sport. I have previously examined sick humor directed toward professional women (Baum, 2006), which has its own gender logic and dynamic. Sport is a particularly interesting area for jokes about athletes, as the sport field is a place where competitors seek personal glory by putting their bodies on the line.

CHAPTER 2

Previous studies have tended to treat sick jokes as innocuous societal outlets (Dundes, 1987b), even minor performances of socialness (Mellencamp, 1992; Penley, 1993). Sick humor is also recognized for various personal and communal efficacies, primarily the emotional release of petty aggravations and interpersonal conflicts. This chapter demonstrates that by employing the interconnected workings of metaphor, race, class, gender, and the grotesque in a sick joke, the individual can experience psychological and physical release. That is, of course, unless that individual is the butt of the joke. Crucially, comic discourses are socially unequal; the target of sick humor is often female. The genre of the sick joke makes possible violent but permissible attack—perceived as a counterattack—upon forces in the greater community against which the individual does not customarily feel personal effects (Freud, 1963). The sick joke principally reconstructs its target, or *butt*, through the mechanism of gender identification. Gender is not confined to genetic structure and biology, but is a performative and performed architecture (Butler, 1993, 1997). Humor's butt is often gendered as "female" (Baum, 2006)[2] despite or especially in the absence of the (con/genital) woman. This chapter observes how humor works to "feminize" (or belittle) through objectification, and how the gaze functions in terms of male athletes. Such positioning of the inferior as female is endemic to limited and limiting notions of gender. Bourdieu (2001) comments on the sociological necessity of fierce role divisions to maintain a hierarchical order accepted as natural to gender:

> The androcentric vision imposes itself as neutral and has no need to spell itself out in discourses aimed at legitimating it. The social order functions as an immense symbolic machine tending to ratify the masculine domination on which it is founded: it is the sexual division of labour, a very strict distribution of the activities assigned to each sex, of their place, time and instruments; it is the structure of space, with the opposition between the place of assembly or the market, reserved for men, and the house, reserved for women. (pp. 9–10)

The following study hones in on key female and male examples of athletes who have been the butt of sick jokes. These are the Olympic skaters Nancy Kerrigan and Tonya Harding and professional football player O. J. Simpson. They fall within the short span of sick joke fame and concomitant public "fall from grace," and allow discussion of the implications of gender and race/ethnicity in the comic (while avoiding criminal determination). The aim is to show how even the princely public icon and famed masculine athlete Simpson could be regendered in the cold light of the comic genre, through linguistic linkage with other objects of sick humor. To facilitate this argument, the issue of gender and masculinity will be revealed to be mobile, a discussion that takes place in the context of the Nancy-Tonya spectacle: Both appear to be women, but their genders are deconstructed via media interventions. (Although theoretical frameworks such as queer studies suggest that gender must be, or is, freed of a congenital, biological focus, the social reality is much less liberating.) The overriding concern in both cases is with a topical pathology of joking. This is not synonymous with dependably constant racial/ethnic slurs or seemingly silly and inoffensive witticisms, such as the "elephant" jokes once so popular in the United States (Dundes, 1977). Rather, it is a syndrome of sick humor attending tragic events popularized by the news media—in this case two disasters from the world of American sport.

Why the interest in a battle between two female athletes when the subject of this book is masculinities? How can the trials of two women in sports—lower paid, less celebrated, under promoted, and with less duration on the national or international circuit—inform the contemporary sports-minded scholar about the more rarefied world of the male athlete? This argument has increasing relevance in the recent recursion of one of the greatest male athletes of modern times. The notion of masculinity itself requires reconceptualization in the dazzling eye of news media, a form of communication that alters its subject, sometimes irrevocably.

## BAD SPORTS

Olympic figure skating is generally considered one of the more sophisticated international sporting events. Basic groundwork and complicated aerials are employed according to professional standards; sequence, frequency, and amplitude are among the essential factors. The event includes solo and double virtuosity and, since the appearance of the Dean and Horvill professional ice skating team, has been highlighted by couples gliding in effortless heteronormative bliss. The male is comfortably taller, stronger and apparently heroic; the female is smaller, slighter, and apparently vulnerable. Costumes are often abbreviated versions of formal evening wear—that is, if one wears knives on one's feet to a party. In short, this sport tends towards a tradition of romantic fiction in which love scenes are played out in calm motility, implacably burning passion depends upon a public metaphorized as ice, and the relationship circles indefinitely until it cools. In the fateful year of 1994, the excitation was reconfigured as a battle between two rival American female athletes and unexpectedly became an increasingly primitive contest.[3]

Kerrigan was the U.S. champion ice skater in 1993 and had received media notice, becoming "one of *People Magazine's* 50 Most Beautiful People in 1993." According to

IMDb.com, she was "shy as a child [and] wanted to be treated like a boy. [She] learned to skate when her older brother, Michael, wanted to learn how to play hockey" ("Biography for Nancy Kerrigan," n.d., Trivia section). Later depictions of Kerrigan reverse this image. In 1992 she earned a place on the U.S. Olympic team, having placed second after Kristi Yamaguchi; Yamaguchi turned professional the next year, and Kerrigan won the U.S. Championships.[4] The third-place winner in 1992 was Tonya Harding, whom media called "powerful" (not "beautiful"); in 1991, Harding was the first woman to receive a 6.0 on technical merit. In the Skate America competition that autumn, she recorded three more firsts:

1. The first woman to complete a triple axel in the short program
2. The first woman to successfully execute two triple axels in a single competition
3. The first ever to complete a triple axel combination with the double toe loop ("Tonya Harding," n.d., Skating Career section)[5]

Despite this series of accomplishments, "the latter part of her competitive career was marked by a series of blunders, causing television commentators to observe that no competition was complete without Harding having a crisis" ("Tonya Harding," n.d., Series of Incidents section).[6]

Shortly before the competition at Lillehammer, the two women burst into the news together in the form of a scandal when a man described as Harding's boyfriend (along with three other men) attacked and wounded Kerrigan.[7] As Laura Bleiberg reported in *The Orange County Register*, "Before the 1994 Winter Olympics, associates of skater Tonya Harding took a metal pipe to rival Nancy Kerrigan and the nation was mesmerized. Figure skating became the hottest sport of the Olympics" (1998, p. 3). The press was delighted to run with this sensational story, identified as the best thing to happen to American sport (Starkman, 2003).[8] In order to differentiate two equally fit and competent women for an extra-attentive audience, however, the media needed a particular way of framing the story. In doing so it effected a symbolic gender operation, masculinizing the manner and even the choreography of Harding by commenting on her "strong, blockish" sweeps and "muscular" leaps, in contrast to Kerrigan's grace, charm, and continuously noted beauty. As Bourdieu (2001) comments,

> Access to power of any kind places women in a "double bind": if they behave like men, they risk losing the obligatory attributes of "femininity" and call into question the natural right of men to the positions of power; if they behave like women they appear incapable and unfit for the job. These contradictory expectations take over from those to which they

are structurally exposed as objects offered on the market in symbolic goods, simultaneously invited to use all means to please and charm and expected to repel the seductive maneuvers that this kind of submission in advance to the verdict of the male gaze may seem to have provoked. (pp. 67–68)

By dramatizing the event as a contest between the powers of nature and forces of evil, all media benefited. So did the Olympics, which acquired another segment of the public sector (news mavens) as part of the television audience. Even viewers who would not ordinarily have watched televised sports tuned in to witness a fight with all the choreography—and most of the *schmaltz*—of a professional "wrassling" (wrestling) match. News and sports producers, should they be familiar with Barthes, would have rediscovered that

> the public is completely uninterested in knowing whether the [wrestling] contest is rigged or not, and rightly so; it abandons itself to the primary virtue of the spectacle. . . . What is expected is the intelligible representation of moral situations which are usually private. (Barthes, 1972, p. 18)

The contest between athletes had ceased to exist in an "Olympic" (utopian) world and had become merely gladiatorial. Although Harding was called by her surname, Kerrigan was becoming "Nancy," perhaps mnemonically linking her with Nancy Reagan's ethical uprightness and Nancy Drew's plucky innocence. Kerrigan was typified as a beautiful, shining princess and as a victim; Harding, whose very surname conspired against her in magnifying negative appeal, was metaphorically (through references to Kerrigan's Disney endorsements) the equivalent of Cinderella's envious, ontologically ugly stepsister. Supermodel Cindy Crawford (as a self-appointed spokeswoman for the social—and athletic—aesthetic) placed Tonya Harding on her list of five women most needful of a hair and facial "make-over."[9] Office workers circulated a (false) ad for Harding's personal liability insurance rates, there being so much paid for a broken nose, so much more for a blow to the leg, and so on. Harding was the "hit man" and Kerrigan a battered woman.

By contrast to the active role Harding played, characterized not so much by choreographic strength (the attribute of any Olympic athlete) as by the fact of her association with violence (typically a male preserve), Kerrigan was depicted in anguish and need of support, a passive player in the Big Game. Her "score" with the media, on the basis of the assault alone, made her the winner in a contest that had not yet been staged on ice. Despite (or because of) this, among her professional deals Kerrigan garnered television commercial contracts with both Campbell's soup and Disney, brands and bywords for the American consumer ideal. In one soupy scene, Kerrigan is presented as the jewel on skates: A somewhat feminist but nonetheless wholly "feminine" character who icily upends a rinkful of coarse, sweaty, and adoring male hockey players. In a Disney clip, dressed in her very own golden fairy costume,[10] Kerrigan is a life-sized Tinker Bell self-consciously quoting her own "Wings on Ice" as a Disney fantasy. Having won the hearts of the American media, which to many audience members spoke as the sports (and culture) authority (rather than as a device of mass distortion), Kerrigan now generated an image of the American dream with the dimensions of a cartoon figure. She could *double* as herself without ever *being* herself.

Harding's "bitchiness" was capitalized upon, even engendered, by news hounds who saw personal conflict between the two figure skaters as a treasure of Olympic proportions.[11] Americans were plastered to their sets, submitting to luge, speed skating (not without its own American success stories) and skiing entries in hopes of a look, clip, or cut-in mention of "Nancy." A contest between Olympians became a beauty pageant constructed on the specific bodies of Harding and Kerrigan, who gradually came to represent structural opposites in the domain of moral order: bad versus good, ugly versus beautiful, unworthy versus deserving. More to the point, these women represented the classically fairytale physiognomic differences between the inappropriately masculine versus properly feminine. This gendered existence prevailed throughout the televised quest for Olympic gold, right up to the stereotypically "feminine" moment when Harding's bootlace snapped on the ice. In that fateful image even inanimate objects seemed to collude with the mediatized image of the Good Woman. Harding, whose nerves were no doubt as frayed as her bootlace, suffered a decisive, "hysterical" breakdown. Kerrigan won the silver medal and Harding took eighth place (having threatened to sue the Olympic Committee were she eliminated from participating in the competition).

Viewers may have felt briefly vindicated: The broken shoestring seemed a test of innocence that Harding had failed. (Establishing guilt by circumstance is historically customary when it comes to "bad women" in literature.) By showing consumer support for Kerrigan, America's spectators had convincingly backed the right horse. Yet chivalry is not dead for the very reason it is still a social problem: Chivalry polices as it protects, curbing dangerous elements, containing not what is weak but that which threatens to become stronger. Tonya had been so vilified as female, and so ill-compared with a "feminine" female, that it was merely a matter of time before she would be rumored to be a lesbian, naturally a "butch."[12] Because lesbian stereotyping does not easily coincide, even for consumer purposes, with the existence of a (biologically) male companion, the virile reputation of Tonya's boyfriend (who later became her husband) was ultimately jeopardized—despite his organization of the attack on Kerrigan. Rumor (including the sources cited herein) determined their public identity as an already-tainted couple. Together they became the subject of pornographic speculation in the not-for-prime-time release of *Tonya and Jeff's Wedding Night,* a B-grade video that made its rounds in pirated copies until the idea was no longer fresh.

> But news—or rather, what makes news—is relative. Not long after the Olympics, one of my female friends in California drove into a Kentucky Fried Chicken outlet and was casually offered the Nancy Kerrigan Special: "One broken leg, and two small breasts."[13]

The joke recalls the Harding-induced injury but immediately remarks upon Kerrigan's feminine attributes in a negative context, emphasizing the (too) small size of her breasts. This joke could not have been employed with a male, as male bodies have "chests" rather than breasts. Most significantly, the joke displays the fickleness of the American public, which altered from worshipful spectatorship to disparaging inventory, in which Kerrigan's body was no longer alluringly female enough. The public's willingness to support Kerrigan as a victim had vanished; Kerrigan was now viewed as weak and served-up for dinner, perhaps the public's comment on its own consumption. (By this time the media had moved on to other fare.) Finally, by being characterized as a chicken, she was gendered doubly female. Thus even Kerrigan, flying into a radiant Disney sky, could crash into the castle, resuming her destiny as Woman when her place as Lady was no longer of interest.

## BAD ACTING

The second case under scrutiny here became a source of national shame with a built-in scapegoat. First, the beginning of the joking:

> *Why is coffee the best drink to have in the morning?*
> *Because 'OJ' will kill you.*

And this one:

> *Why shouldn't you invite O. J. Simpson for Thanksgiving?*
> *He only carves white meat.*

Both jokes draw upon the distinguishing features of Orenthal James (hence the nickname "O. J.") Simpson as a Black man, something immediately and visually perceptible to the viewing public. The calm suggested by the first part of the ditties is arrested by the jokes' endings, when O. J. is identified as American (in the second joke at least) and darkly violent (in both). Although both sick jokes depict Simpson as a killer, wielding the coffee cup, juice glass, or carving knife, the second joke suggests a definition of violence specifically directed at White people—the "meat" of the punchline. The theme of consumption is again relevant. Where Simpson had previously enjoyed a celebrity status and wealth exceeding typical racial limitations, in these jokes he became (again) an African American male—*coffee-colored,* the antithesis of white meat—and prey to stereotypical White fears with respect to negative identifications associated with many Black American men.

The Simpson case and its extra-judicial speculation was a tragedy (Editorial, 1994)—the self-ruin of a national hero—in which, as with the two female athletes discussed before, everyone seemed anxious to take sides. On one hand lay the evidence reportedly stacked up against O. J. Simpson, evidence that could not be used or that, in its usage, perplexed a jury that could not understand it. On the other hand was the body of the athlete-turned-actor himself, hunted and captured on national television in a high-speed, hyperdramatic chase scene reminiscent of hundreds of television police movies. After this histrionic activity—albeit of the accused's own making—O. J. went on trial and into prison amid fears that he would fail to receive due process of peer review or "impartiality" anywhere in the world.

The prominence of television in generating a realm and material for public humiliation and joking bears resemblance to the centrality of professional sport in viewers' lives. As with images of the Olympic athletes, the Simpson case captivated the public. George Lipsitz (1997) has commented,

> If something happens over and over again on television, then it certainly "happens" to all of us. Television played the key role in the Simpson case in many ways. The trial was telecast live, and its details were aired endlessly on new and entertainment programs. The case opened up whole new television markets with gavel-to-gavel coverage on cable and broadcast outlets. It helped spur the development of new programs and the creation of new celebrities through specialized discussion on cable channels. It provided a constant frame for reference for late-night comedians, talk shows, and news features, and even served as the source of a new line of Halloween masks featuring the case's central "characters." (p. 8)

Here, joking moves into the representational field of costume (as it had previously for controversial public figures like Richard Nixon), with children encouraged to play a part in adult fantasies and *scopophilia*.

Studying the marketing of the Simpson trial, Lipsitz (1997) has noted the conflation of products (not issues) that made the O. J. trial successful as a media fetish commodity:

> Stories about the O. J. Simpson trial enjoyed a powerful presence in the market, in part, because they would draw on the main themes that organize television discourse in the United States: The primacy of products as the center of social life, the stimulation and management of appetites, and alarm about the family in jeopardy. A story linking any two of these categories will always make the news (i.e., a news event that resembles a popular motion picture). A story that links all three is even better. . . . One reason why the O. J. Simpson trial became so prominent in the media is because it contained all these elements necessary for televisual representation. (pp. 12–13)

Toni Morrison and Claudia Lacour (1997) have voiced concern about the cultural politics of the "race card" and readings of Simpson as a Black man in a White world, not just *a* White world but the upper echelon of White Los Angeles—as far economically from his gang-land childhood as a working-class boy might run. For at the heart of jokes about Simpson he is clearly, all too clearly, Black. Like an American Oroonoko (the Surinam prince in Aphra Behn's novel *Oroonoko: Or, the Royal Slave, A True History,* 1688), the so-called "Juice" was a prince among White savages: Homegrown, handsome, intelligent, charming—the closest one can come in the United States to being (rather than marrying) royalty. As a professional athlete he outranked even Olympians in status, largely a facet of his economic strength but also a reflection of his physical beauty and charisma. Both a man's man and a lady's man, Simpson occupied a place to which few men, and certainly no women, could aspire. Indeed, in terms of sport and celebrity status, many fine female athletes have found themselves battling the negatively applied label of "lesbian" (Brown, 1983; Cohen, 1993).

Simpson himself appreciated the power of a joke to displace or disarm public criticism. As David Roediger (2002) has noted, "A quarter-century ago [in the 1970s] O. J. Simpson told of his strategy for responding to racial taunts. It consisted of a sharp jab to the offender's chest, accompanied by a literal punch line: 'Hertz, don't it?'"(p. 68).

## CHAPTER 2

Roediger and Johnson (2002) have explained that

> the humor rested on the bitter contrast of Simpson's tremendous success as an athlete who crossed over to become a beloved corporate icon, advertising rental cars among much else, with his continued facing of racial hurts and desiring to strike back against them. . . . Simpson surely knew that he briefly stepped out of character in telling the joke. He followed the remark with laughing reassurances that such jabbing was of course unnecessary . . . [pointing] out that "The Juice" so transcended white racism that he scarcely faced bigotry. [14] (pp. 68–69)

These circumstances were evidently altered by the events of his trial for murder, when jokes about (rather than by) Simpson performed fundamentally as those about Harding and Kerrigan, to regender, delimit and reclass. This was not so far a leap because Simpson is a Black man and, in the American economy of the body, Black power arguably remains closer to a notion of femininity (in Bourdieu's terms of diminution and inferiority) than White masculinity—regardless of what Simpson experienced, or feels he experienced, earlier in his career. Canny Francis (1992) has put it this way:

> As with the exploitation of working-class and young men, the exploitation of black men is a function of political vulnerability in a white, bourgeois, ageist society, and serves to reinforce not only the exploitable position of blacks but, also by its reflexive attack on white (in)security, the distrust between men of different colour and/or culture. Characteristic of patriarchy, it reinforces competition, insecurity, inflexibility, hardness, non-engagement, and (in other ways) sexual rapacity. . . . [It is the] patriarchal subject to objectify those men who, like all women, are potentially victims—young men, working-class men, non-Anglo, nonwhite, men. (pp. 113–114)

Shorn of positive celebrity, Simpson resumed what might be termed *racial status*: negative recognition of his Blackness. The reversal of his public image from hero to villain is symbolized by the fall from esteem, as opposed merely to a (different or other) type of characterization, as Simpson himself clarified, according to Francis:

> As early as 1969, he triumphantly reported that O. J. was thought of as a man, not as an African American. He told reporters that the American

public happily saw him as "colorless." In making the latter claim, Simpson also invoked Hertz. The marketing division of the firm, he observed, has generated data that proved his transcendence of race. (Roediger & Johnson, 2002, p. 69)
For Simpson (as Daniel Herwitz has said of President Barack Obama),

> The process . . . and the expectations [of the American media] . . . become illegible and unreal. He is set up to disappoint. . . . The media is not containable [but] grows through its own genius. . . . It's a market system."[15]

Herwitz has also noted Lynne Siegel's codification of American television as "domestic and feminine."[16] Feminization—to be exact, emasculation and re-racialization—became more apparent in the early months of the first public trial, although the startling conclusion reversed most of the signs, or at least their meanings. Simpson's eventual full exoneration from criminal guilt for murder of his wife and his wife's lover erased the (re)production of Simpson as part of an "underclass," a man who, because stigmatized as Black, could not be fairly tried by either Blacks or Whites and had therefore become a "victim" of the system.

The following lengthy sick joke, circulated widely on the Internet during the sensational murder trial, reveals the extent to which its author (anonymous, of course) and intended public (anyone with Internet access) inveighed against a judicial system in which it appeared that proof—even proof of violence—seems circumstantial, and therefore only partly admissible. The chagrin of the blogger is evident in the use of a child's nonsense tale to emphasize the comic absurdity of Simpson's testimony.

The OJ trial as told by Dr. Seuss
*I did not kill my lovely wife.*
*I did not slash her with a knife.*
*I did not bonk her on the head.*
*I did not know that she was dead.*

*I stayed at home that fateful night.*
*I took a cab, then took a flight.*
*The bag I had was just for me.*
*My bag! My bag! hey, leave it be!*

*When I came home I had a gash.*
*My hand was cut from broken glass.*

## CHAPTER 2

*I cut my hand on broken glass.*
*A broken glass did cause that gash.*
*My friend, he took me for a ride.*
*All through LA, from side to side.*
*From north to south, we took a ride.*
*But from the cops we could not hide.*

*My trial lasted for a year.*
*A year! A year! just sitting here!*
*The DNA, the HEM-The HAW!*
*The circus-hype the viewers saw!*
*A year! A year! just sitting here!*
*And lawyers charge by the hour I fear!*
*If I'm found guilty I will appeal!*
*Appeal! Appeal! I will appeal!*
*I'll wheedle and whine—I'll cut a deal!*
*If it's "not guilty" so glad I'll feel.*

*Did you do this awful crime? Did you do this anytime?*
*I did not do this awful crime. I could not, would not anytime.*
*Did you take this person's life? Did you do it with a knife?*
*I did not do it with a knife.*
*I did not, could not kill my wife.*
*I did not do this awful crime.*
*I could not, would not anytime.*

*Did you hit her from above? Did you drop this bloody glove?*
*I did not hit her from above.*
*I cannot even wear that glove.*
*I did not do it with a knife.*
*I did not, could not kill my wife.*
*I did not do this awful crime.*
*I could not, would not, anytime.*

*And now I'm free, I can return*
*To my house for which I yearn.*
*And to my family whom I love.*
*Hey now I'm free—Give back my glove!!!!!*

## Emasculating American Athletes Through Sick Humor

This joke is unusual among sick humor for its length, as well as its adherence to a form—here, Theodore Geisel's iambic tetrameters. The joker rarely loses sight of the Dr. Seuss stories' rhythm or humor, and repeats key phrases, such as "could not, would not" and "I did not do it with a knife," suggesting that another instrument might have been used. But the ditty breaks down in the "trial" stanza, only to be restored "under oath" in the stanza following. As "Dr. Seuss" comments on the media event, the narrator ceases to tell the story of the murder and tells instead the story of the *observed* media event. The "it" referred to is the murder, but because from the outset the narrator remarks that "he" (the ersatz Dr. Seuss) was unaware that something had happened, use of the unspecified "it" sounds odd. Also odd is the fact that the narrator does not answer specific questions—denies the events of the crime—complaining about treatment and threatening to appeal a trial when its outcome is still in doubt. The narrator never evinces remorse. Among other things, the joke's teller predicts the liberation of Simpson, who then has the nerve to demand the return of a glove he has just denied belonged to him, thus falsifying or recanting.

Sick jokes featuring Simpson referred to either the murder charge or the athlete's color—or both (as in the white meat joke). The extended "Dr. Seuss" story conjures up images of strange characters existing only in storybooks, animals whose stripes or spots comically change. Thus, the O. J. of the third joke is a grotesquely comic beast. Jokes involving Simpson's nickname of "Juice" (rhyming with "Seuss") naïvely and absurdly link beverage with crime; color jokes in which an American holiday figures prominently, posit Simpson as a menace to White society, a renegade Black who lives as a star among stars, rather than as a man who *might* have killed his ex-wife and her lover. For a celebrity, public disapproval is a severe form of prosecution, and the public suspected long before the second civil trial reached its due course that Simpson was a batterer, a violent man who expressed dominance rather than love in the presence of his ex-wife Nicole. Nicole Simpson is now and forever dead, and the real tragedy of the O. J. Simpson saga, unmentioned in any joke, is that women must die before the public notices that they are being beaten, while men, including the hypothetical O. J. of the Seuss joke, can return to what is left of the families they help to destroy.

By now the similarities of the murder case of "Blade Runner" Oscar Pistorius should be obvious. As this book goes to press the conviction in that trial was recently pronounced (by the Black female judge)—and contested by feminists worldwide. The Olympic runner Pistorius's "race card" is also visible: He achieved his first racing victories as a Paralympian. Throughout the trial, the defense invoked his minority status as a man destroyed by his disability. The White Pistorius, too, has been

# CHAPTER 2

de-classed and feminized by the press. In fact, in Pistorius's case the effeminization was of his own making, an effort to diminish a history of domestic abuse, public violence and now murder (regardless of intent) by comparing him with a woman (specifically, a woman's scream)

One of the more repulsive jokes then circulating about O. J. reminded listeners of his children, left motherless and (at the time of the trials as Simpson sat in jail) potentially fatherless. While it offered no sympathy, this joke managed to link Simpson's tragedy with another, somewhat earlier American catastrophe, one in which the public was far less lenient with another media star:

> *What did Michael Jackson say to O. J. Simpson?*
> *"The kids? Don't worry about them. I'll take care of them."*

Although it may be going too far to call this joke explicitly racist, the joke invokes the tragic Jackson, Black king of pop. The sense of a larger family (delineated by race) therefore seems implicit. Although White men kill and molest women and children every day, there is no comparative joke involving two *White* men. The joke demonstrates the extent of the public's outrage when its celebrities are involved—and its readiness to feed on the remains.

Through their associative magic, jokes—like metaphors—create alchemy, corrupting ordinary categories. People who repeated this joke could visualize Black men, especially famous and wealthy Black men, as a fraternity of criminals. For many tellers, this touched up a picture of society already hanging permanently on the wall back home. The racism in the following joke is inescapable:

> *Shapiro, O. J.'s top lawyer, sees O. J. in at the airport, carrying his luggage. He says: "Hey, Juice, where are you going?" O. J. replies: "I'm doing what you told me; I'm flying down to Baja." Shapiro looks puzzled. Says O. J.: "Remember? You told me I should go to Cancun." "No," says Shapiro, "I said 'you're going to the can, Coon.'"*

Color should have no connection to criminality, particularly in the context of one whose record indicates that color long since ceased to be a barrier; yet here the darkness of Simpson's body is again cited as a factor in his intended escape. O. J.'s self-perception of a "colorless" existence as a celebrated American entity is shattered in the type of jokes that emerged at the time, centered on race, bestiality and loss of status, confirming that Simpson was neither colorless nor White, but a "fully racialized commodity, brilliantly positioned to be marketed to middle-class white men" (Roediger, 2002, p. 70). Just as Nancy Kerrigan's body has no bearing on chicken, except in the context of a gendered slur, such jokes fulfill a need that ranges across society and rely upon stereotyping, racial and gender differentiations, and imposed limitations.

Through the alembic of powerlessness in and through these jokes, Simpson becomes reclassified and loses class, face, and even the metaphor of economic success. Roediger and Johnson (2002) note that "all thinking about Simpson now is read as reflecting on 'the case'—that books about him are now not shelved in sport or business aisles but in the 'True Crime' sections of bookstores" (p. 70). While to be gendered female is a *categorical* alteration that has no permanent physical effect, the virtual procedure is feminization—conversion to a female position. For this reason, Aphra Behn's sojourn in Surinam and the aforementioned tragedy of Prince Oroonoko is pertinent. By the end of Behn's story, the African prince is gendered female and carved like Thanksgiving meat. Proven not guilty in his first trial, O. J. Simpson emerged again a prince in spite of previous physical violence towards his wife and its more than circumstantial associations with her murder, and his (motherless) children remained in his custody. Michael Jackson, already suspiciously "feminine"—the media having conveniently forgotten that androgyny was always a part of his appeal—had no representational "manliness" to prop up his scandalous reputation, and could not escape his class fall until he "proved himself" a man in the public eye—most ironically, by siring his own child. Unfortunately, he also produced the proof of marriage to a woman, thus reifying the definition of woman as not-man by use of a formal institution. (Later his patrimony would be held suspect, as well as his suitability as a father for his own children.)

The public was slowly coming to grips with the once startling revelation that football heroes and rock musicians (by American standards, *gods*) had private lives with shameful secrets, hidden boxes locked away and hedged 'round by privilege and status. The genre of sick jokes (Huang, 1995), presenting outcries of rage acceptably masked as humor, neutralizes that status. A folk type of relatively clever construction, the sick joke is of higher status than unwritten, or un-rote, gossip—that is, oral transmission that has not crystallized into a specific pattern, length, or word choice. Because of this it is not considered to be mere gossip (the type of "idle chatter" with which women have long been identified, while men are said to partake in "men's talk") and is therefore suitable for all to transmit. Communicating anger, distrust, and shame through violent language, people circulate sick jokes at the office, at social parties, on golf courses—everywhere professionals meet. Sick jokes are thus effective media for reclassifying—in Harding's case, as masculine, in Simpson's, as black—of an Other carefully delineated by the joke itself. The object of public vitriol may even be seen as a sacrificial victim, thus fulfilling the ancient role of scapegoat (Girard, 1977).

CHAPTER 2

The media commentary on Tiger Woods indicates that status can only protect an American athlete for so long before his sexual proclivities are declared open season. Yet Woods, an African American reared from childhood to become a champion golfer—a sport previously dominated by white men and women—indicates how fruitful and feminizing the genre of sick humor remains, as these "friendly" contributions from Twitter show:

> Tiger Woods says he still loves his wife very much. And he wants his three iron back.

Or this one:

> Tiger Woods told friends today how he is not his wife's punching bag as the media has made him out to be. "I can take care of myself in a fight with Elin. Last night I showed her how tough I really am. I snapped my chin down on her fist, then I hit her in the knee with my stomach, and finally smashed her in the elbow with my nose!"

The following demonstrates the continuing correlation between motor vehicles and masculinity:

> What's the difference between a car and a golf ball? Tiger can drive a ball 400 yards.

The next makes the connection between driving and penetration as masculine sport:

> Tiger crashed his car because he was in a rush to move on to the second hole.

What is most noticeable about the sick humor surrounding Tiger Woods's extramarital affairs is that the jokes employ the language of golfing (putter, iron, wood) and sexuality (the same words) rather than race. For instance:

> Tiger sounded very contrite in his speech and is back in rehab for sex addiction. As part of his treatment, they're trying out a new patch to combat his addiction. . . . Apparently it's working: he's now down to just two butts a day.

Even the jokes playing on his first name eschew racial imagery,[17] focusing instead on more generalized sexually based comparisons:

> In case Tiger Woods doesn't return to golf, he has a future with [American sewage drain company] Roto Rooter, which says: "If Tiger can't snake your drain, no one can."

These jokes[18] are also relatively tame. To date, only one joke has come my way that might be suggestive of an African context, given the provenance of the animals involved:

> Tiger will have to change his first name to "Cheetah."

But this joke also clings to the region of naming—here the Tiger is a "cheater" (hence, cheetah)—and does not capitalize on a potential racial context. Has the Obama presidency generated this much change? Or is it because Tiger Woods, in playing an effete white game, never challenged the American public to reflect on (and condemn) black virility?

## DENYING SPEECH

This chapter has made a journey from rink to sink, retelling the joke about "women" athletes as Olympians of the domestic, women who rise to sports acclaim only to be reduced to butts of sick humor. The joke on women is (almost) as easily transmuted into a joke on men: That is, on a man (Simpson) whose fall enrages his audience, a man who falls so far and so hard that he is reconstructed as a black inferior—in terms of Bourdieu's economy, a feminization. Such a fall, while it transports television executives, transgresses the sacred in the public imaginary. The public demands that its stars light the firmament (albeit a sky of billboards, tabloids and Twitter feeds) and shows no charity when the star plunges to earth.

As this examination of gender suggests, female presence is often symbolically rather than physically realized, abstracted rather than concretized as female. In reducing women to their bodies, one does not simply renounce female intellectualism, including the capacity for scientific thought; this may also renounce the body itself. That is a singular mistake given that the Harding-Kerrigan conflict involved the physical contest of female super-athletes, just as the saga of Simpson was constructed on the body of a super-man. Once the chase scene is over, and the big man has been brought down—like an animal, that is, by other men—the joking begins. It is a joke on gender, class and, in this case, race, but then race is always a matter of class and gender, as these jokes dramatically demonstrate.

The architecture of gender is a crucial structure rocked by such crises, social earthquakes in which public personages are made over into the Other through sexual implication. Progressive perspectives might challenge the sick joke as a social carrier of the disease of feminization, a condition in which masculinities are empowered as the tellers, or not present. As a category of the larger rubric of class, gender is a means to subjugate individuals and groups, excluding what is not understood, and retaining systems of privilege intact and unchallenged. Definitions of gender, race and class that fail to recognize social inequalities are sadly uninformed, thereby justifying an application of revolutionary tactics to the politics of identity. Openly voiced expressions would be better served by guiding the public toward seeing and hearing differently, rather than insulting others with a smile.

# REFERENCES

Associated Press. (1994, September 3). Photographs of "sign-bearing death penalty supporters." *Santa Barbara News-Press,* p. A5.

Barthes, R. (1972). *Mythologies.* (A. Lavers, Trans.). New York, NY: Hill & Wang. (Original work published 1957.)

Baum, R. (2006). Navigating the narrative space of women: Gender and sick humour. *Gender Forum: Gender Romours I,* pp. 1–12. Retrieved from http://www.genderforum.unikoeln.de/space1/article_baum.html

Behn, A. (1688). *Oroonoko: Or, the royal slave, a true history.* London, England: Canning.

Biography for Nancy Kerrigan. (n.d.). *IMDb.com.* Retrieved from http://www.imdb.com/name/nm0449872/bio#trivia

Bleiberg, L. (1998, December 22). A look at how Feld Entertainment produces the Disney on Ice shows. *The Orange County Register,* p 3.

Bourdieu, P. (2001). *Masculine domination.* (R. Nice, Trans.). Stanford, CA: Stanford University Press.

Brown, R. M. (1983). *Sudden death.* Toronto, Canada: Bantam Books.

Butler, J. P. (1993). *Bodies that matter: On the discursive limits of sex.* New York, NY: Routledge.

Butler, J. P. (1997). Critically queer. In S. Phelan (Ed.), *Playing with fire: Queer politics, queer theories* (pp. 11–29). New York, NY: Routledge.

Cohen, G. L. (Ed.). (1993). *Women in sport: Issues and controversies.* London, England: Sage Publications.

Cranny-Francis, A. (1992). *Engendered fictions: Analysing gender in the production and recepetion of texts.* Sydney, Australia: New South Wales University Press.

Dundes, A. (1987a). Jokes and covert language attitudes: The curious case of the wide-mouth frog." *Language in Society, 6,* 141–147.

Dundes, A. (1987b). *Cracking jokes: Studies of sick humor cycles & stereotypes.* Berkeley, CA: Ten Speed Press.

Editorial. (1994, June 27). An American tragedy. *Time Magazine.* p. 26 and cover.

Freud, S. (1963). *Jokes and their relation to the unconscious.* New York, NY: Norton.

Girard, R. (1977). *Violence and the sacred.* (P. Gregory, Trans.). Baltimore, MD: Johns Hopkins University Press.

Huang, T. (1995, April 23). Hey—that wasn't funny! *Santa Barbara News-Press,* p. D1.

Lipsitz, G. (1997). The greatest story ever sold: Marketing and the O. J. Simpson trial. In T. Morrison & C. B. Lacour (Eds.), *Birth of a nationhood: Gaze, script, and spectacle in the O. J. Simpson case* (pp. 3–29). New York, NY: Pantheon Books.

Mellencamp, P. (1992). *High anxiety: Catastrophe, scandal, age & comedy.* Bloomington, IN: Indiana University Press.

Morrison, T., & Lacour, C. (Eds.). (1997). *Birth of a nationhood: Gaze, script, and spectacle in the O. J. Simpson case.* New York, NY: Pantheon Books.

Nancy Kerrigan–winning ways. (n.d.). *JRank.* Retrieved from http://sports.jrank.org/pages/2485/Kerrigan-Nancy-Winning-Ways.html

Penley, C. (1993). Spaced out: Remembering Christa McAuliffe. *Camera Obscura, Special Issue on Imaging Technologies/ Inscribing Science, 29,* 179–212.

Robertson, L. (2000, December 27). Women enjoy great moments in year. *The Miami Herald*.
Roediger, D. R. (Ed.). (2002). *Colored White: Transcending the racial past*. Berkeley, CA: University of California Press.
Roediger, D. R., & Johnson, L. (2002). 'Hertz, don't it?' White 'colorblindness' and the mark(et)ings of O. J. Simpson. In D. Roediger (Ed.), *Colored White: Transcending the racial past* (pp. 68–93). Berkeley, CA: University of California Press.
Starkman, R. (2003, March 25). A skater's fine edge. *The Toronto Star*, p. 42.
Tonya Harding. (n.d.). *Absolute astronomy*. Retrieved from http://www.absoluteastronomy.com/topics/Tonya_Harding
Williams, A. T. (2001, March 24). Women's NCAA lost in hubbub over Madness. *The Charlotte Observer*, p. 10H.

## ENDNOTES

[1] See "Not fat, just a full tank, says Hackett's defender [Ky Hurst]," *The Sydney Morning Herald* (May 7, 2008). http://www.smh.com.au/articles/2008/05/06/1209839647469.html

[2] For an extension of this form of simulacrum, visual pleasure, and sick jokes, see Baum (2006).

[3] "Women's figure skating, arguably the most anticipated Winter Olympics event, had been strong even before that ugly 1994 skirmish between Tonya Harding and Nancy Kerrigan drew millions of viewers, lots of them men, who were looking-hoping-for an Olympic catfight" (Williams, 2001).

[4] "Feeling the pressure of her standing and her new role as a media darling, Kerrigan began to falter. In 1993 at the World Championships in Prague, Kerrigan, favored to win, was in first place after the short program, but she fell apart in the long program. Missing her first jump, she lost concentration and turned two triple jumps into unimpressive singles. She finished ninth in the long program and fifth overall. It was a devastating loss for Kerrigan, who sobbed in defeat after the competition" ("Nancy Kerrigan–Winning Ways," n.d., para. 3).

[5] See "Tonya Harding," n.d.

[6] Some examples:
- Skating magazine reported that at Skate America in 1991, Harding was stranded in heavy traffic just before her event was scheduled to begin, and had to hitch a ride with people who drove her backwards through traffic to the arena.
- In the short program at the 1993 U.S. Championships, Harding had to ask permission from the referee to restart her program after the back of her dress came unhooked as she began to skate.
- At 1993 Skate America, Harding stopped midway through her free skate and complained to the referee that her skate blade had become loose. She was allowed to resume her program after her blades were checked by a skate technician.
- In late 1993, Harding was scheduled to compete in a regional qualifying competition for the U.S. Championships. However, before the event, its organizers received an anonymous assassination threat against Harding, which led the United States Figure Skating Association (USFSA) to tell her to stay away, excluding her from having to qualify.

- The medal ceremony at the 1994 U.S. Championships had to be delayed because Harding could not be found backstage after the competition.
- At the Hamar Olympic Amphitheatre during the 1994 Winter Olympics, Harding almost failed to appear on the ice when her name was called for the free skating because she was scrambling to replace a broken shoelace. The replacement shoelace turned out to be too short, and after missing the opening jump in her program she again had to ask the referee for permission to find a new lace" ("Tonya Harding," n.d.).

7  The assault took place on January 6, 1994. Harding publicly apologized for her part in the kneecapping on January 27. Jeff Gillooly pled guilty to the attack on February 1, 1994. That Tonya Harding was Gillooly's ex-wife subsequently surfaced.

8  From an interview:
Q. The Tonya Harding-Nancy Kerrigan scandal. The best or the worst thing to happen to figure skating?
A. I think it was the best thing. A lot of people tuned in that would never have watched figure skating in their entire lives. It was a bit of an obvious trashy, tabloid kind of thing. But so many guys watched figure skating for the very first time. It happened out of an unfortunate incident, but I think it was a really good thing for our sport."

9  From an interview with *TV Guide,* in which Crawford proposes to make over Tonya Harding, Vince Neill, Meat Loaf, and Michael Jackson. Reported by Liz Smith: "Finally, victims were recognized" (in the *Toledo Blade,* July 12, 1994, p. 18). Interestingly, the title of Smith's article refers to Nicole Simpson and Ronald Goldman, the two "almost-forgotten and ignored victims in the O. J. Simpson case" (*ibid*). For locating many of these sources, originally citations from popular culture, I acknowledge the incomparable help of Gillian Morgan, Librarian at University of Cape Town; for hunting down articles for final proofs, thanks to Lyudmila Ocholla, Librarian at University of Zululand.

10  Kerrigan's outfit from the Olympics has its repeat performance in the commercial.

11  Another element of humor: "The friendship between two of the gods of sport—the world's fastest men, Maurice Greene and Ato Boldon—is so strong they jokingly refer to themselves as being members of the Tonya Harding track club." Found in Brian Burke, "Goodwill bonds sprint kings" (in *The Australian,* May 4, 2001).

12  See Bourdieu (2001) on the relationship between gender and sexuality, particularly gay and lesbian sexuality (e.g., pp. 119–120).

13  Contributed by Marilyn Romine, Santa Barbara.

14  They add parenthetically, "The same Hertz/hurts punning was repeated endlessly on O. J. jokes websites during Simpson's later trials" (Roediger, 2002, p. 68).

15  Public lecture for the Gordon Institute for Performing and Creative Arts, University of Cape Town, March 4, 2010.

16  Compare Patricia Mellencamp on the "gender base" for television in "Situation and Simulation: An Introduction to 'I Love Lucy,'" *Screen, 26* (1985), p. 31.

17  As before, see Dundes (1993) on the origins of the elephant joke.

18  All the foregoing jokes were found on Twitter. The next (and last) joke included was contributed by Carolina Ponce de Leon, San Francisco.

# ON BEING A WARRIOR: RACE, GENDER, AND AMERICAN INDIAN IMAGERY IN SPORT[1]

C. Richard King

## INTRODUCTION

The playing fields of North America have become battlefields as Native American sports mascots, once celebrated symbols, increasingly foster intense conflicts over history, culture, and identity. Consequently, scholars and commentators have seized upon these struggles to consider the changing articulations of race and power in American culture. Importantly, an expansive literature has offered critical analyses of Native American sports mascots, stressing that they can facilitate the creation of identity, community, and history (Connoly, 2000; Davis, 1993; King, 2002; King, 2004; King & Springwood, 2004; Pewewardy, 1991; Slowikowski, 1993; Spindel, 2000; Staurowsky, 1998).

A concern for race, especially "Indianness," has anchored these interpretations. And while Eitzen and Zinn (1989, 1993) have rightly highlighted the gender implications of naming and imaging sports teams, both on and off the playing field, gender has received little attention in accounts of Indian imagery in sports (Davis, 1993).

Indeed, most studies of Native American sports mascots have foregrounded race at the expense of gender. Native American political leader Dennis Banks has even unequivocally rejected the significance of gender for efforts to understand and undermine such icons (Banks, 1993).

The neglect and dismissal of gender is most unfortunate because it has obscured a full understanding of the complex meanings of Native American sports mascots. More specifically, scholars to date have failed to build on Laurel Davis's (1993) work. She argued that on the one hand the use of Indian imagery reinforced dominant notions of masculinity, citizenship, sport, and tradition, while on the other hand the controversy over mascots derived in part from efforts to defend traditional formulation of identity in the United States, especially its foundations in race (whiteness), gender (masculinity), nationality (Americanness), and history (the myth of the frontier). Consequently, the intense attention to race in the absence of gender has caused scholars to overlook the troubling discourses that sanction racialized team spirits by marshaling dominant ideas about gender.

This chapter seeks to redress this oversight through an examination of the place of gender and racial differences in the development and the more recent defense of Native American sports mascots. It focuses on the writings of three neoconservative commentators: Dave Shiflett, Richard Poe, and David Yeagley—especially the ways in which they explicitly and implicitly employ masculinity and femininity in their assessments of cultural ideals, coding of ideological perspectives, and evaluations of race, nation, and politics. To contextualize this analysis, the discussion begins with a consideration of the changing uses and understandings of Indian imagery in athletics, and then it turns to the gendered meanings of Native American sports mascots. It ends with a consideration of the importance of including gender in analyses of the history and significance of American Indian imagery in sport.

## A BRIEF HISTORY OF NATIVE AMERICAN SPORTS MASCOTS

Native American sports mascots first began to appear as modern America crystallized, notably coinciding with the rise of intercollegiate and professional athletics. During this same period, a crisis in white masculinity that was itself associated with the closing of the frontier, urbanization, industrialization, and the subjugation of Native America also occurred and contributed to the adoption of such symbols (Churchill, 1994; Davis, 1993). These appropriated indigenous symbols became a ubiquitous feature of American culture precisely because of the pleasures, possibilities, and powers they granted to nonindigenous performers. At the end of the 20th century, the sports teams at more than 2,500 schools used Native American names, imagery, or references, including more than 80 colleges and universities (Rodriguez, 1998; Staurowsky, 1999).

Native American sports mascots draw on clichéd images of Native Americans that are rooted in the imperial imagination (Bird, 1996). They promote a set of cultural features that are too often wrongly associated with the indigenous peoples of North America: the feathered head-dress, face paint, buckskin pants, warfare, dance, and the tomahawk (chop). They make use of these elements to create moving, meaningful, and entertaining icons that many people take to be authentic, appropriate, or even reverent. The condensed versions of Indianness rendered through signs and spectacles confine Native Americans within the past, typically within the popular image of the Plains warrior. Whatever the precise image or reference (real or imagined), mascots trap native nations within the many overlapping tropes of savagery. At one extreme are romantic renditions of bellicose warriors, such as the University of Illinois (Chief Illiniwek and the Fighting Illini), Florida State University (the Seminoles with Chief Osceola), and the University of North Dakota (Fighting Sioux). At the other extreme are perverse burlesque parodies of the physical or cultural features, such as Runnin' Joe at Arkansas State University or Willie Wampum at Marquette University (King, 2001; Landreth, 2001).

Native American sports mascots are derived from a long tradition of "playing Indian" (Deloria, 1998; Green, 1988; Huhndorf, 1997; Mechling, 1980). EuroAmericans have long known, invented, and expressed themselves by casting themselves as Indians, using the trappings, props, and symbols they associated with indigenous peoples to make powerful statements about themselves that they might not be able to otherwise enunciate. Native American sports mascots build on a long tradition dating back at least to the Boston Tea Party that persists in popular culture, from the Y-Indian princesses and the Boy Scouts to the ongoing appropriation of indigenous spirituality, dubbed "white shamanism." Significantly, Native American sports mascots are meaningful only in the context of American imperialism, where EuroAmericans simultaneously sought to control and remake Native America, feeling nostalgic for that which they had destroyed. Thus, EuroAmericans banned Indian dance and traditions while also appropriating them, from the late 19th century onwards, as essential elements of their athletic events (Springwood & King, 2000). Moreover, with the rise of public culture, the production of Indianness in spectacles, exhibitions, and other sundry entertainments proliferated, offering templates for elaborations in sporting contexts (Moses, 1996). Because of comments by fans or sportswriters, historic relationships between institutions and indigenous peoples, and regional associations, Native American sports mascots crystallized as institutionalized icons, encrusted with memories, tradition, boosterism, administrative investment, financial rewards, and collective identity.

Over the past 35 years, Native American sports mascots have increasingly become subject to debate (King & Springwood, 2001; Spindel, 2000). Individuals and organizations have challenged Indian symbols in sports, forcing broader discussions and change. Some institutions, like Stanford University, have retired their mascots, while others, like the University of Utah, have opted to revise their imagery. At the same time, many school boards have encouraged schools to change them. Meanwhile, religious groups and professional organizations, including the United Methodist Church, the National Education Association, and the Modern Language Association, have denounced Indian symbols in athletics. And, in April 2001, the United States Commission on Civil Rights issued a strongly worded statement condemning such mascots.

Importantly, individuals and organizations have made a difference. The number of mascots has declined over the past three decades. By one estimate, nearly 1,500 mascots have been changed, retired, or reworked since 1970 (Harjo, 2001).

## RACE, GENDER, AND SPORTS MASCOTS

Native American sports mascots have much to teach about race, while at the same time offering valuable lessons about gender. First and foremost, they underscore that sports, like public culture more generally, remain predominantly homosocial, heteromasculine spaces centering on men and their exploits, and celebrating masculinity (or those traits and ideals defining what it means to be a man in American society) such as aggression, independence, and competitiveness (Davis, 1997; McKay, Messner, & Sabo, 2000; Messner & Sabo, 1990; Scraton & Flintoff, 2002). The prevalence of teams named the Warriors, Braves, and Red Raiders conforms to this pattern; so too does the previously discussed imagery used to represent such teams and schools.

Significantly, Native American mascots do not simply reflect and reinforce hegemonic masculinity, but they have deep entanglements with struggles over what it means to be a man. Laurel Davis (1993) has argued convincingly that the usage of such symbols emerged in response to a crisis in white masculinity during the late 19th century in association with efforts to reformulate what it meant to be in man through (misleading) ideas about the American West—namely, the myth of the Frontier. The idealized connection between masculinity and the West, often cast in terms of Indianness, remained hegemonic for much of the 20th century, until challenged as part of broader social movements, including feminism and cultural and political resurgence across Native America. Many Americans, whether consciously and unconsciously, interpret the critique of Indian imagery in athletics as an assault on American values, identities, and traditions, including hegemonic forms of masculinity. Consequently, Davis concludes that struggles over mascots are also struggles to redefine what it means to be a man and, hence, are met with fierce opposition. Clearly, as discussed in the next section, this is a central element of the conservative response to mascots (Davis, 1993; Kimmel, 1990; Messner, 1992).

Importantly, Native American sports mascots do not merely clear a space for the perpetuation and performance of hegemonic masculinity. They also offer important interpretations of femininity and gender relations as well, including the image of women; roles open to women; the kind and quality of gender relations; and inequities and limitations imposed by the symbols, performances, and narratives at the heart of sport. In fact, the use of Indian symbols has resulted in the devaluation, oppression, erasure, sexualization, and empowerment of women.

Eitzen and Zinn (1989, 1993) suggest that the naming of sports teams is often a sexist practice. They have identified six such practices: (a) taking a nongendered name of a male sports team and adding "lady" (Lady Indians); (b) double gender marking (Lady Chocs when the men are Choctaws); (c) male name with female modifier (Lady Braves); (d) paired polarity (Warriors/Squaws); (e) use of feminine suffix for women's teams; and (f) the use of physical markers emphasizing femininity. Clearly, these practices extend to teams with Native American sports mascots. Such practices suggest that women are secondary, supplemental, dependent, lesser. Men are the central actors: the norm. They literally degrade women and, importantly, demarcate the kinds of roles to which they might aspire. The use of racialized words, most notably *squaw*, can intensify the injuries associated with team names, precisely because they simultaneously inscribe ethnic stereotypes and gender norms (Eitzen & Zinn, 1989, 1993).

Native American sports mascots also erase women. The University of Illinois has a long history of Playing Indian at half-time, centered around a figure known as Chief Illiniwek, a white male student who performs in Indian regalia. Each performer has had his name recorded for posterity. During the Second World War, an Indian Princess replaced Chief Illiniwek. Dressed in a short skirt, a female student cheered the teams to victory. After the war, when Chief Illiniwek made his triumphant return, subsequent chiefs literally effaced the names of the young women who had performed in their absence, scratching individual names from the ceremonial placard. In addition to the manner in which they position women as supplemental, marginal, and invisible, Native American sports mascots allow for individuals and institutions to fashion images of women as well. For several decades, the sports teams of Arkansas State University have represented themselves at home games not through a solitary dancing Indian, but through an ensemble cast known as *the family*. A chief, a maiden, and a brave constitute the family, but this is more than a domestic unit: While bellicosity characterizes the portrayal of the male figures, sexuality (suggestive dress and flirtation) defines the maiden (Landreth, 2001).

Arkansas State University has not been alone in its usage of Native American sexuality. Many secondary schools, colleges, universities, and professional sports teams use Indian imagery to clothe their cheerleaders as well as their athletes. The Stanford University Dollies and the Washington Redskinettes are but two of many examples that might be cited. Wherever they appear, young women in short skirts and/or revealing tops, often reminiscent of indigenous regalia, sometimes with feathers or face paint, jump about, dance, and perform routines, using their objectified bodies to delight, titillate, and excite the crowd. More disturbing, perhaps for their explicitness rather than their effect, are t-shirts worn by supporters of North Dakota State University (home of the Bison), the in-state rivals of the University of North Dakota Fighting Sioux. One bears the phrase "Buck the Bison," accompanied by an image of an obese Indian copulating with a buffalo from behind. Another shows a Native American on his knees with mouth open, beneath a larger, fiercer buffalo, the caption completing the message: "Blow us. We saw, they sucked, we came." From the normalized display of the female body as an object for male pleasure to more obscene visions of bestiality, sexualization is fundamental to what Indian imagery means in sporting contexts and to what ends institutions and individual can put it.

Oddly, Native American sports mascots have not simply reproduced gender hierarchies, as they have on occasion opened spaces within which EuroAmerican women have laid claim to power and equality. When Saint Bonaventure University became a coeducational institution in the 1960s, the new women's teams needed a symbol and mascot. To complement the Brown Indian, the Brown Squaw was chosen. Many women at the time were pleased with the moniker. One commented, "We were so proud to be Squaws. . . . I'm ashamed of it now, but it was part of my identity—it made us feel equal to the men" (Quoted in Staurowsky, 1999, p. 382).

Indian imagery obviously has facilitated engagements with gender in changing social worlds (from crises in masculinity to quests for equality for women) that have accentuated, elaborated, and occasionally interrogated the contours of masculinity and femininity in American culture. Significantly, gender also accentuates how some commentators talk about Native American sports mascots, thus directing attention to the prominence of sexual rhetoric in the controversy over such symbols.

## THE (NEOCONSERVATIVE) RETURN OF THE NATIVE

In the wake of the Vietnam War, struggles for social justice and associated governmental remedies, economic realignments, a rising tide of feminism, and a renaissance in Indian Country, a neoconservative movement coalesced, intent to challenge what it saw as an assault on American values, institutions, and traditions. In the subsequent culture wars of the 1980s and 1990s sparked by this backlash, neoconservatives sought to reestablish American identity, refusing negative critiques that had linked white masculinity with exploitation and exclusion, while reframing social problems, the role of government, and the meaning of history. In the process, they successfully shifted the discourse around gender, sexuality, race, and class, rehabilitating whiteness and masculinity through a coded language that referenced issues of difference and domination without naming them explicitly, and hence "implicitly reproduce[d] and protect[ed] the practices, institutional arranges, and social relations that enable the central and normative position of white masculinity to be produced" (Hodgson, 2004; Kusz, 2001, p. 397; Savran, 1998).

Native American mascots, created during an earlier crisis around white masculinity, have proven central to neoconservative efforts to resolve a more recent crisis and defend America against multiculturalism and other assaults on traditional identity and hegemonic white masculinity. Commonly, this has meant that supporters of mascots turn attention away from questions of racism and victimization, extolling instead the virtues of convention and the positive values expressed through such imagery (Davis, 1993; King, 2003). And increasingly, they weave together reactionary understandings of race and gender to defend such team spirits and the values, identities, and relationships embodied by them. In one striking example, in 1999, the Chief Illiniwek Educational Foundation (CIEF), an organization dedicated to the retention of said mascot at the University of Illinois, planned an essay contest focused around the theme: "How does Chief Illiniwek best exemplify the spirit of the University of Illinois?" Significantly, CIEF sought not only to defend Chief Illiniwek, but also to link its defense of an imagined Indian with the struggles of embodied Native Americans insofar as it planned to donate the prize money to a Native American organization that would support its cause (King, 2002; Spindel, 2005). To get at the shape and significance of the broader discursive field anchoring and animating this failed project and more general efforts to save "their Indians," the remainder of this chapter focuses on the writings of three neoconservative commentators: Dave Shiflett, Richard Poe, and David Yeagley.

CHAPTER 3

**Dave Shiflett**

In his short essay "The Mascot Wars" in *Women's Quarterly,* Dave Shiflett offers an argument in support of the continued use of Indian symbols in athletics, noting: "As a certified relative of Pocahontas, the famed Indian Princess, I am not without a cock in this fight." Rarely does an authentic descendent of Pocahontas announce her/his ancestry when s/he participates in a public debate, but such was the extraordinary circumstance marking Shiflett's entrance into the ongoing controversy—or, as he might prefer, cockfight. In the face of opponents "on the warpath," Shiflett doubtlessly advances such a claim in his online article published by the Independent Women's Forum to legitimize his position. Believing it contributes to an argument that in the words of the headline "scalps" those protesting Native American sports mascots, Shiflett employs a discourse shared with many others who defend team spirits like the Washington Redskins and the sociohistorical conditions that make them possible, imagining that such symbols are "meant as a hat-tip to courage, bravery, skill, and power." In other words, mascots honor Native Americans, precisely as they enshrine indigenous masculinity in the form most familiar to Americans, the figure of the aggressive, proud, indomitable warrior. He asserts that critics of mascots, in turn, rely on emotion, projection, and exaggeration—in short, irrationality. Indeed, those opposed to mascots—dismissed here as activists—refuse "reasonable discussion" and opt instead to use "hysteria" as their "weapon of choice" (Shiflett, 2002).

Shiflett employs a complex and troubling sexual rhetoric to defend Native American sports mascots. He makes three arguments. First, such symbols are good because they celebrate idealized masculine qualities. Second, any reasonable—that is, heteromasculine—interpretation will conclude that mascots are appropriate, even honorable. Third, arguments against Native American sports mascots expose themselves to be weak, pathological, and feminized/feminist constructions.

**Richard Poe**

Like Shiflett, conservative columnist Richard Poe marshals gender to defend racialized symbols and spectacles. In his essay "Why Aren't Sports Teams Ever Named After Blacks?," Poe responds to critics who have suggested that the names, symbols, and practices associated with such mascots injure Native Americans. Moreover, he claims that if other ethnic groups were subject to such stereotyping and racism, such mascots would surely be understood as offensive and quickly retired. In particular, he refutes *Denver Post* columnist Reggie Rivers (2002), who had argued, "If Colorado had a high school team named the Niwot N-ggers [sic], with a big-lipped spearchucker as a mascot, we all know that African-American groups would demand the school change the name." Poe (2002) rejects Rivers's thinking, arguing instead that it has much to do with how Americans understand race and masculinity: "White Americans have not named their sports teams after blacks because white American have not viewed blacks as exemplars of the warrior spirit. Indians, on the other hand, are remembered in popular legend as brave and worthy foes on the battlefield." Hence, there is the honor of having sports teams named after them.

Poe (2002) proceeds from these troubling, implicitly racist sentiments to assert that the real problem with the warrior as mascots for "liberal commentators" is that they "promote an 'aggressive' image...[and by implication] are insulting." Individuals opposed to mascots, he continues, "have swallowed the line that aggression is evil... popular among Ivy League feminists...[but] foreign to ordinary folks, who admire a fierce and warlike spirit, on the battlefield or the football field." Quite simply, African Americans do not have teams named in their honor, he concludes, "because Americans, in general, do not envision blacks as fighters. . . . They imagine blacks in pathetic roles, as slaves and descendants of slaves" (Poe, 2002; Rivers, 2002).

In the process of elaborating his argument, Poe shifts the ground of the discussion from racism, discernible in the structures and symbols of American culture, to the convoluted intersections of race and gender. Blacks, he implies, are not aggressive or fierce or fighters (one might wonder, as an aside, about the forms of policing and warfare directed at urban Black America advocated by neoconservatives since Reagan if this is really the case); by extension, they are not fully masculine, and thus do not merit respect. Moreover, those who would speak out against mascots are not championing an antiracist project, but rather are weak agitators (that is, liberals opposed to aggression) who have been brainwashed (having "swallowed a line") by elitists (Ivy League) or, worse, feminists (that is, anti-male activists) working against accepted norms and values (held by ordinary folks) or the common good (Poe, 2002; Rivers, 2002).

In sum, Poe engenders Native American sports mascots in a number of subtle and pronounced ways. First, he feminizes Blacks and critics of mascots for not being aggressive or masculine and for not valuing aggression or masculinity. Second, he insists that the idealized traits associated with masculinity demand celebration, not critique. And third, he rehabilitates Native American sports mascots by connecting the supposed aggression and bellicosity of indigenous peoples with the honor and respect accorded to them by such mascots. In essence, as he uses masculinity to absolve the insults and stereotyping commonly detected in such mascots, he refutes charges of racism as well.

CHAPTER 3

## David Yeagley

The writings of Shiflett and Poe offer glimpses into an increasingly common defense of Native American sports mascots, but it is in the work of David Yeagley, a conservative Comanche commentator, that this discourse finds its fullest expression. Yeagley has been a prolific and vocal defender of pseudo-Indian sports symbols, authoring numerous opinion pieces for David Horowitz's online forum, *Frontpage Magazine;* delivering dozens of lectures on college campuses and to community groups; appearing on news-talk programs; and offering expert testimony in newspaper articles. Along with Shiflett, Poe, and many others, he not only believes that Native American sports mascots honor indigenous peoples, particularly men, but that attacks against them expose more fundamental ruptures within (Native) American society as well. His views on society, gender, and race provide an important foundation for more fully understanding his interpretations of mascots.

For Yeagley, Native American men are best understood and appreciated as warriors; for him, mascots reflect and respect the heritage and ideals of indigenous communities, offering rare occasions to value Native American men and educate a broader public. Sadly, according to the Comanche commentator, the native warrior has fallen and the remaining imagery rightly celebrating the warrior has come under siege by feminists and leftists. Even renowned leaders come under suspicion. He criticizes Lakota Russell Means, a Native American political leader best known for his work with the American Indian Movement, for, amongst other things, his rejection of the ideals of the warrior, particularly aggression; he claims, "I cannot follow a man who denies the warrior tradition of my Comanche people" (Yeagley, 2002b). In this time of crisis, he echoes fundamentalist groups like the Promise Keepers, asserting that many of the problems in Indian Country derive not from racism (which he reads as an "excuse") or sociohistorical structures of power and oppression, but from the weakness of men: "When men fail to be men, everyone suffers" (Yeagley, 2002d). In turn, change, betterment, or salvation is attainable only through the actions of men: "We Indian men must finally face our worst enemy: our own irresponsibility" (Yeagley, 2002d). Yeagley not only accepts that (Native) American society rises and falls on the actions and characters of men, for good and for ill, but (as discussed momentarily) he endorses a corollary position as well: Images of men, namely the warrior mascot, hold the promise of saving America in its time of need as it fights wars on terror.

Native American women, in contrast, threaten tradition, society, and men. Yeagley has grave concerns about the number of American Indian women marrying non-Indians, which he sees both as a sign of the weaknesses of Native American men and as an indication of Native American women's lack of dedication to their people. In

## ON BEING A WARRIOR: RACE, GENDER, AND AMERICAN INDIAN IMAGERY IN SPORT

fact, he questions the Indianness, integrity, and intention of Elise Meeks, member of the United States Commission on Civil Rights and key proponent of their collective statement against mascots, noting that she married a white man (something Yeagley's own mother did as well): "While she had every right to do, her choice does indicate a less than passionate commitment to the preservation of Indian heritage and bloodlines" (Yeagley, 2001a). And while miscegenation troubles Yeagley, he writes, "Some [Native American women] find other, more inventive ways of humiliating, punishing, emasculating, and otherwise rejecting Indian men" (Yeagley, 2002d). Here, specifically, he seeks to condemn the efforts of an all-female drumming group to participate in a pow-wow in Minnesota, claiming it runs counter to tradition and works to dissolve one of the few remaining sources of strength and power for Native American men. In this context, it is important to note that Yeagley understands the movement against mascots to be "the latest campaign to emasculate society's last remaining symbols of strength, the Indian warrior mascot" and that often women, sometimes referred to as "socialist women," have taken a leading role in this destructive project (Yeagley, 2002g).

Whereas women trouble Yeagley, threatening his vision of the social order, leftists alarm him, intent as they seem to be on dismantling what he sees as the virtues of modern society and his beloved warrior imagery as well. He does not view them as political rivals or adversaries but as enemies: enemies of common sense and decency, enemies of the American way, enemies of the state, enemies of the warrior tradition. Repeatedly in his writings he castigates those with whom he disagrees and those working against mascots as "Leftists" (always capitalized). Most commonly, he links those he labels as leftists with women generally, and specifically with socialist women, liberal female and minority professors, and feminists. In effect, Yeagley feminizes the perspectives of individuals concerned about Indian imagery and its effects. This rhetorical move is meant to delegitimize social criticism through gender.

Yeagley's thoughts about race are no less troubling. To date, he has spoken only about whiteness, blackness, and Indianness. His comments are revealing. Not surprisingly, he has great praise for indigenous traditions, especially the warrior heritage of the Comanche. He regularly defends conventions and the past in the face of degradation that for him tends to come from leftists and feminists. In a piece titled, "Leftists Rape Indian Barbie Doll," he interprets Patricia A. MacCormack's critique of Native American Barbie as an example of leftists trying to "humiliate Indians" (Yeagley, 2002c). Elsewhere, he asserts that Leftists are "making Indian images a crime" (Yeagley, 2002a). And he speaks of the struggle against Native American sports mascots as ethnic cleansing. While defending Indianness, he also strategically deploys his heritage to advance his position, regularly noting that he is Comanche. In essence, his ethnicity legitimizes his arguments. At the same time, he uses Indianness to delegitimize the claims of other Native Americans; to offer but one example, "My sources tell me that the Indian Students and faculty who oppose the mascot are almost all Ojibwa and Arikara. Not Sioux" (Yeagley, 2001g). While his Indianness grants him legitimacy in broader discussions, particularly when the warrior (as image and ideal) demands an advocate, other Native Americans do not have the same possibility or privilege to speak for themselves or on behalf of other indigenous peoples.

Yeagley suggests that Native Americans are worthy and honorable, yet under attack; African Americans are pitiful at best. He describes them as contemptuous, pathetic, and weak. While Yeagley finds that, "Superior beauty is in the white race . . . in the darker races, everything is always the same, dark brown and black a beastly bore" (Yeagley, 2002f). More than this, though, he fears that Native Americans have begun to walk "the *black* man's path," that is, "the familiar strategy of *black* civil rights leaders, who bait, belittle, provoke, and bully white people, then run for cover, screaming 'racist' when their white victims react" (Yeagley, 2001d). Yeagley reads social justice movements as efforts to transform once-proud people into victims; victimization, to him, in turn suggests weakness and a lack of dignity. By association, he imagines African Americans as weak, undignified victims: the antithesis of the warrior. This is something he makes clear in "It's a Warrior Thing. You Wouldn't Understand," an essay in which he chastises an African American who questioned his failure to recognize the irony of mascots and the decimation of indigenous peoples during the colonization of the North America. He claims that while the EuroAmerican "took [my land] like a warrior fair and square…[and] treated my people harshly . . . he never denied their bravery, never besmirched their memory as warriors. You did" (Yeagley, 2001e). Again, African Americans are seen as weak complainers. Their attention to race and racism strips them of dignity; their claims of harm make them weak.

While Yeagley expresses contempt for African Americans, he celebrates EuroAmericans. That is, he accords the white warrior great respect, implicitly legitimating the conquest of Native America. In large part this derives from his sense that EuroAmericans are like Native Americans; they are warriors. He admires them for defeating the Comanche and for doing what the Comanche would have done to their foes (Yeagley, 2001e). In fact, he believes that "the white man won the Indian warrior's image with his own blood" (Yeagley, 2002e). Thus, EuroAmericans won the right to use Indian imagery by besting indigenous people on the battlefield. Might makes right. Yeagley regularly expresses admiration for EuroAmericans. More implicitly, he accepts EuroAmericans as superior aesthetically (as noted above), militaristically, and perhaps even culturally, precisely because of their triumphs and conquests.

Against this background, Yeagley's take on mascots becomes clearer. Native American sports mascots, for him, are all about race and gender; Indian imagery, he asserts, honors Native Americans, particular their warrior ancestors. Speaking specifically about the mascot controversy at the University of North Dakota, he suggests that the Fighting Sioux moniker "shows an admiration for the courage and manliness of the Sioux warrior, who laid so many whites in their graves just a few generations ago " (Yeagley, 2001d). For Yeagley, those who want to change the school spirit betray and disrespect Lakota warriors as they display their disinterest in masculine virtues and the indigenous people who so boldly brought them to life. Not surprisingly, for Yeagley, "Mascots provide an opportunity to re-educate America, as well as Indians, on the virtues of being a man" (Yeagley, 2002g). In fact, the warrior is not simply an antiquated ideal, but the foundation for the future: "I'm looking to the future. It seems to me that modern American Indians have very little imagery to deal with. We have pre-reservation imagery of the warrior, the brave, the man that's courageous, the man that lives for his people, the man that will sacrifice his life for his people. This side of the war days our imagery is quite different. We have the Indian alcoholic, the Indian suicidal, [etc.]" (Yeagley, 2001c).

Nostalgically, Yeagley continually joins race with gender to sanction the warrior. In fact, during the recent debate in the Californian legislature over a bill intent to remove Native mascots from the state, he insisted the legislation was the work of socialists and man-haters, suggesting it would "fell both the Indian and the white man" simultaneously (Yeagley, 2002e). For Yeagley, like many other conservatives, Native American sports mascots honor indigenous peoples, precisely because they code Indianness in terms of hegemonic masculinity.

Yeagley's rhetoric quickened after the events of September 11, 2001. He let out a war cry, inflected with race and gender. Not content with the administration's action, he called for a stronger response: "We've heard glorified condemnations before. We're tired of hackneyed adjectives, and effeminate, poetic dramatizations. . . . We want action" (Yeagley, 2001b). He casts Bush as feminine, promoting a more bellicose reaction to the attacks. Oddly, symbols center Yeagley's call to arms; in particular, he sees the post-9/11 world as one primed for the proliferation of Native American sports mascots: "Where are the warriors? Since February [2001], I've argued that the warrior images of American Indian mascots should remain forever in American schools and universities. If ever there was a time warriors were needed, it's now! . . . Keep every mascot there is! Make more of them! Educate the country about warrior-hood. Let the people know what the great Indian warrior did for their people. If Americans really want to use Indian images on army badges, helicopters, police cars, and sports teams, then let's remind them all what Indians really can be" (Yeagley, 2001b).

In sum, David Yeagley elaborates a multilayered argument in favor of Native American sports mascots, anchored in sexual and racial rhetoric. His uses and understandings of gender allow him to simultaneously celebrate masculinity, the warrior, and mascots, and at the same time question the fidelity of women, dismiss his opponents, and call for a renewal of hegemonic masculinity, colonial imagery, and national pride in the wake of colossal tragedy. Connecting gender to race, in common with Poe and Shiflett, he uses sexual rhetoric to devalue and feminize African Americans, social justice movements, and critics of Indian imagery.

## CONCLUSIONS

Clearly, gender has everything to do with Native American sports mascots and the ongoing controversy over them. As a rhetorical toolkit, gender affords authors a set of strategies to ground their perspectives, attack their opponents, and craft a vision of the world. The entanglements of race and gender make the use of sexual rhetoric to defend Indian imagery all the more powerful.

Dave Shiflett, Richard Poe, and David Yeagley reflect a more general trend in the ongoing mascot controversy. On the one hand, they celebrate hegemonic masculinity, particularly as embodied by Native American sports mascots, protecting white male privilege as they defend antiquated, stereotypical renderings of indigenous peoples. On the other hand, they feminize others (Blacks, critics, leftists, liberals) in an effort to devalue them and dismiss their perspectives. Sexual rhetoric is so central to this discourse precisely because what is at stake in the mascot controversy is not just the names of sports teams or the imagery used at athletic events, but the meanings of gender and race in the contemporary United States as well. In fact, the defense of mascots, as the authors discussed in this chapter reveal, is in many ways a defense of masculinity, a response to a crisis regarding what it means to be a citizen, a subject, and a man.

Recognizing the prominence of sexual rhetoric in debates over Indian imagery and the sociohistorical conditions animating them should encourage scholars to rethink the mascot controversy. Gender must be placed at the center of future analyses to gain the fullest appreciation of the history and significance of such symbols and spectacles. At the same time, individuals working against controversial mascots must commit themselves to discerning the ways in which gender intersects with race. This entails understanding the gendered meanings of mascots as well as the sexual rhetoric employed by supporters, and in turn devising strategies to effectively counter them.

# REFERENCES

Banks, D. (1993). Tribal names and mascots in sports. *Journal of Sport and Social Issues, 17,* 5–8.

Bird, S. E. (Ed.). (1996). *Dressing in feathers: The construction of the Indian in American popular culture.* Boulder, CO: Westview Press.

Churchill, W. (1994). *Indians are us? Culture and genocide in native North America.* Monroe, ME: Common Courage Press.

Connolly, M. R. (2000). What's in a name? A historical look at Native American related nicknames and symbols at three U.S. universities. *Journal of Higher Education, 71,* 515–547.

Davis, L. R. (1993). Protest against the use of Native American mascots: A challenge to traditional, American identity. *Journal of Sport and Social Issues, 17,* 9–22.

Davis, L. R. (1997). *The swimsuit issue and sport: Hegemonic masculinity in Sports Illustrated.* Albany, NY: State University of New York Press.

Deloria, P. (1998). *Playing Indian.* New Haven, CT: Yale University Press.

Drinnon, R. (1980). *Facing west: The metaphysics of Indian-hating and empire building.* Minneapolis, MN: University of Minnesota Press.

Eitzen, D. S., & Zinn, M. B. (1989). The de-athleticization of women: The naming and gender marking of college sport teams. *Sociology of Sport Journal, 7,* 362–369.

Eitzen, D. S., & Zinn, M. B. (1993). The sexist naming of collegiate athletic teams and resistance to change. *Journal of Sport and Social Issues, 17,* 34–41.

Green, R. (1988). The tribe called Wannabee: Playing Indian in America and Europe. *Folklore, 99,* 30–55.

Hodgson, G. (2004). *More equal than others: America from Nixon to the new century.* Princeton, NJ: Princeton University Press.

Huhndorf, S. (1997). *Going native.* Ithaca, NY: Cornell University Press.

Kimmel, M. S. (1990). Baseball and the reconstitution of American masculinity, 1880-1920. In M. A. Messner & D. F. Sabo (Eds.), *Sport, men, and the gender order: Critical feminist perspectives* (pp. 55–65). Champaign, IL: Human Kinetics Books.

King, C. R. (2001). Uneasy Indians: Creating and contesting Native American mascots at Marquette University. In C. R. King & C. F. Springwood (Eds.), *Team spirits: The Native American mascot controversy* (pp. 281–303). Lincoln, NE: University of Nebraska Press.

King, C. R. (2002). Defensive dialogues: Native American mascots, anti-Indianism, and educational institutions. *Studies in Media & Information Literacy Education, 2,* 1–12.

King, C. R. (2003). Arguing over images: Native American mascots and race. In R. A. Lind (Ed.), *Race/gender/media: Considering diversity across audiences, content, and producers* (pp. 68-76). Suffolk, MA: Allyn & Bacon.

King, C. R. (2004). Re/Claiming Indianness: Critical perspectives on Native American mascots. *Journal of Sport and Social Issues, 28,* 1–87.

King, C. R., & Springwood, C. F. (2001a). *Beyond the cheers: Race as spectacle in college sports.* Albany, NY: State University of New York Press.

King, C. R., & Springwood, C. F. (Eds.). (2001b). *Team spirits: The Native American mascots controversy.* Lincoln, NE: University of Nebraska.

Kusz, K. (2001). 'I want to be the minority': The politics of youthful White masculinities in sport and popular culture in 1990s America. *Journal of Sport and Social Issues, 25,* 390–416.

Landreth, M. (2001). Becoming the Indians: Fashioning Arkansas State University's Indians. In C. R. King & C. F. Springwood (Eds.), *Team spirits: Essays on the history and significance of Native American mascots* (pp. 46–63). Lincoln, NE: University of Nebraska.

McKay, J., Messner, M. A., & Sabo, D. F. (Eds.). *Masculinities, gender relations, and sport*. Thousand Oaks, CA: Sage.

Mechling, J. (1980). Playing Indian and the search for authenticity in modern White America. *Prospects, 5,* 7–33.

Messner, M. A. (1992). *Power at play: Sports and the problem of masculinity*. Boston: Beacon Press.

Messner, M. A., & Sabo, D. F. (Eds.). (1990). *Sport, men, and the gender order: Critical feminist perspectives*. Champaign, IL: Human Kinetics.

Moses, L.G. (1996). *Wild West shows and the images of American Indians, 1883-1933*. Albuquerque, NM: University of New Mexico Press.

Pewewardy, C. D. (1991). Native American mascots and imagery: The struggle of unlearning Indian stereotypes. *Journal of Navaho Education, 9,* 19–23.

Poe, R. (2002, April 19). Why aren't sports teams ever named after Blacks? Retrieved from http://www.richardpoe.com/2002/04/19/why-arent-sports-teams-named-after-blacks/

Rivers, R. (2002, April 18). Odd ways to show respect. *Denver Post,* p. B7.

Rodriguez, R. (1998). Plotting the assassination of Little Red Sambo: Psychologists join war against racist campus mascots. *Black Issues in Higher Education, 15*(8), 20–24.

Savran, D. (1998). *Taking it like a man: White masculinity, masochism, and contemporary American culture*. Princeton, NJ: Princeton University Press.

Scraton, S., & Flintoff, A. (Eds.). (2002). *Gender and sport: A reader*. New York, NY: Routledge.

Shiflett, D. The mascot wars. *The Women's Quarterly*. Retrieved from http://www.unz.org/Pub/WomensQuarterly-2002q2-00016

Slowikowski, S. S. (1993). Cultural performances and sports mascots. *Journal of Sport and Social Issues, 17,* 23–33.

Spindel, C. (2000). *Dancing at halftime: Sports and the controversy over American Indian mascots*. New York, NY: New York University Press.

Springwood, C. F. (2001). Playing Indian and fighting (for) mascots: Reading the complications of Native American and Euro-American alliances. In C. R. King & C. F. Springwood (Eds.), *Team spirits: The Native American mascots controversy* (pp. 304–327). Lincoln, NE: University of Nebraska.

Springwood, C. F., & King, C. R. (2000). Race, power, and representation in contemporary American sport. In P. Kivisto & G. Rundblad (Eds.), *The color line at the dawn of the 21st century* (pp. 161–174). Thousand Oaks, CA: Pine Valley Press.

Staurowsky, E. J. (1998). An act of honor or exploitation? The Cleveland Indians' use of the Louis Francis Sockalexis story. *Sociology of Sport Journal, 15,* 299–316.

Staurowsky, E. J. (1999). American Indian imagery and the miseducation of America. *Quest, 51,* 382–392.

Yeagley, D. (2001a). Can a 'breed' lead? *FrontpageMagazine.com* Retrieved from http://www.frontpagemagazine.com/Articles/Printable.asp?ID=280

Yeagley, D. (2001b). Comanche war cry. *FrontpageMagazine.com*. Retrieved from http://www.frontpagemagazine.com/Articles/Printable.asp?ID=1692

Yeagley, D. (2001c). David Yeagley vs. Russell Means. *FrontpageMagazine.com*. Retrieved from http://www.frontpagemagazine.com/Articles/Printable.asp?ID=1271

Yeagley, D. (2001d). Don't walk the Black man's path. *FrontpageMagazine.com*. Retrieved from http://www.frontpagemagazine.com/Articles/Printable.asp?ID=1952

Yeagley, D. (2001e). It's a warrior thing. You wouldn't understand. *FrontpageMagazine.com*. Retrieved from http://www.frontpagemagazine.com/Articles/Printable.asp?ID=1950

Yeagley, D. (2001f). Make more Indian warrior images. Retrieved from http://www.geocities.com

Yeagley, D. (2001g). Who is more Indian than whom? *FrontpageMagazine.com* Retrieved from http://www.frontpagemagazine.com/Articles/Printable.asp?ID=1951

Yeagley, D. (2002a). An Indian mascot wins again. Retrieved from http://www.badeagle.com/html/indian_mascot.html

Yeagley, D. (2002b). I'm more Indian than Russell Means. *FrontpageMagazine.com*. Retrieved from http://www.frontpagemagazine.com/Articles/Printable.asp?ID=275

Yeagley, D. (2002c). Leftists rape Indian Barbie doll. *FrontpageMagazine.com* Retrieved from http://www.frontpagemagazine.com/Articles/Printable.asp?ID=270

Yeagley, D. (2002d). The failure of Indian men. *FrontpageMagazine.com*. Retrieved from http://www.frontpagemagazine.com/Articles/Printable.asp?ID=274

Yeagley, D. (2002e). The new Indian killer. Retrieved from http://www.theamericanenterprise.org/hotflash020523.htm

Yeagley, D. (2002f). What's up with dark men? *FrontpageMagazine.com* Retrieved from http://www.frontpagemagazine.com/Articles/Printable.asp?ID=273

Yeagley, D. (2002g). Where were the fighting Whites? *FrontpageMagazine.com* Retrieved from http://www.frontpagemagazine.com/Articles/Printable.asp?ID=265

## ENDNOTE

[1] This article was originally published in *The International Journal of the History of Sport*. Vol. 23, No. 2, March 2006, 315–330.

# "Other" Masculinities: Equestrianism in Uruguay

Luiz Rojo

## INTRODUCTION

Upon asking what it means to be a man from a social perspective, Miguel Vale de Almeida alerts his readers to the fact that "being a man in Pardais [where he wrote his ethnography] is not the same as being one among the Lisboan literati with whom I associate" (Almeida, 1998, p. 129). Starting with that assumption, this chapter is not a study of *the* Uruguayan man, nor even Uruguayan masculinities per se. This is because the notion of "being a man" in an equestrian context is not the same as asserting manliness in other domains, such as carnival or politics, in Montevideo. Instead, what I intend to analyze are the processes of building masculinities in a specific and unusual sociocultural situation. I do so from the perspective of a Uruguayan man, though not someone immersed in equestrianism.

In the many Olympic events, men and women normally square off exclusively against people of the same sex, and in virtually all events men achieve the best times (in swimming, track and field, cycling, and others), the farthest distances (track and

CHAPTER 4

field), or the highest scores (shooting, archery, weightlifting). However, in one of them—equestrianism—male and female riders compete in all of the events without separation of men and women competitors. Equestrianism is multifaceted: It includes jumping, dressage, and eventing (the Olympic equestrian disciplines), as well as reining and endurance riding. Uruguay is a country where the presence of women in sports—and especially in high-performance sports—is particularly low.[1] Men have a powerful and dominant place in the Uruguayan sport culture; the co-involvement of women in equestrianism therefore appears to be an exception. This chapter explores the negotiation of gender identities in equestrianism; though, as mentioned at the outset, with a particular focus on notions of manliness. The presence of females in the sport means that ideas of masculinity are conceived, at least in part, in relation to ideas of femininity.

From the end of 2006 to June 2008 I conducted comparative research into gender relations in equestrianism in Montevideo (Uruguay's capital city) and Rio de Janeiro (Brazil). There I had the opportunity to follow a number of jumping and dressage competitions and to conduct a series of interviews with current and former riders with ages varying from 12 to 70 years old. Directors, course designers, and judges were also interviewed in order to broaden the field of observations about the sport. Prior to beginning this study, my familiarity with equestrianism was limited to watching a few competitions on television, so I sought the advice of these experts to better understand the sport. Finally, based on the contacts made during my field work, I gained access to a set of books and documents put out by equine federations and confederations, which did not amount to an organized historic archive, but nonetheless provided valuable background information.

Hence, as this work uses an ethnographical methodology, it highlights the "locals' points of view." This approach distinguishes it from other research that has approached gender issues in equestrianism, such as the work of Plymoth (2012), who has looked at equestrian sports in the press, as well as Jönsson (2012), who has approached gender from a philosophical perspective. These are valuable contributions, both in methodology and objectives. My approach, I hope, adds to this body of literature by attempting to understand gender contexts and issues that arise among riders who experience equestrian sports and who play out the gender identities associated with that subculture.

Using these ethnographic and documentary approaches, including the collection and analysis of relevant data thereof, I shall present the primary social traits of the two equestrian disciplines under focus here (jumping and dressage). Next, I shall discuss how gender identities are built from emotional discourses; this follows the perspective of Abu-Lughod and Lutz (1990) who investigate gender differences and the production of multiple masculinities. Finally, through a dialogue with the Uruguayan historian José Pedro Barrán (2004), I shall attempt to establish how these equestrian-specific masculinities relate to broader movements in the construction of gender identities in Uruguayan society.

## EQUESTRIANISM

Equestrianism is divided into seven disciplines: show jumping, dressage, and eventing (the three Olympic events) as well as reining, endurance, vaulting, and driving.[2] Of these, as mentioned above, I opted to research the first two because I was interested in making comparisons, and both of these disciplines were performed in the cities I had direct access to—Montevideo and Rio de Janeiro. In both cases, too, the equestrianism competitions were conducted in private riding clubs, so the social contexts for the study were similar.

Show jumping, considered the most important discipline in equestrianism, takes place on a course with ten to fifteen obstacles of varying height and length, depending on the level of the competition. The horse and rider must leap over these obstacles without knocking them down (each knockdown results in a loss of four faults), both without "refusing a jump" (called "refusals," with a loss of four faults for the first refusal and elimination for the second), and without falling (immediate elimination) within a specified time limit (some competitions set out an ideal range of minimum and maximum time within which the course must be completed).

The varying height of obstacles is one of the main indicators of a horse and rider's advancement. Yet there are underlying aspects to gauging development. The age of both rider and animal places them in particular categories (a rider, with differently aged horses, can be in different categories). Additionally, there is a distinction between *amateurs* and *open*. From my field observations, the competitions started at a height of 0.60 meters in the *School* category, with the highest obstacles reaching 1.80 meters in international competitions (where there are obstacles of different heights, normally going from 1.40–1.45 meters to 1.75-1.80 meters, as well as a "stream"—a water obstacle—that is seen as a higher degree of difficulty owing to the possibility of the animal's negative reaction to this element).

Dressage, for its part, involves competitions held in a small arena (a rectangular area marked off with points at which the horse and rider must begin and end their course) where each competitor has to demonstrate complete control over his or her horse during a series of choreographed moves. Unlike show jumping, the scoring in dressage is extremely subjective and based on a decision by a group of judges who

CHAPTER 4

observe the quest for perfection of movements and harmony between horse and rider. Advanced performance categories require a progressive rise in the level of difficulty of a *reprise* (as the set of movements is called that is performed in each test). The plan of the rider's routine must be given to the judges in advance; the performance is therefore not spontaneous.

In historical terms, the unique characteristic of equestrianism, where men and women take part jointly in competitions, took place gradually. Indeed, women were only admitted into equestrian Olympic events for the 1952 Olympic Games (four female riders participated in that competition, with one earning a silver medal in dressage). As Pat Smythe[3] reported in her autobiography, there was still pressure for them to remain separated, and from her point of view, one of the reasons for that was a certain fear (and associated prejudice) that some of the women might demonstrate superiority over many of the men. She notes that at the end of the 1940s, the presence of two female riders among the first three places at the King George V Cup resulted "in the following year, the Princess Elizabeth Cup being introduced for ladies, and the men remained protected by their competition being exclusively for male riders" (Smythe, 1992, p. 31).

To reflect on these issues in terms of the Uruguayan context, we have to keep in mind that the participation of women in high-performance sports is very small (in the last three Olympic Games, women only accounted for an average of fifteen percent of participants in the national team), and that this has been the same for many decades. One of the effects of this low participation is the fact that even today, of the ten Olympic medals won by Uruguayan athletes, none have been won by a woman. Even at the Pan American Games, where Uruguay has a larger contingency, of the seventy-five medals won, only thirteen were won by women (to date, no Uruguayan woman has taken home the gold at these Games) (Rojo, 2007).

In equestrianism specifically, Uruguay has participated in two Olympic Games (Rome 1960 and Sydney 2000), with five men and no women, and in the Pan American Games (São Paulo, 1963—four men; Winnipeg, 1967—one man; Indianapolis, 1987—three men; Mar del Plata, 1995—six men; Winnipeg, 1999—eight men; and Rio de Janeiro, 2007—three men). Based on this data, we are able to identify how the assumption of equestrianism enabling equal participation of men and women in its competitions was not realized, even more so in the Uruguayan context. By comparison, Brazil, with the recent addition of the female rider Camila Mazza, now has had five women in its equestrian Olympic history, specifically in show jumping. In dressage, the Brazilian team for Beijing 2008 had two women and a man.

## "Other" Masculinities: Equestrianism in Uruguay

It is important to acknowledge and investigate hierarchies of status among the equestrian disciplines themselves. Throughout my research, I found that dressage contests attracted fewer riders and spectators, and they received less attention than show jumping. I discussed these differences in an impromptu conversation with a member of a horse club while we were waiting for a competition to begin. We were commenting on how few spectators and participants there were in the dressage tests, which led to his asking, in a joking tone, if I knew what dressage was called in Uruguay. When I told him no, he responded: *"la hermana puta"* ("the slutty sister"). Dressage was, in this pejorative sense, second-class as an equestrian event *because* of its association with the genteel, the sensitive, and the feminine. Notwithstanding the place of men and women in this event, it was a locus for misogynistic discourse.

## DISCOURSES REGARDING EMOTIONS & THE PRODUCTION OF EQUESTRIAN MASCULINITIES

Ever since the seminal work of Fredrik Barth (1969), the dominant definition in social sciences for the concept of *identity* has been that it is a relational construction; that is, "there is no identity per se, nor solely for its own sake. Identity always exists in relation to 'another'" (Cuche, 1999, p. 183). Applying this conception to studies of gender identity, both Bourdieu (2007) and Vale de Almeida (1998) called attention to the fact that, in a significant number of social interactions, the "other" person against whom masculine identity is built is not primarily given by females, but rather by other males. Thus, for Bourdieu, "virility has to be validated by other men, in its truth of real or potential violence, and proven by the recognition of being part of a group of 'true men.' . . . Virility, as one can see, is an eminently relational notion, constructed in light of other men, for other men, and against femininity, by a type of fear of the feminine" (2007, pp. 64–66). Similarly, Vale de Almeida, in his ethnography on active masculinities in the village of Pardais, shows us how these are built in a complex game of antagonisms and friendships that simultaneously establish a "masculine fraternity" that begins to delineate a specific male gender, with "other" males feminized by not acting within the standards hegemonically established by that gender.

In this way, it is possible to think that almost all sports, when played by each gender in separate competitions—though in accordance with the objective of this chapter, I shall focus mainly in terms of men—symbolically reproduces this struggle for the affirmation of masculinity. In this case, being faster, stronger, more agile, more resistant, or more skillful than other men involved in sport implies not only a pursuit of medals, but also an increase to masculinity that can be demonstrated both by the increase in prestige associated with the victorious, and by the joking, and in certain

## CHAPTER 4

contexts, explicitly offensive ways in which the defeated are "feminized" (*perdeu de enfiada; se fudeu; caiu de quatro*—sexualized Portuguese expressions mocking defeat and other means of deprecation that apply to sexual impotence [Scharagrodsky, 2002]).

The peculiarity of equestrianism in combining women and men in a single competition—in this sport the focus is the rider and horse[4]—modifies this relationship. It makes sense to compare the various interviews conducted on this subject with the more informal conversations that I had while attending competitions, which normally occurred over two or three full days and provided numerous opportunities (mainly during meal breaks) for more relaxed interaction among competitors and spectators (who generally tend to be relatives, friends, and people involved in the sport in some way). These moments, therefore, provided excellent chances to observe riders as they talked to their peers rather than responding directly to my questions. In addition, after an interview, we would keep on talking, and occasionally, with the recorder off, some very interesting comments about this subject would result.

Thus, in terms of whether or not a parallel dispute exists among the sexes during competitions, some of the interviews pointed to their nonexistence or irrelevance:

Q: *How is it, for you, to compete in a sport in which there is a direct dispute [competition] between men and women?*

A: [Man, soldier, show jumping competitor] For me, personally, it doesn't affect me. For me it's generic, the group is all the same, whether it's a man or a woman, it's all the same. So, if a woman wins that's okay, if a man wins, for me, it's the same thing. It doesn't bother me if a woman beats me.[5]

Q: *How is it, for you, to compete in a sport which is characterized by not having a separation between men and women?*

A: [Man, soldier, show jumping competitor] It's all the same. First, when you're in there, it's a single unit, it's you with the horse, and it's you versus yourself, trying to improve your performance, to ride without knocking down obstacles. There isn't direct confrontation, there's no contact, everyone enters the course and tries to do their best. So there's no difference whether it's a man, whether it's a woman, whether it's a horse [gelding or entire], whether it's a mare.

Q: *And do you think that everyone has this same view?*

## "Other" Masculinities: Equestrianism in Uruguay

A: [Woman, show jumping competitor] Whether or not they have this view I don't know, but on the course or in the paddock,[6] it's all the same. I've never felt that I was treated differently because I was a woman.

However, when this issue was addressed in informal conversations, the focus changed considerably, especially from women's point of view, as two passages from my field diary, transcribed below, demonstrate. The first was with a woman who had come back to compete in Uruguay after spending time abroad, which gave her a comparative look between the sport's situation and gender-related issues, and between her country and both the United States and Europe. We talked during a break shortly after her contest, while she was having lunch, mainly about the sport performances that day. I noted that, as often occurs in jumping competitions in that country, the number of women has been declining as the height of the obstacles has gone up, to the point where no more women were competing above 1.30 meters. From there, we started talking about the issue, or indeed the assumption, of men having more courage to jump over higher obstacles (which is one of the most generalized statements made by male and female riders in Uruguay). This led to a change in conversation in order to include an issue of disputes among men and women in Uruguayan equestrianism:

> A: There's a group of men here who, when they're jumping over 1.20 meters, they immediately want to move on to 1.30 meters in order not to compete with the women, because they don't like it. [Why?] They're kind of chauvinistic. One day they're competing and suddenly a woman wins and they don't like it, especially the military guys. They get jealous of the women, and you see, it's one of the few sports where men and women are together. So, if you go out there and beat a man, imagine if this happened in a test at 1.30 meters, or 1.40? How awesome . . . that'd be a real blow, especially here in Uruguay. If you're abroad, no. But here? There's still a lot of chauvinism here.

The second discussion took place at the home of a female show jumper who was around 45 years old. After an interview with her, I realized that her answers indicated many more issues that she did not seem comfortable talking about publicly with the recorder on. So, in a less formal environment, we discussed the reaction of men to the possibility of being beaten by women,

> A: These types of comments exist, in a friendly tone, joking, but a little of this always appears, of men that 'ah!' when a woman beats them . . . even though this normally appears to be a joke, joking around, but there's

## CHAPTER 4

always some comment made. [*I ask why she thinks that this happens.*] Men have been suffering lately a bit from losing the pedestal that they used to stand on in society; everything is balancing out in a different way, so they're adapting a little to the drops in status that they take as we move towards operating in a much more egalitarian manner. There is still the legacy that they, the men, [are] used to being superior to women in everything, to command, to order, to win, and to participate on their own, so a little of that sensation still exists.

As such, we can therefore identify how this sport imposes an even greater threat to traditional notions of masculinity; this longstanding sense of male dominance is challenged by losing to a woman in sport. The field work pointed to two main paths through which hegemonic masculinity seeks to react to this threat: The first is explicit in the expression "he's got balls," which is normally used for men who demonstrate a lot of courage and willingness for everything that they do (in these cases, they say *"poner los huevos"*), but occasionally for women who, acting this way, would mimic these male traits. With this, the "masculinization" of women who, in jumping contests rival the men, enables a symbolic shift propitiated by the value placed on the difference in gender (men and women who "have balls" as opposed to men and women who do not) in detriment to the difference in terms of gender. At the same time, there is a constantly restated discourse of gender-specific emotions (mainly men's courage and women's greater sensitivity) and the performance of male and female riders, both in show jumping and dressage, that suggest a balance between gender archetypes in this sport.

This way, we can say that masculinities, in the context of Uruguayan equestrianism, are produced predominantly through a dual sense of achievement with respect to courage. On the one hand, as an essential masculine virtue, it must be constantly exalted. On the other, the need is emphasized for permanent control of this courage in the pursuit of excellent athletic performance, thus avoiding procedures that might result in knocking down obstacles and consequently losing points in show jumping tests.

This was made clear through many statements by both men and women, who expressed and reinforced local representations regarding emotions in this sport:

Q: *I've observed that, even though there are many women in the lower categories, this number drops considerably in the tests with higher obstacles. In your view, why does this occur?*

## "Other" Masculinities: Equestrianism in Uruguay

A: [woman, around 25 years of age, show-jumping competitor] I think that it has something to do with men's strength. You get to a certain height where a little more strength helps make the jump, but it's much more a question of courage. Men have more of this risk-taking, of enjoying the adrenaline, and women hold back a bit more. Now, this is mainly here too, because in the United States, women are there from childhood and there's none of this fear business. They're as courageous as the men.

Q: *I've heard, in many interviews that I've done, of the importance of courage in jumping tests. What do you think is the impact of this trait on the performance of men and women?*

A: [military male rider, around 35 years old] There's no doubt that you have to have courage to jump over the higher obstacles, but you have to know how to use it too, because there's a lot of people who take risks unnecessarily. You see that for women fear makes women pay more attention when getting close to the obstacles, and so they approach them with more technique.

A: [former female ride, around 45 years old] Women are more careful because they're afraid of the obstacle. Men, since they can't demonstrate this fear, attack them with abandon, and with this, many times they make a lot more faults than they would if they had respect for the obstacles.

In a previous paper (Rojo, 2007), I undertook a comparative analysis of these considerations about courage, the focus being Montevideo and Rio de Janeiro, where the former attributed greater importance to controlling these emotions, while I found among the latter that they placed value on outward emotional expression. In the interviews above, beyond the importance given to this control—loss of which would result in decreased technique when performing a test—the unsuitability of this courage should also be emphasized. Thus, for one of the interviewees, fear and courage were consequences of differences in the socialization of children with this sport, explicitly saying that a gender-differentiated education, as occurs in Uruguay, produced different emotions. However, as expressed in the last interview above, the issue for the female rider is not the emotion itself, since men feel fear too, but the impossibility of its expression for males without running the risk of losing one's sense of virile manliness.

At the same time, the emotions that involve a relationship with the horse appear to reinforce the "feminization" of dressage and the "masculinization" of show jumping. Due to the characteristics of dressage, as presented at the outset of this section, there is an emphasis on etiquette, poise, and the harmony required between riders and the animal:

## CHAPTER 4

A: [woman, dressage] Equestrianism, whether show jumping or dressage, but in dressage it's even more important, has to be like a symphony, an orchestra. If this union doesn't exist, this rhythm between maestro and orchestra, if there is not a profound understanding, one cannot ride well. So you have to know how to conduct the animal, dialogue with it, explain what you want at each stage of the test, so that it can go on. If you, on top of the horse, want to be 'macho' and not feel what the animal is feeling, then you should go be a boxer, and not a rider.

A: [man, soldier, dressage, emphasis added] In dressage, unlike show jumping, every little detail makes a difference between victory and defeat. In jumping, you can jump poorly over an obstacle, even making the bar shake, but if it doesn't fall, then you have [lost] zero points, just like if you had jumped over it perfectly. In dressage, any unforeseen reaction of the horse penalizes you, so you need to have much more control, over yourself and the animal. It's not by chance that even the women who are better at dressage are a little bit older than those who are show jumpers, because in some way they've learned to control their emotions more, but even so, men are steadier.

This valuation of the capacity to control emotions, as well as its perception as being common sense with masculinity, has been widely discussed by Lutz (1990). In the considerations above, we can identify how this association is not made with an abstract "male," but can be thought of as a producer of specific genders, including in its relationship with the age issue. Thus, even more emphatically than in jumping tests, in dressage the "macho"—which in this case appears as that man who "exaggerates" his performance of masculinity—seems to be devalued in comparison to a man who is "steadier." This differentiates two distinctly different norms of masculinity within the male gender: machismo and daring, versus gentility and composure. The sportive tasks in equestrianism are so different, notwithstanding them both being about horse and rider. The associated assumptions about masculinity reflect these structural and performative differences. Intriguingly, though, a rider can be adroit at *both* jumping and dressage, thus underscoring the masks of manliness that are worn in specific contexts.

These different identities of male gender not only appear in the interviews I conducted, they can also be found in many nonverbal expressions during long-term ethnographic field work (even when, due to the specific characteristics of this field, this

## "Other" Masculinities: Equestrianism in Uruguay

is done fundamentally through *nonparticipant observation*). According to Malinowski, this is a "series of very important phenomena that cannot possibly be recorded through questionnaires or statistical documents, but have to be observed in their full actuality" (1986, p. 42), something he has called the "imponderability of real life."

Key among these phenomena, both of which were unfamiliar to me, were two elements: the use of the riding crop during contests, and the ways in which riders "thanked" their horses after competing with them. Thus, as I familiarized myself with the rules and practice of this sport, I was able to expand and train my view to observe aspects that, at first, went unnoticed by me. If, during the first trips to the field, I was more concerned about jotting down the number of men and women in the tests with different heights of obstacles—which led me to realize that as these heights increased, the number of women contestants fell off sharply—then the final period of my eighteen months of observation found me much more attentive to the little gestures in which I was able to identify significant variations, not just among men and women, but among different masculinities and femininities.

Even though it is not normally mandatory (save for a few specific competitions), the riding crop is considered an integral part of the accessories that one must have when starting the course, whether for jumping or for dressage. Specifically in the case of show jumping, its function, according to some of the trainers with whom I spoke, is to "correct" the animal after it makes a mistake (normally after a "refusal") or, if possible, to correct its step before a fault is committed (mainly in the case of transition for obstacles with water, where some horses have greater difficulty). However, many times I found that this accessory, when in the hand of certain men, was transformed into a punitive tool. In this sense, it was employed in the manner more closely associated with a type of absolute power associated with a colonial and patriarchal past (such as in the treatment of slaves or children), in which "correction" acquires its double meaning more explicitly.[7] Though I do not have the technical background for differentiating when a fault might be attributed to a rider's poor performance or to a mistake made by the horse (there are people who I know who attribute all faults to mistakes made by the rider, though most admit that the horse is also able to contribute occasionally to them), I did start to be able to differentiate between different types of "correction." Thus, all of the women I was able to observe, as well as a few men, either did not use a crop (some did not even enter the course, when not explicitly required by the test's regulations, with this accessory) or they gave one or two quick and dry hits that, according to them, would not hurt the horse, but only "alerted" it to some greater difficulty or "reprimanded" it after a refusal to jump over a certain obstacle. On the other hand, a significant number of men, mainly after a

## CHAPTER 4

refusal, used the crop repeatedly, such that they even occasionally caused comments of disapproval among spectators, such as one from a woman, shortly after what she interpreted as a "discharge of rage" by the rider due to his mistake: "Look at that! He must feel like an all-powerful 'macho' man!" Upon hearing this exclamation, I could not help but walk over to her and tell her of my research in order to stimulate a conversation about this issue, which really seemed to please her because she was able to express her complete disapproval (she seemed very irritated by the way in which the horse had been "punished," in her own words):

> A: Having to hit a horse for it to jump over an obstacle isn't pleasing for it or for me! You don't have to hit it.
>
> Q: *So why do some people do it, do you think?*
>
> A: Ah! At times, there are men who look at a course and want to feel as if they dominate the horse, and there are also many who look at them and see them as "men" and say, "That's right, that's a real man." Like the butchers at a slaughterhouse, the men who do the cutting see themselves as the most valiant. It may be that some men have this as an example, but anyone who uses a whip like that, at times hitting the horse's most sensitive parts, I'd like to get that guy and grab him by his most sensitive parts and put a tourniquet on him so that he can see what it feels like.

I also talked to men about this issue of using a riding crop; many associated it with one's age. Thus, these *"arroubos"* ("demonstrations," as one of them called it) of masculinity were more likely among the young, who through immaturity do not realize that, as one interviewee put it, this often "irritates the animal unnecessarily; a rider has to show control over the animal, not oppress it." With these statements, we return once again to the possibility of realizing how, in this context, the construction of gender identities occurs in lockstep with the age issue.[8] In this process, returning to discussions already presented by Lutz, the capacity to control emotions, a characteristic fundamentally associated with "adult men," is highlighted in opposition both to females and the "young."

The second of these "expressive gestures" I was able to observe frequently is the "thanks" or "appreciation" offered to the horse after a test, either in jumping or dressage. After some time spent video-recording[9] how they were done, I was able to group them into three main categories: "little taps," "caresses," and "kisses." Even though the same person might, depending on their performance in the competition, change the type of "thanks" with respect to the horse, the material I accumulated and analyzed allowed me to establish a few of the most relevant trends, which once again reinforced the importance of age in relation to gender differences and expressions of masculinity.

Thus, the most common "thanks" were given with two light taps on the side of the horse, near its head. It is rare for male or female riders, after a contest, not to make at least this type of gesture, even when the performance was completed with a result considered very bad or that led to disqualification (due to a fall or two refusals). A greater number of taps generally resulted from a contest in which the rider liked its performance better or where, for some reason, he identified that the horse had contributed to overcoming a trickier obstacle (some animals, based on what I heard while accompanying reconnaissance laps[10] with competitors and their coaches, apparently had a harder time with certain types of obstacle). Occasionally, these little taps were replaced by (or given in addition to) "caresses," in which the rider gently caresses the animal, sliding his or her hand on its side or mane. This type of affection is much more common among women than men, and at least during the entire field work that I did in Montevideo, it never occurred among male riders under the age of twenty. Finally, only female riders were caught kissing their animals after a competition. If for no other reason than it was a much less frequent gesture, normally associated with a performance well beyond expectations, I was unable to identify if there were any differences in terms of age among the women who did so.

These observations thus seem to reinforce the analyses conducted by Lutz in terms of the greater possibility of women's emotional expression. According to the hegemonic emotional considerations of gender "common sense" in the West, studied by this author, women "by nature" supposedly have a greater capacity to establish and maintain relationships and to use their emotions for this purpose. In his interpretation, which the results of my research corroborate, this association between femininity/emotion/relationship reinforces the perspective of positioning women in a private space, with an emphasis on home and family, rather than being a pivotal part of the public sphere.

My observations can also enable a fruitful dialogue with the work of Birke and Brandt (2009). These authors bring to the equestrian social research agenda several important topics, such as the relationship between human and animals, particularly horses; and they feature in these relationships gender and age issues, as they consider those essential for the understanding of the mutual corporeality that arises from human/horse relationships.

In the words of many Uruguayan female riders with whom I interacted, this consideration acquires a metaphorical expression at times, associating the horse with a child, and at others it serves as one of the central elements for explaining the reasons why many women typically abandon equestrianism at a much younger age than men:

> A: [Female show jumper]: It's often true, in this thing of getting too involved with horses, that we end up spoiling them too much, and when a bit more has to be demanded of them, the women aren't able, out of pity, to force the horse beyond what we imagine that they're capable of doing. We end up treating them like children, from whom we accept everything, while the men are able to get much more from them.

> A: [Former female show jumper, who accompanied the tests and collaborated in the organization of some of them; italicized text indicates emphasis given by the interviewee]: I used to jump really well, I even jumped 1.30 meters, but for me equestrianism was always just a sport, something that I liked to do, but not my life. So, when I married and had my children, I stopped. Now I enjoy coming here to watch, seeing the younger girls, but in Uruguay, women . . . *we have other priorities*.

## CONCLUSION

In a paper on the possibilities of anthropology in urban settings, Magnani (1996) points to the danger of the "'village temptation,' which means looking at the object under study as a closed and self-centered unit . . . Delineating a research object or subject in the city does not mean cutting the ties that it has with other dimensions of the urban dynamic, in particular, and modernity in general" (p. 47). In this sense, though it was clear that the masculinities observed in the equestrian context of Montevideo do not represent all of the possible male gender identities of Uruguay, I feel that the delineation proposed in this paper allows one to establish a few ties with the issue of gender relations in the country, as well as to establish comparisons, which is one of the objectives of the broader research of which this text is a part, with the construction of gender identities in the equestrianism practiced in Rio de Janeiro.

To further detail these ties, there is nothing more eloquent than the last quote presented above. A woman's placement of value on marriage and maternity, as expressed by her statement that "in Uruguay . . . we have other priorities," seems to go well beyond what occurs in the microcosm of equestrian sports. To interpret this statement more densely, though, it is fundamental that we recall that this sport is not only practiced, but also highly valued as a hobby of the dominant social and economic sectors. The costs involved in learning how to ride horses, especially when equestrianism is no longer a pastime but becomes a competitive sport, make the involvement of people from lower or even middle classes of the population practically infeasible.[11]

As such, the position expressed in the final quote by the former female rider reinforces the traits stressed by Barrán (2004) regarding the process of the "civilization of customs" that supposedly occurred in Uruguay between the end of the 19th and start of the 20th centuries. Following a perspective very close to that developed by Elias (1989) regarding the Western civilizing process, Barrán discusses how certain sectors of the Uruguayan elite have sought to modify what has been called "barbarian customs," not only among lower classes, but in the heart of the elite as well, "civilizing" the various spheres of society (i.e., politics, education, Carnival, games, parties, attitudes towards death). In this process, the "control of impulses" and the decline of public space allocated for women have been mutually reinforcing. Thus, for instance, until the period of 1870-1880, both in Carnival and in games, there was practically no distinction between spectators and the spectacle, with men and women in the streets actively participating in both. Starting at that time one is able to note a progressive differentiation in these and other spheres of society. In the first place, women were increasingly relegated to a passive role of watching, while men occupied both realms (participating in spectacles, especially young men, but also spectators, given that the new "sobriety" required of adult male behavior did not match up with certain practices that society sought to define as "civilized"). In the second place, the replacement of unchecked games, without predefined rules and full of laughter and enjoyment, with regulated sports in which passions must be contained to achieve a result that becomes more important than the enjoyment of the game itself, contributes to a sense of a "discourse about emotions" in Uruguayan society, which has deeply shaped gender identities, social classes, and age groups.

It is notable that these spaces traditionally associated not only with the male world, but also with the location of "containment of oneself," offer greater resistance to this repositioning of the gender issue. In this way, though the data presented here do not allow one to deduce that the hegemonic pattern of masculinity developed in the context of equestrianism in Montevideo *represents* Uruguayan masculinity, I believe that it is possible to identify that it acts strongly in the sense of maintaining and reinforcing certain power relations between the genders in this society. As this chapter set out to explain, this action occurs mainly through a naturalization of the association between certain discourses regarding emotions and gender identities. It is further aided by its expression in the only sport in which there is no formal separation between men and women. This naturalization of gender differences—which are promoted in these realms—does not seem to be easily questioned without a deeper critique of both the academic and common-sense discourses on emotions.

# REFERENCES

Abu-Lughod, L., & Lutz, C. (1990). Introduction: Emotion, discourse, and the politics of everyday life. In L. Abu-Lughod & C. Lutz (Eds.), *Language and the politics of emotion* (pp. 1–23). Cambridge, England: Cambridge University Press.

Barrán, J. P. (2004). *História de la sensibilidad en Uruguay*. Montevideo, Uruguay: Ediciones de la Banda Oriental.

Barth, F. (1995). Les groupes ethniques et leurs frontières. In: P. Poutignat & J. Streiff-Fenart (Eds.), *Théories de l'ethnicité* (pp. 203–249). Paris, France: Le sociologue.

Birke, L. & Brandt, K. (2009). Mutual corporeality: Gender and human/horse relationships. *Women's Studies International Forum, 32*, 189–197.

Bourdieu, P. (2007). *A dominação masculina*. Rio de Janeiro, Brazil: Bertrand Brazil.

Cuche, D. (1999). *A noção de cultura nas Ciências Sociais*. Bauru, Brazil: EdUSC.

Elias, N. (1989). *El proceso de la civilización*. México DF: Fondo de Cultura Económica.

Jönsson, K. (2012). Humans, horses, and hybrids: On rights, welfare, and masculinity in equestrian sports. *Scandinavian Sport Studies Forum, 3*, 49–69.

Lutz, C. (1990). Engendered emotions: Gender, power, and the rhetoric of emotional control in American discourse. In C. Lutz & L. Abu-Lughod (Eds.), *Language and the politics of emotion* (pp. 151–170). Cambridge, England: Cambridge University Press.

Magnani, J. G. (1996). *Na metrópole: Textos de antropologia urbana*. São Paulo, Brazil: Editora da Universidade de São Paulo, FAPESP.

Malinowski, B. (1986). Introdução: O assunto, o método e o objetivo desta investigação. In: E. Durham (Org.), *Bronislaw Malinowski* (pp. 2–15). São Paulo, Brazil: Ática.

Plymoth, B. (2012): Gender in equestrian sports: an issue of difference and equality. *Sport in Society: Cultures, Commerce, Media, Politics, 15*, 335–348.

Rojo, L. F. (2007). Relações de gênero no hipismo: Um olhar comparativo entre Rio de Janeiro e Montevideo. In M. C. Coelho & C. M. Rezende (Eds.), *Antropología social y cultural en Uruguay* (pp. 163–172). Montevideo, Brazil: Editorial Nordan.

Scharagrodsky, P. A. (2002). Los grafittis y los cantos futboleros platenses: O acerca del proceso de configuracion de diversas masculinidades. *Brazilian Journal of Sports Science, 24*, 179–197.

Smythe, P. (1992). *Leaping life's fences: An autobiography*. London, England: The Sportsman's Press.

Vale de Almeida, M. (1998). *Senhores de si: Uma interpretação antropológica da masculinidade*. Lisbon, Portugal: Fim de Século.

Websites visited:
Uruguayan Olympic Committee: www.cou.org.uy
Uruguayan Federation of Equestrian Sports: www.fude.com.uy

## ENDNOTES

1. In order to compare data on Uruguayan athlete participation in the Pan American and Olympic games, see Rojo (2007).
2. There are also equestrian events for athletes with disabilities who compete, for example, at the Paralympics. They participate in modified forms of equestrianism.
3. Pat Smythe was the first female rider to win an Olympic medal in show jumping (the bronze for teams, in the 1956 Olympic Games).
4. The observations made did not reveal any significant correlation between the rider's sex (male/female) and the animal's sex (entire or gelding/mare).
5. I am responsible for all translations of interviews and conversations.
6. Paddock is where the horse and rider wait to be called to the course. During a competition there is always a horse and rider competing, a horse and rider in the paddock–where the last contact can be made with the trainer or other assistants–and lots of others warming up on an auxiliary course.
7. "Correction" can be used both simply as the act or effect of correcting something that is not right and be associated, as in "correctional facility," with the punitive measures used for this purpose.
8. Equestrianism not only brings men and women together in the same competitions, it is also considered one of the sports with the broadest range of ages. This is true even in the most important competitions, such as the Olympic Games. In Beijing 2008, for instance, this range went from the 16-year-old Brazilian rider Luiza Almeida, to the 67-year-old Japanese rider Hiroshi Hoketsu.
9. By using little videos taken on a digital camera, I was able to record the different types of "thanks" given, resulting in better quality material for the sake of comparison.
10. Thirty minutes before a test begins, the courses are open for the competitors to run around on foot, in general accompanied by their trainers, in order to become familiar with the location of each obstacle in the sequence, and the distances between them, which varies from test to test. At the times I was able to accompany these inspections, I found that advice is given indicating the types of tests for horses that jump better over higher obstacles, or wider ones, and that have more or less trouble with obstacles that include water.
11. It should be pointed out that certain exceptions may occur. Since horses need constant exercise to stay in shape, it is common that part of these exercises are performed by paid employees. Occasionally, one of these employees may stand out for their ability, which enables this person to have access to the more restricted space of the competitive sphere, in general backed by "sponsors" who finance the expenses involved and achieve a financial return with the sale of the animals that stand out due to the performance of the person who has been "adopted."

# Football, Cinema, and New Sensibilities in the Masculine Territory: An Analysis of Asa Branca, a Brazilian Dream (1981) and New Wave (1983)

Jorge Knijnik and Victor Andrade de Melo

## INTRODUCTION

Football (soccer) has featured in well-known films led by renowned directors. Perhaps the best known examples are *Die Angst des Tormanns beim Elfmeter* (The Goalkeeper's Fear of the Penalty Kick), directed by Wim Wenders, released in 1971, and *Escape to Victory*, directed by John Huston, released in 1981. These films exceeded the borders of basic sport cinematography, for social issues were confronted in their story lines. In a similar vein, we argue that the art of cinema and the art of football can coalesce in both aesthetics and narrative. They can help us to think about certain representations of culture and society in context, and thus to analyse the spirit of a time.[1] The aim of this chapter is to capture that spirit within a particular moment in Brazilian society through the analysis of two films that have football as an essential part of their plot.

The films are *Asa Branca: Um Sonho Brasileiro* (Asa Branca: A Brazilian Dream, 1981), directed by Djalma Limongi Batista, and *Onda Nova* (New Wave, 1983), directed by José Antonio Garcia and Ícaro Martins. These films deserve attention because they deal with issues connected to sexuality and gender, bringing sport into a territory where it had never been before—at least not in such an explicit way. The films shocked (and still shock) Brazilian society, as they were bringing to the cultural agenda issues such as the role of women and female/male homosexuality in a field (both sport and its culture) that has always been seen as a male territory.

What are the ideas of gender worked into these productions? Why were those themes incorporated into these films, with football the key vehicle for discussion? What does it tell us about the Brazilian society and ideas of manliness and masculinity at that time?

## FOOTBALL AND GENDER: THE BRAZILIAN CONTEXT

In Brazil, football is seen as something much bigger than a sport phenomenon; it is a fundamental part of the nation's socio-cultural heritage. Brazilians see themselves as belonging literally to the "country of football," and the Brazilian team represents the "nation in football boots." The journalist Roberto Pompeu de Toledo, writing about football metaphors used in public speeches by Brazilian national authorities and celebrities, states,

> If it was not for football, how could we understand each other? If it were not for the football popular sayings, the famous sentences, the metaphors it inspires, we would find ourselves, when communicating with each other, more helpless than a goalie in a penalty kick. (2002, p. 134)

However, in Brazilian society, football has always been a "male business." Whether on playing fields or in the very social representations of football, it has always been configured as male territory. Knijnik (2003) alerts us to the spatial dimensions of this male territory. In big housing conglomerates and even in the *favelas* (slums):

> Often built on invaded land, the houses overlap each other but no one dares to invade that rectangular terrain that would be good for building dozens of small houses, but that is, in fact, used by 22 people to practice their "holy" football. (p. 20)

Knijnik emphasises that those "22 people" are men. Women scarcely have the chance of invading this terrain that, both symbolically and in practice, is male space. Indeed, many Brazilians still see football as too physically arduous for women and thus inappropriate in respect of women's "frail" biology. Votre (1996) notes that "according to the social beliefs, football is a sport that demands virile endurance and strong muscles, which without a doubt show a stereotype attributed to the football player" (p. 46). These social perceptions are more important than the physiological reality that women are perfectly capable of playing football.

That is why both *Asa Branca* and *New Wave* are important symbolic turning points in terms of cultural production in Brazil. These films represent signs of change to gender identities that could be seen in sport during the later decades of the 20th century. Other studies, such as Goellner (2005) and Knijnik (2012) have already discussed modifications in the idea of femininity and their repercussions in sport, particularly football, in this period. It is now timely to focus on changes to masculinity in society and implications for football; *Asa Branca* and *New Wave* provide cinematic windows through which to do this.

## TRANSITIONS IN BRAZILIAN MASCULINITIES IN THE 1980S

Brazil, at the end of the 1970s and beginning of the 1980s, was going through a period of political and cultural effervescence. The country was looking for new paths. In 1979, the amnesty law made possible the return of many who had fled from the bloody dictatorship imposed by the military in 1964.[2] Therefore, traditional political leaders from the old left of politics, like Leonel Brizola[3] and Miguel Arraes,[4] started to reappear on the national scene, with a left-wing discourse that appealed to those who espoused democratic rule and liberalism. But when it came to behaviors and moral values, this alternative mode of leadership demonstrated male dominance and a sexist discourse that was not dissimilar to that of the conservatives or fascists they opposed.

At the same time, there was something new in the air: Strike movements were taking place in the country, and this is where many important national political leaders started, including Luiz Inácio Lula da Silva, who would later become elected president in 2002 and govern Brazil until 2010. The counterpoint to what the generals represented—the authoritarian, conservative, violent, and anti-democratic behavior—came neither from traditional political leaders nor from the strike leaders. Those, each in their own way, had produced what Connell (2005) calls hegemonic masculinities. Their dress and gestures displayed aggressive manliness, with body postures and discourses that were close to the generals' rigidity, arrogance, and supreme sense of self. There was no room for contestation or dialogue about alternative forms of masculinity within these hegemonic movements, behaviors, and discourses.

Resistance to this hegemonic way of articulating masculinity came from a former revolutionary who had been exiled and had returned with the amnesty: Fernando Gabeira.[5] He came back to Brazil with a new political agenda and, as part of this crusade, presented an alternative view of the male body. The striking images of him wearing crocheted thongs at beaches in Rio de Janeiro in the early 1980s still endure in the social imagination, being an iconoclastic and provocative symbol of new possibilities for "being a man" and aesthetically displaying the masculine body. Gabeira's images in newspapers and on television were very popular at that time, as they were showing to a wider Brazilian audience new ways to demonstrate and perform what Anderson (2009) has since called "inclusive masculinity."

The consequences to the gender order that such revolutionary corporeal practices represented were huge. By performing a new embodied masculinity (Coad, 2008) and subverting the notion of hegemonic masculinity, the body of the former guerrilla (refashioned for nonviolent resistance) acquired notoriety and profile in a counter-hegemonic social process (Connell, 2005).

In the arts, an atmosphere of change was also evident. Caetano Veloso[6] and Gilberto Gil,[7] musicians from the state of Bahia and creators of Tropicalismo,[8] were acknowledged as politically reformist Brazilian pop music icons. Rita Lee,[9] considered the national voice of rock, brought irreverence, irony and political criticism to national radio. On the "disco" tracks, the Frenéticas[10] appeared, challenging taboos about women and sexuality with provocative lyrics such as: "I will drive you crazy, real crazy, inside of me."[11]

Just as importantly, new types of male rock bands brought novelty to traditional practices of masculinity in popular music. For example, *Titãs* were a group of eight boys who refused to have a leader, so each member had a central moment on stage, showing that it was possible to live around alternative, nonhierarchical masculinities (Anderson, 2009; Connell, 2005) without the necessity of having members circle around a dominant male.

Other rock bands, like *Barão Vermelho* and *Legião Urbana,* had figures (the lead singers and songwriters Cazuza[12] and Renato Russo,[13] respectively) who portrayed heterodox sexual behaviors (they liked "boys and girls" as one of Russo's songs said), escaping from the compulsory heterosexuality that the traditional gender order imposed and thereby presenting to the country, especially to the urban youth, new ways of being a man (Anderson, 2005; Louro, 2000). Those models of manliness were certainly very different from those imposed by the generation of American foreign films in the cinemas in that period, where "Rambos" and "Terminators" displayed their muscles and their hypermasculine violence.

During this era, the Brazilian sport scene was undergoing huge transformations. Football, the national passion, was enduring a crisis. It had experienced two defeats in World Cups (in 1974 in Germany and in 1978 in Argentina), and after those another epic tragedy would follow: the incredible defeat to Italy in the "battle of Sarriá" in the 1982 World Cup (Spain). According to the Brazilian national team's coach, Telê Santana, this defeat spelled the end of the "football-art era." The coach was bemoaning the death of the true Brazilian style; the defeat in Spain was, to him, the death of poetry in the nation's football, which was played with flair and imagination unlike the "mechanical" European style, which was more like inelegant prose (Maranhao & Knijnik, 2011). So people were asking, what would happen now to Brazilian football?

Even with those defeats, a new configuration would emerge within Brazilian football. The Corinthians[14] Democracy, an innovative political movement inside the club, was led by one of the best Brazilian footballers from the 1982 national squad, "Doctor" Sócrates,[15] alongside the well-known players Casagrande and Wladimir. They questioned, among other things, the practice of isolating the players in a hotel before official matches (known as the "concentrations"). These concentrations were, and still are, meant to control the players, to force them to rest and avoid them "hanging around" with girls and having sex and parties before matches. It was a movement that certainly left a legacy in the gender order in the country, for it questioned the authority of coaches and managers in controlling the athletes' bodies. It is one of the corporeal practices well established by hegemonic masculinity, which intended to maintain control over a male body assumed to be heterosexual, and in this logic, an insatiable sexual predator.[16]

In football there was another great novelty. In 1979, during the same year that the amnesty law[17] was signed, women achieved a victory with legislation allowing their participation in previously gender-proscribed sport practices. Act 3.199 from April 14, 1941,[18] which prohibited women from playing football and several other sports, was overturned. This reform opened a legal space for women so that they could finally enter football fields. The gender order in sport was starting to feel the winds of change (Knijnik, 2011).

In the 1980s, a new sporting wave swept the country. Male volleyball attracted big crowds, notable especially for the presence of young girls. The attraction was the so-called "Silver Generation" that achieved second place at the 1984 Olympics. Xandó, Renan, Bernard, and others were feted as Olympic celebrities, but were also admired by young women for their bodily attractiveness. Their profile was a sign of the success that would follow. Thousands of young men started attending the volleyball court and beaches, playing a sport that was historically labeled a "game for queers." Those sport idols, with their legion of teenage fans, contributed to the reconfiguration of masculinities, displaying new uses for the male body and new ways of appearing and participating in Brazilian sport (Oliveira and Costa, 2010).

Elsewhere, changes were evident in the new holistic and gymnastic practices that were becoming more common at the time in Brazil.[19] The middle class started to join in practices like aerobic gymnastics, weightlifting, or even practicing alternative body practices, such as tai chi chuan and yoga. This movement toward novel body practices was increasingly being incorporated into the habits of the middle class, creating new forms of body awareness and embodied performance, and helping to reshape gender identities.

Masculinity is incorporated and observable in its actors (Coad, 2008; Connell, 2005), being experienced in the body and in its practices. These practices directly influence the construction of new models, which are alternative or even marginalized in relation to the hegemonic standard. It is in this picture of profound transformation that *New Wave* and *Asa Branca—A Brazilian Dream* were produced: political, cultural and socioeconomic changes involving many layers of the Brazilian population, influencing and also being influenced by new gender configurations.

## ASA BRANCA[20] (1981)

*Asa Branca* focuses on Antônio dos Reis, a poor child in an average-income, devout Catholic family in Mariana do Sul, a countryside city in the state of São Paulo. The period, the 1950s and 1960s, can be discerned by the picture of Juscelino Kubitschek[21] on the wall of the local church. Antonio's mother dresses him in an angel outfit (a costume that to her, and according to the nuns' reprimand, would be used during Carnaval). This costume will generate the nickname that follows him for the rest of his life: *Asa Branca* (White Wing).

Football is part of this family. At the breakfast table, Asa's older brother complains that his younger sibling does not study, does not work, and takes his radio, not letting others listen to the football match. The boys' father, reading the newspaper, starts discussing the changes in the oldest son's way of playing football. Their sister tries to give her opinion but is severely reprimanded by their father: Football is not for women; it is a man's game! We soon find out that Asa (as he is usually called) wants to be a footballer. His mother is worried about this confidence in his future, but Asa calms her down. He assures her that he will be Brazil's greatest player. He dreams of the improbable: leaving the humble country life behind, being a famous champion, having a sports car and girls—or even better, one girl, the most beautiful girl in the city. Asa also has a good mate, Poca, a friend from childhood, who is a partner in his dream—a dream which, it must be said, is the same for many Brazilian boys: becoming a famous and rich footballer.

**Football, Cinema, and New Sensibilities in the Masculine Territory**

This is the initial scenery of *Asa Branca: A Brazilian Dream* (1981), the full-length movie debut of Djalma Limongi Batista, a filmmaker graduate of the University of São Paulo, Brazil's biggest university. Curiously, Batista had already made another debut in the football theme, which can be seen in his short-length debut, *Um clássico, dois em casa, nenhum jogo fora* (a derby, two at home and none away—1968), where football is used as a metaphor to represent male bonds in Brazil. The match itself is only in the background. The film focuses on a homosexual relationship between two male characters, and causes reflection for both about their situation in a country under severe censorship and authoritarian control. Batista's works are varied but generally considered both rebellious and transgressive. Some people regard him as one of the main gay film directors in Brazil, a title he rejects not out of shame, but because he is not fond of labels or formulas. With Batista it is curious and interesting to see football as a central theme in one of his films. Not surprisingly, homosexuality has major importance in *Asa Branca's* plot; it is, as we will see, a turning point in the drama.

Asa Branca starts training, and his talent stands out in a small local team, the *Comercial*. However, he is soon transferred to *Sport Club*, the team of a rich businessman in the region. Thus from the beginning, he will have to deal with commercial trickery in the world of football: the power of the money that paid his contract and bought his rights as a player, preventing him from joining another club. The film shows that Asa is very confused and sad, as he wanted to stay at his original club (the *Comercial*), with the blessings of his first coach who was like a father to him. At this stage, Asa is rebellious and initiates several undisciplined acts. However, the *Sport Club's* owner does not want to know about Asa's feelings or complaints; he wants his star player on the field. That said, the businessman is a pragmatist and appreciates that a polemical, undisciplined, *and* brilliant athlete attracts audiences and generates income. The journey of the compromised hero thus begins.

Asa already shows signs of a strong personality. He hits the new coach when reprimanded for drinking, smoking, and hanging around with women (even though it was, in fact, an exaggerated accusation at the time). Asa, who was ridiculed by teammates when he first got to *Sport*, is now the leader and the star of the team, and his controversial off-field persona gives the club added profile. The small town boy is now a celebrity in his hometown, admired and loved by everyone, even by Cleise, "Miss Mariana do Sul," the daughter of the president of *Sport*, a beautiful lady that used to constantly say she hated footballers. However, Cleise, like everybody else, could not resist the charm of the football star. The plot therefore becomes romantic.

New situations will arrive and define a turn in the path of the character. Poca, Asa's best friend and partner in his boyhood daydreaming, gives up his career to get married and find a job. Asa is transferred to a big football team called *Bandeirantes*, which is situated in São Paulo, Brazil's biggest city. In the following four-year period, he learns again how to be a man. When Asa gets to the big city, he is taken to a group room in an old hotel, something which was very different from his humble but cosy home. He does not know how to get around the city and, as he is still a "nobody," no one helps him in this arduous mission of wandering through the paths of the "concrete jungle." Even when he is recognized by reporters who cover the daily news in *Bandeirantes*, he runs away from the press just as the coach advised him to. He is a boy from the country; he does not know how to deal with so many new things at once.

The atmosphere in the club is just as daunting. The training, more professional and intense, scares him. He has trouble relating to his new teammates. During his first match for *Bandeirantes*, Asa experiences something completely new: being seated on the bench instead of starting on the field. When he gets the chance to play, he can't perform well due to the aggression and competitiveness. He then loses his temper and starts a fight and is hit in the face in retaliation. He leaves the field humiliated and bleeding. The coach, who nonetheless believes he will be a top player, faces the managers and keeps him on the team, but in a lower rank. His first match had been a complete disaster.

In his journey as the filmic hero, Asa will still have to prove himself worthy. Different ways of configuring his masculinity are presented to him, and he slowly reconfigures his gender identity, or at least incorporates the one most suitable to his new context. At first the confusion in his head and in his life is overwhelming. Asa receives a very affectionate letter from his mother. In spite of the comfort it gives him, it is not enough to provide emotional balance. Fragile, he gives into temptations. Multiple women and a seedy nightlife deviate the heroic character from his path of glory and lead him to his downfall. Asa starts arriving late for training at the club, stops practicing for weeks, becomes a regular in the nightclubs, and has prostitutes as his usual companions. Big dreams are susceptible to potentially big risks. The film shows that it is necessary to learn how to resist and how to overcome big problems and temptations. Lost and alone, Asa is caught between the wish of returning to Mariana do Sul, playing for *Comercial* with his old friend Poca as his partner, or aspiring to wear the glorious golden jersey of the Brazilian team, with the hope of having a great footballer, Garrincha,[22] as a teammate.

Chance will present him with the opportunity to overcome his problems, but only so long as the hero shows he is worthy. He goes down to the coast with some teammates for a promotional match on the shore, delighted with the chance to see the ocean for the first time. Freed from urban shackles and happy, he plays like never before, getting the attention of his colleagues, who had never seen him perform like that, and also from Isaias (played by Walmor Chagas),[23] a rich publicist who seems to be fascinated by the "kid."

At night, in a Carnaval party, dressed with the same angel costume from his childhood (Carnaval and religion, festivity and discipline will always leave a mark on his path), the hero falls, drunk and wasted. Isaias picks him up, takes him home and looks after him. There is an insinuation of a possible homosexual relationship. This is the turning point of the hero; it is when Asa will start to learn a different lifestyle, and how to express his new masculinity. Isaias helps Asa adjust to a new life. He is a rich and powerful man who has commercial connections and a web of political and economic relations. Isaias teaches Asa how to "wear" his new life style, as he now has the clothes (and the body) of a winner—both on and off the field. At that time, footballers were beginning to assume a higher financial status in Brazilian society, receiving money as never before. Isaias wants Asa to be at the top of his profession, and the movie continues with insinuations that Isaias and Asa are more than just friends. For the first time, a football movie is touching upon the issue of homosexuality inside this so-called macho, and therefore strictly heterosexual, sport.

By the end of the 1960s, Asa is no longer a short-tempered troublemaker. He has been transformed into a competent, hard-working professional who does not give in to temptations; he wears suits, smiles, and always says the right things. Asa's story holds all the classic conflicts, phases and journeys of a hero, transitioning from a boy to a man. But the film insinuates that it is another man who is instrumental in Asa's "coming of age." Isaias establishes with him a relationship that surpasses friendship; it reconfigures the hero's masculinity, and is therefore provocative.

It is Isaias, with all his contacts, who arranges for Asa to again start a match. Feeling more confident, Asa plays very well, surprises everyone, and is the highlight of the match. Under the benevolent gaze of his protector, Asa also performs capably with the press, regains his confidence, and finally learns the "rules of the game"—on and off the field. He now advertises sponsor products and is interviewed for newspapers and appears on radio shows. It is the beginning of his ascent to widespread public popularity. However, there are still risks on this pathway. The hero cannot relax, for he must be alert to the dangers of the (social) game and its strict rules, which are narrow and elitist when it comes to issues of status, class, and race. When Asa is invited to a party hosted by the fashionable elite, in the house of the president of the club for which he plays, he takes some colleagues with him. His friends are uneducated and, despite being athletes, relatively poor. Asa's group also includes a black-skinned friend who, just like him, feels out of place in a big mansion crowded with wealthy, white, elite people. Upon their arrival, the players inadvertently cause a commotion.

The club president refuses to greet the black athlete and only allows his entrance after Asa's insistence—and even so he warns them: "You boys better behave yourselves, you are not in a pigpen . . . or you will return to the hotel concentration!" In spite of the warning, the footballers do not behave; they drink copiously and make too much noise, and are kicked out of the party. Asa does, however, make an impression on someone very important. Just before he and his colleagues are thrown out, Asa clandestinely has sex with Sylvia, the president's young and beautiful wife. This is at the same time an act of defiance against an authority figure, a demonstration of Asa's sex appeal, and a reassertion of the hero's heterosexuality—something that had been dormant owing to his intense friendship with Isaias.

However, Isaias remains Asa's guardian. He organizes a birthday party for Asa in the presence of his loyal friends both new and old (Poca is there) and his family. Asa misses them and thinks about his journey. The hero feels weak—his masculinity seems to be in conflict—but he decides to keep on going. His mother thanks his protector, and the audience then finds out that Asa and Isaias are in fact living together. The insinuation of a relationship is clear when, during the party, the athlete and the publicist discretely exchange tender looks. However, in the party there is also Marta, an innocent young woman who is introduced to Asa by his family, and who would later become Asa's bride. To add to the complexity, Isaias is happy for Asa to have a woman at his side, so he can fit in with the heterosexual social profile expected of a footballer.

Near the end, in Maracanã,[24] the great temple of football religion, Isaias tells Asa that the door man at the stadium was once a football star, reminding him that many heroes end up failing at the end of their journey. They talk about legislation regarding footballers and the need to plan for a future beyond the game. Asa becomes aware that he needs to effectively take on certain roles to embody the outer layer of the renewed hegemonic masculinity and keep a "low profile" if he wants to remain at the peak of his football career. Isaias will continue to be Asa's "protector," advising him on and off the field. So Asa remains under Isaias's influence, both personally and professionally. The homosexuality in the life of the footballer, even if behind the scenes, remains core.

At the end, in an atmosphere of dreams, and with the same angel outfit, Asa definitively gets to the top: After being a part of the 1970 World Champion National Team (in Mexico, with Pele), he flies over the city, looking back at his victorious journey, filled with obstacles. A new man arises, centered, with controlled emotions,

## Football, Cinema, and New Sensibilities in the Masculine Territory

as a "real man" should be, at least in terms of his outward social profile. This is the end of the film. Asa's *Brazilian Dream* was successful. By paradoxically resisting and complying with the gender order, he became a professional footballer.

Asa Branca himself, who at first fights the dominant gender order, questioning authoritarian coaches and wanting to impose his way of being and playing, later on holds on to the hegemonic masculinity, becoming (outwardly at least) both a great athlete and a womanizer. This hegemonic masculinity incorporated and represented by Asa Branca is not a steady model; it does not have "fixed characteristics" (Connel, 2005, p. 76). It is the one seen at the top of the social scale, but it can always be contested in the gender relations field. Induced both by his desires and the pressures he is faced with due to his social status, Asa chooses and is chosen by a determined set of male behaviors. Those changes and choices come because of his relationship with another man—an idea that, no matter how subtle, remodels the idea of masculinity built around the player.

## NEW WAVE (1983)

The second film under discussion, *New Wave,* is part of a set of film experiences that were typical in the 1980s, a time when the Brazilian cinema, as well as the society as a whole, was going through fundamental political and social changes. The film is the second of a trilogy[25] directed by José Antonio Garcia and Ícaro Martins. Garcia had already approached the sport world in his debut short film, *Hoje tem Futebol* (There Is Football Today—1976), a fictional story about the preparation of a team for a match, with an experimental language about "alternative sexualities." It is with this background and all these cultural influences that Martins and Garcia made *New Wave*. They were absorbed in the cultural and political changes of the 1980s: new sexual and gender behaviors, the political amnesty, and the slow and gradual political openness that would influence their work.

The beginning of *New Wave* prepares the audience for what will come. The credits are presented on bed line, painted by the characters, an innovation and an alignment with the rise of graffiti culture. The place is the Ibirapuera Park[26] and the plot is a match in which men dressed as women and women dressed as men to celebrate the creation of the *Gayvotas Futebol Clube,* a women's football team sponsored by a professional male club. The name *Gayvotas* is a wordplay combining the Portuguese word for seagulls—*Gaivotas*—and the word gay.

This beginning also anticipates a strong erotic atmosphere that will be seen throughout the film. The sex scenes are intense. As mentioned before, there is indeed a relation with the *Pornochanchada*[27] experiences, a major success among audiences at the time. However, in spite of the combination of comedy and eroticism, *New Wave* has a more profound connection (even though it has no intention of being a sociological study) with the new sexual engagements of a society in transition. Virginity, abortion, free sexual relations, adultery and betrayal, male and female homosexuality, threesomes, gender changes—these are the issues that the film approaches, in a straightforward way, as daily facts that should be neither hidden nor denied.

It is interesting to notice how football is chosen to start and support the conflicts of the plot. In the early sequences there is an explicit subversion of the most usual senses of this sport. Two professional footballers, Wladimir and Casagrande,[28] dressed as women, are submitted to a questionable interrogation by two women. The key words are said in an ironic tone by the character played by Regina Casé[29]: "I love masculinizing sports." The actors use the words with double meanings and the presence of wordplay is constant; they discuss their menstruation period with the professional men players (now cross-dressed); they say they do not care about menstruation anymore—they just think about the football championship. On their sacred football ground, the men seem to be subdued.

Casagrande, who was a very attractive young man, a player with alluringly long and curly hair who was the dream of many female fans, will return later on in the film as a simple object of a woman who chooses him to take her virginity. This is a very significant change of roles. It is not the man anymore who tries to convince her; it is she who chooses him and brings him to her place. This portrayal of new sexual conduct, visible during the entire film, displays something that is still very shocking for many people: feminism. Feminism introduced a wide spectrum of new ways to experience sexuality, for both men and women. The message was that men should learn how to behave differently in the face of those changes.

As the plot goes along, the film depicts sport as its counterpoint, seeing the feminine as a way of opposing masculine hegemony and its rigid behavioral standards, and emphasizing issues that are typically hidden in this context. If football is a festive space, it is also a space of desire and, therefore, of potential liberation. There is an escape from the aseptic ideal of the sport practice (the constant references to drug use by the athletes is an important symbol of this view), as well as the more complex view of the identity construction of gender regarding this practice. An example of the articulation of these two dimensions are the changing room scenes, filled with sensuality: In these spaces, the female footballers live and enjoy their bodies, distanced from the shame that surrounds men in those exposed moments, always delicate about what is related to their masculinities and in their strict rules regarding pleasures associated with their bodies.

## Football, Cinema, and New Sensibilities in the Masculine Territory

A sequence toward the end of the movie deals with homosexuality as well as with new configurations of sexual desire. After a long homosexual relationship, Rui and Marcelo, two young men who were friends with the Gayvotas team, decide to play Russian Roulette. Though it is played as an act of love, Rui dies tragically. Desperate, Marcelo dresses in Lili's clothes. Lili, a woman and the goalkeeper of the *Gayvotas*, was in a love triangle with both young men. Marcelo looks for her in the stadium, but it is the final match day and he is not allowed to enter there after the start of the game. He wanders, feeling devastated, alongside the huge river *Tiete*, with its rubbish and its *favelas*, until he finds some street boys playing football on the road. He joins their game, still in women's clothes, in a pathetic yet strong image that definitely challenged the macho representations surrounding Brazilian football.

The film's clothing, music, slang, and expressions remind us that Brazil was indeed living a "new wave." The cast itself, featuring young actors who were icons of the underground and who did not belong to the mainstream broadcasts or TV shows seems to have a strong relation to this moment of cultural transition. The film shows in a powerful and shocking way that football was a part of this new wave, and the relationships in the game were contributing to the establishment of a new sexual and gender order.

It is important to highlight the fact that famous and important footballers such as Wladimir and Casagrande took part in this film; this can be seen as a sign of boldness and even confrontation in the traditionally conservative environment of Brazilian football. Their club, Corinthians, is one of the most popular in the country, with more than 30 million fans. Therefore, the intention of the directors by having them in the opening of the film wearing women's clothes is more than clear: to challenge the notions of heteronormative masculinity. Moreover, it is possible to see that the Gayvotas team has various symbolic meanings. First, there is an evident relationship between the Gayvotas and the *Radar*, a Brazilian women's football team that was trying, in the early 1980s, to consolidate football among women, thereby challenging prejudice against women in sport and society (Knijnik, 2011). Gayvota's final match is also symbolic, as they play and win against the "Italian" team, which is a clear payback of the 1982 World Cup defeat and death of "football-art."

This scenery, the articulation between a new political context, the distension in manners and social habits, and the new football experiences were represented at the very time that the sport was conservative. This may help us to understand how provocative the presence of football was in a film that has been often called a "gay" movie. Besides the homosexual relations scenes (male and female), many symbols of the gay culture are present, such as the name of the team, the Gayvotas—the seagull

CHAPTER 5

is a symbol usually connected to homosexuality and, in this case, the name of the team starts with "Gay." The Ritz, one of the scenarios of the film, is a bar/restaurant that since the 1980s has been seen as gay friendly.

On one hand, the use of football (the bastion of hegemonic masculine cultural power in Brazilian society) as an axis of the plot allows the creation of interesting counterpoints to the sexual roles established by heterosexist hegemonic rule. There are no typical male or females in the production; neither gays nor lesbians follow the common sense model. On the other hand, a few stereotypes are reinforced during the film. Some of them are occasional and may be interpreted in the opposite way. For example, the Gayvotas are coached by a man. Jorge, the coach, is married to the team's captain, Neneca, who is also one of the best players on the team. He runs all the training sessions and uses the same coaching strategies applied to male teams. He screams a lot and makes the players undertake strong physical efforts. If these female footballers subverted logic when entering a masculine sacred ground, the football field, it is the men who continue to be in charge, at least on the field. In another scene of evident stereotype, in the middle of a match some players lose interest; they talk or dance ballet, as if they did not know what the game was about. There is a moment when the club's manager and the team's sponsor complain about the players' inappropriate behavior. Jorge, angry with these occurrences and with their weak athletic performance, supposedly due to problems of the "feminine nature," states: "Football is a men's game!"

The women who try to play football face many conflicts. For example, Lili has a misunderstanding with her mother (a hilarious performance by Patrício Bisso),[30] who does not want her playing football. Aggressively, Lili reminds her that her father knits, and her mother defends him, saying he is following the doctor's orders and it is not a reflection of his masculinity. The tensions between the players and their parents have many facets, but conflicts within their families are usual and always feature gender/sexual behaviors.

*New Wave* is not a documentary. It is a fictional story inserted in a historical period, and especially because it is a comedy, it allows us to notice something about its time from the perspectives of its directors. New models of masculinity were under construction; these models are in constant interaction with a new female posture and public presence, and in the first moments of a greater visibility of the homosexual struggles for the respect of different sexual orientations. As we have seen, football, as resistant as it is, would not be completely invulnerable to this set of changes, both in the film and in real life, with the experiences of Corinthians and Radar. Those tensions are captured not only in *New Wave*, but also in *Asa Branca: Um Sonho Brasileiro*, in spite of their different approaches.

## CONCLUSION

Football and cinema were arts and techniques of the 19th century that permeated the 20th and 21st centuries, not only registering social changes, but also being part of them or even provoking them. The cinema incorporates representations, often contributing to a reconfiguration of the social life. Movies come up with new proposals and, by the spread of new images and ideas, generate perturbations and tensions. These renewed social views are certainly felt in the sport environment, showing that football is also a social sphere where is possible to resist the established gender order. Those tensions are clearly identified in the films analyzed in this chapter. On the one side, a boy leaves the country life, moved only by his skills and passion for the ball. He opens up to the world and becomes aware of other possibilities for being a man in a heartless world of appearances, with no space for losers—the world of the hegemonic masculinity so far dominant in Brazilian football.

Asa gives in to this world and is victorious without forgetting what is most precious—his humble and pure feelings, and his origin. He must hide them, but his feelings are always there, showing the breaches and the cracks in this order that appears to be solid. The presence of male homosexuality itself, subtly presented in the film, almost subliminally, shows that the fissures in hegemonic masculinity go further than could be tolerated years before, and that new models of men may appear or are already in the making, while old models start to collapse. The new models will quietly and politely infiltrate social relations, influencing other types of masculine behaviors.

On the other side, what was subtle and insinuated in *Asa Branca* is out in the open in *New Wave*. The women invade the area of male symbolic power—the football field. What will they do with their newly conquered space? How are they supposed to deal with this situation? What are the possible answers regarding this feminine presence in a space that has always been in absolute control of men, into which the women were always denied entrance? The film answers in the most ironic way, dressing football stars as women in an inversion of roles that says men will have to change. The masculine hegemony is gone, and the gender relations will be more equal. The free sexuality presented in the film is one of the facets of this new era and is an important aspect, but not its only facet. In fact, the film and the plots, with homosexual men and women, free sex, women in charge kicking balls (an ideal metaphor for transforming hegemonic masculinities) make powerful male footballers into sexual objects—bodies to be used and dumped. They show that the body behaviors in Brazil, both in sport and sexual practices, were undergoing intense changes, influenced by major modifications in the social relations of gender in Brazilian society. Such changes do not occur only on the part of women—modifications in many social scenarios force men to reconfigure their own performances, their feelings, their behaviors, and their ways of relating socially among themselves, with women, with work, with their bodies, and with sport.

In short, new masculinities in transition were appearing on the horizon in Brazilian society. The traditionally hegemonic man—brutal, violent, and insensitive to the needs of others—will give way to a new type of man with the profile of the modern businessman: sensitive, but competent and mindful. At the other end, women advance with postures and behaviors that were formerly exclusive to men. They are de facto masculine and, even when questioned, go ahead on their own way. Both *Asa Branca* and *New Wave* capture those changes. They are films that, due to their social sensibility, deserve to be watched and analyzed through gender-attuned lenses as being representative of the new order that was being set up in Brazilian life during the 1980s, in spite of the major resistances that it still faces on many social fields, and especially in football.

## REFERENCES

Anderson, E. (2005). *In the game: Gay athletes and the cult of masculinity*. Albany, NY: State of New York Press.

Anderson, E. (2009). *Inclusive masculinity: The changing nature of masculinities*. London, England: Routledge.

Bellos, A. (2002). *Futebol: The Brazilian way of life*. London, England: Bloomsbury.

Coad. D. (2008). *The metrosexual: Gender, sexuality and sport*. New York, NY: SUNY Press.

Connell, R.W. (2005). *Masculinities*. Crows Nest, Australia: Allen & Unwin.

Dias, C. A. (2008). *Urbanidades da natureza*. Rio de Janeiro, Brazil: Apicuri.

Goellner, S. V. (2005). Mulheres e futebol no Brasil: entre sombras e visiblidades. *Revista Brasileira de Educação Física, 19*, 143–51.

Knijnik, J. D. (2003). *A mulher brasileira e o esporte: seu corpo, sua história*. São Paulo, Brazil: Editora Mackenzie.

Knijnik, J. D., & Vasconcellos, E. G. (2005). Les femmes en crampons à coeur ouvert au Brésil. In T. Terret (Ed.), *Sport et genre: v1—La conquête d'une citadelle masculine* (pp. 295–308). Paris, France: L' Harmattan.

Knijnik, J. (2013). Visions of gender justice: 'Untested feasibility' on the football fields of Brazil. *Journal of Sport and Social Issues*, special issue *Transforming Sport: Visions of Social Justice/Strategies for Change, 37*, 8–30.

Knijnik J. (2011).From the cradle to Athens: The silver-coated story of a warrior in Brazilian soccer. *Sporting Traditions, 28*, 63–83.

Louro, G. L. (2000). Por que estudar gênero na era dos cyborgs? In T. M. G. Fonseca & D. J. Francisco (Eds.), *Formas de ser e habitar a contemporaneidade* (pp. 121–136). Porto Alegre, Brazil: Ed. Universidade/UFRGS.

Maranhao, T., & Knijnik, J. (2011). Futebol mulato: Racial constructs in Brazilian football. *Cosmopolitan Civil Societies Journal, 3*, 55–71.

De Melo, V. A. (2006). Futebol e cinema: Relações. *Revista Portuguesa de Ciências do Desporto, 6*, 270–362.

De Melo, V. A. (2006). *Cinema e esporte: diálogos*. Rio de Janeiro, Brazil: Aeroplano/Faperj.

De Melo, V. A., & Fortes, R. (2008). *O surfe no cinema e a sociedade brasileira na transição dos anos 1970/1980*. Rio de Janeiro, Brazil: Mimeo.

Oliveira, L. P., & Costa, V. L. M. (2010). Historias e Memórias dos pioneiros do volei de praia na cidade do Rio de Janeiro [Stories and memories from the forerunners of beach volley in Rio de Janeiro]. *Revista de Educacao Fisica/UEM, Maringa, 21*, 99–113.

Salles, J. G. C., Silva, M. C. P., & Costa, M. M. (1996). A mulher e o futebol—significados históricos. In S. Votre (Ed.), *A representação social da mulher na educação física e no esporte* (pp. 79–94). Rio de Janeiro, Brazil: Editoria Central da Universidade Gama Filho.

Soares, A. J. (1999). História e a invenção de tradições no campo do futebol. *Estudos Históricos, 13*, 119–146.

Soares, A. J. (2003). Futebol brasileiro e sociedade: A interpretação culturalista de Gilberto Freyre. In P. Alabarces (Ed.), *Futbologías: Fútbol, identidad y violencia en America Latina* (pp. 145–162). Buenos Aires, Argentina: CLACSO.

Sócrates, & Gozzi, R. (2002). *Democracia corintiana: A utopia em jogo*. São Paulo, Brazil: Boitempo.

Toledo, R. C. (2002). Aviso aos incautos: o Brasil continua. *Revista Veja*, 1776, p. 134.

## ENDNOTES

[1] For detailed discussion about relationships between sport and cinema, see Melo (2006b).

[2] The dictatorship lasted 21 years. In 1985 the Parliament elected the first nonmilitary president after this period, Tancredo Neves, who died before he took office. However, that was a nondemocratic election; it took until 1989 for Brazilians to be given the chance to vote to their first elected President. The dictatorship has lasted 25 years.

[3] Brizola, 1922-2004. He went into exile in 1964, but ended up being unique in Brazilian politics by being elected to govern in two different states (Rio Grande do Sul—before the military dictatorship, and Rio de Janeiro, after returning from exile).

[4] Arraes, 1916-2005. He was three times governor of the northeast state Pernambuco. After the military coup in 1964 he went to jail, staying there 11 months before going to exile in Argel.

[5] Fernando Gabeira (writer, journalist, and politician) was born in 1941. He was a representative in the National Parliament and is now with the leftist Greens party.

[6] Caetano Veloso (singer, composer, and guitarist; known as Caetano) was born in 1942. He has been awarded five Latin Grammy Awards and is widely regarded as one of the great songwriters in the contemporary world. His style of music, its lyrics, and his behavior (long

hair, left-wing political opinions and progressive ideas) were threatening to the dictatorship. He was arrested in 1969 and later exiled, living two years abroad in London.

[7] Gilberto Gil (singer, composer, and guitarist; known as Gil) was born in 1942. He was seen as a political threat to the military regime, having been arrested in 1969 and imprisoned for nine months before going into exile in London. He made a triumphant return, serving as Brazilian Minister of Culture for five years (2003-08). He is an innovative musician and received a Latin Grammy award in recognition of his talent.

[8] Tropicalismo (or 'Tropicália') is a Brazilian art movement that arose in the 1960s, led by Caetano and Gil. It encompassed several forms of art, however is best known for a distinctive musical expression, which is a fusion of Brazilian rhythms, rock and roll, African and Caribbean rhythms.

[9] Rita Lee (singer, composer, and cultural personality) was born in 1947. She wrote three children's books, had her own comedy show on radio, and had a talk show on TV. She was also the recipient of the Latin Grammy Award and sang with Gilberto Gil.

[10] The Frantic, a female vocal group, performed during the 1970s in the Frenetic Dancing Days a disco house that was extremely popular in Rio de Janeiro's nightclub scene.

[11] The original words in Portuguese are "eu vou fazer você ficar louco, muito louco, dentro de mim."

[12] Cazuza (1958-90; singer, composer, and poet, and one of the most beautiful male voices in Brazilian pop music) was a self-proclaimed bisexual.

[13] Renato Russo (1960-96; singer, and one of the most important composers of Brazilian rock music) also wrote about drugs, politics, and bisexualism.

[14] Corinthians is one of the most popular football teams in Brazil.

[15] Doctor Socrates had this nickname as he was also a medical doctor.

[16] For more information, see Sócrates and Gizzo (2002).

[17] Amnesty Law gave freedom to all the politicians who were exiled by the dictatorship, allowing them to return to Brazil.

[18] The Act prohibited women from playing sports that were deemed "incompatible with their nature." The deliberation 7/1965 of the National Council of Sport decreed the following sports unsuitable for females: judo, water polo, rugby, weight lifting, baseball and, of course, football (indoor, outdoor, or beach).

[19] For more information, see Dias (2008).

[20] Asa Branca is the name of the main character of the film. It means literally "White Wing." Those who knew him personally simply called him Asa.

[21] Juscelino Kubitschek (1902-1976) was Brazilian President (elected) from 1956 to 1961.

[22] Garrincha (1933-83); known affectionately as the Joy of the People, was one of the best players in Brazilian football history. He was part of two World Cup victories (1958 and '62). Playing with Pele in the national team, they never faced a defeat while together. But he had a difficult life off the field, including alcohol problems, and his story may have partially inspired the filmmaker of Asa Branca.

[23] Walmor Chagas was born in 1930; he was one of the most brilliant actors during the 20th Century in Brazilian theatre, TV shows, and movies.

## Football, Cinema, and New Sensibilities in the Masculine Territory

[24] Maracana, the biggest football stadium in Brazil, is located in Rio de Janeiro. It was opened in 1950 on the occasion of the Football World Cup.

[25] The other two are *O Olho Mágico do Amor* (The Peephole of Love–1981) and *Estrela Nua* (Nude Star–1984).

[26] A huge green area in Sao Paulo. It could be said the *Ibirapuera* is Sao Paulo's version of New York's Central Park.

[27] Pornochanchadas were soft-core sex comedies popular in Brazil in the early 20th century.

[28] Both Wladimir and Casagrande were protagonists of the Corinthians Democracy, as mentioned earlier, and at the time of filming were playing as professionals in Corinthians. They were very popular footballers and played in the Brazilian National Team for a brief period.

[29] Regina Case was born in 1954; she is a famous actress in Brazilian TV shows and theatre, best known for comedy.

[30] Patricio Bisso is an Argentinean who went to live in Sao Paulo in the 1980s. He created several female comical characters in theatre movies and TV shows (as the Russian sexologist *Olga del Volga*), always dressing in women's clothes.

# I Am Dancing on the Courts: Masculinities in Brazilian Sports

## 6

Jorge Knijnik

*Dance is the art of combat, everywhere and in every position. Early on, ever since you are a small child, you struggle—if you are a boy, you need to confront the family in order to dance. Later on, it's the way people, who fit you into a stereotype, look at you. Then, you become a dancer and realize that you are . . . less than a musician, less than a painter, less than everything.*
—Angelin Preljocaj, Albanian choreographer

### MASCULINITIES AND SPORTS: A LONGSTANDING RELATIONSHIP

As Knijnik and Adair argued in Chapter 1, masculinity is a very complex and multifaceted concept. Despite such varied ideas and heterogeneous approaches to masculinity, there is one issue that remains constant: the strong relationship between sports and masculinity. Brazil provides an intriguing sociocultural context for research of this kind. First, discourses about masculinity in Brazilian sport have been hidden from public discussion for many years; it is a subject without debate. Yet the tensions are very real. Second, Brazil will be hosting two major sports events in the forthcoming years (FIFA World Cup, 2014; Rio de Janeiro Olympic Summer Games, 2016) and they will both bring attention to the Brazilian sports scene, providing global inputs to the discussion of gender norms.

## MY FOCUS AND METHODOLOGY

In focusing on sport and masculinities in Brazil, I have chosen to explore the life experience of one person to illustrate a sense of the transition from boyhood to manhood. Although a biographical approach is limiting in that the discussion centers on an individual, it can also be illuminating if the in-depth experiences reveal key facets of wider social structures, norms, and values. My goal is to reconstruct the sports life of a well-known handball player in São Paulo, Brazil's richest state. My approach is to narrate this player's story and, while doing so, interweave sociological theory as an interpretive frame, drawing particularly from the work of Connell (1995) on masculinities. I also infuse the ideas of philosophers into the discussion, thereby allowing me to reflect broadly on the nature of the body, the mind, and masculine performance in sport.

At the end of the 1980s, men's handball in São Paulo was the most sought-after sport modality. In the highest-level competitions, there were two tiers with a total of twenty-two clubs competing in both. The top-10 clubs made the first tier of the state competition, and participation in the first tier was clearly a core aspiration of teams and players. One Saturday night, however, two teams were playing to avoid relegation the following year. On one side, there was a well-structured club with highly skilled, professional, and physically imposing players; on the other side, there was a small-club team, with mostly amateur players, who loved to get together, practicing and playing in a social sense. Despite these disparities, the small club won the game, sending the other team to the lowest division. The next Monday, on the defeated team's court, almost twenty strong, tall, unshaven, ill-tempered, and crestfallen men sat and listened for over one hour to a dressing-down from their coach, who could not accept their defeat and consequent downgrading to second division. At one point, enraged, the coach confronted them:

> And what about Lukas? How come we didn't mark him? Everyone knows that he is the "handball dancer," he jumps from one side to the other and doesn't do anything? Not even individually marked were you able to stop him?

## I Am Dancing on the Courts: Masculinities in Brazilian Sports

Inadvertently or unknowingly, and in an attempt to articulate an insulting nickname, the coach had just complimented an athlete who, until then, had not found his identity within the court and had great doubts about continuing to play. This is despite the fact that he loved to play handball and had done so since childhood.

The "Handball Dancer," who will be referred to in this study as *Lukas*, is the subject of this research. Lukas confided in me, thereby allowing insights into his world. He had actually been very pleased when learning through a player from the opposing team that the other coach had thus nicknamed him. Right then, Lukas had an insight and realized something that the world of sports had already come to realize: In fact, Lukas danced on the court, his steps were light, long, and beautiful leaps, like those of a dancer—and handball does allow for many steps and leaps; there is a rhythmic step that allows three steps, or sometimes a combination composed of a double rhythmic step, twice three steps (Knijnik, 2009).

Gard (2008) has argued that dance "has long been seen as something which boys and men, particularly in Western countries, do reluctantly if at all" (p. 184). He reported that for most of the boys he talked to about dancing, dance was rarely seem "as a normal part of life." It was a physical activity that brought boys and men feelings of unease, as dance is in most of the cases was wrapped with gendered stereotypes, as being appropriate for girls, effeminate boys, or something that interested gays, in contrast to sports that were unrelated to any type of feminine trait.

It is interesting to note, though, that in the story of modern ballet, many choreographers have designed defensive strategies to "protect" the male body, by showing "positive"—meaning heterosexual—images of the male body on stage (Burt, 1995). As Melo and Lacerda (2010) have argued, even with different historical trajectories, sport and dance, as physical activities, were structured in order to reinforce hegemonic masculine representations. And they ask, Are there connections and interactions between these fields that might allow gender stereotypes to be challenged and transformed? Melo and Lacerda (2010), using historical examples, showed many dissonant models that defied the hegemonic model of masculine embodiment. Defiance is one thing; normative gender relations are another.

Lukas was conscious of the offensive meaning of "handball dancer" in the homosocial sports environment where he played. By accepting with pleasure a meant-to-be-hurtful nickname, Lukas was embracing a defiant attitude towards hegemonic models of seeing and representing the male body and physicality. Would the consequences of his stance be positive or negative? Relying in the powerful metaphor of a sport body who dances, and through an intense relationship with Lukas, this

## CHAPTER 6

research examines the formation of sports masculinities and the dialogues and tensions that exist between the masculine bodies in the sport of handball in São Paulo.

The ideas presented here were initially based on the thoughts inspired by my reading of philosophers and sociologists, who raised questions that prompted my interest in critically observing masculinities in sport. Initially, Butler's (2002, 2006) research, wherein she argued that bodies become tangible entities consistent with their social existence, circumstances that give them identity and legitimacy but also the possibility of being exploited by others, sparked my interest. I then studied Rial (2000), who discussed the relationship between sports and masculinity based on the examples of judo and rugby, suggesting that in these sports there is an actual incarnation of the masculine *habitus*, which is incorporated and literally becomes part of the practitioner's flesh. I was also inspired by the scholarship of Connell (1995) and Terret (2004), who stated that neither is there a universal and single masculinity that travels through all periods and cultures, nor would this be a natural masculine norm to be followed; rather, they found that in present societies, several kinds of masculinities coexist in a hierarchical order where some are more highly valued than others, sparked my interest. According to these authors, all forms of masculinity are parts of social and historical scenarios, which, while they define those forms, are also influenced by them.

Based on the insights of these authors, as well as the research context I had identified, I decided to employ a rather unique methodological approach. Having been his friend for over ten years, during his sports-practicing youth, I happened to meet Lukas again approximately nine years after we both left the courts and resumed our old friendship amid long conversations after work hours. Often the subject of our chats inevitably fell back on our lives in sport, recalling stories and interesting facts, until we reached the summary on the "Handball Dancer" presented earlier. That day, it was proposed to him that these conversations be written down or recorded for academic purposes. Lukas thought about it for some time, asked how the research would be conducted, and eventually gave his consent in writing.

Conversations then took another direction, for we agreed that once a week we would tape the depositions to be employed in the studies, and subsequently the full transcription would be presented to Lukas for his evaluation and approval. Those authorized transcriptions formed a kind of sports life history of the subject herein interviewed, which was later organized around two pivotal issues—one thematic and the other chronological. This article presents and discusses elements of these depositions, which begin in elementary school and go through several moments in Lukas's adolescence and youth, and onto the present.

### I Am Dancing on the Courts: Masculinities in Brazilian Sports

## Becoming a Young Man

> *Ever since I became aware of myself, I felt as if the whole world was staring at me. . . . The simple idea that there could be a conjunction of body and spirit called 'I' made me ashamed. . . . I wanted to suppress other people's gaze. Or just suppress myself.* (Kenzaburo Oe, "Seventeen")

This first section of Lukas's story draws upon his childhood, his first experiences of being, and, as his father would early define him, a "little man" who could take care of himself and handle situations in the streets of São Paulo. So, as a little man as young as six years old, until his prepubescent years, Lukas started to experience how his gender performance (Butler, 2006) was already being policed and shaped by gender expectations and constraints (Connell & Messechmidt, 2005).

Lukas told me a little about his childhood. A city boy residing in a good neighborhood in the city of São Paulo, he lived at a time when the streets were a territory comparatively free from today's violence that terrorizes the urban population of São Paulo. Until he was six years old, Lukas would go with his mother to preschool, only four blocks and a 15-minute walk away from home. At seven, when he began elementary school, his older brother, who was in fifth grade, started to accompany him. When school was over, Lukas would wait at the door for his brother so they could walk home together. This went on throughout the year, until one day his brother didn't show up. Tired of waiting, he took his knapsack and walked home by himself, losing his way around a few times, but eventually making it home. Waiting for him in the street, his parents were frantic: "Where were you?" yelled his mother, almost crying, while his father vociferated: "Now, he's a little man, he can come home by himself!"

That was perhaps the first gender-related experience our hero remembers—he was allowed to walk home by himself; now he was a little man! And men have the space of the street all to themselves. His sister, three years older than him, had been chaperoned to school by her parents for a few years, but he was going all alone. Lukas played ball and had lots of fun in the quiet neighborhood where he lived. But the girls, he couldn't remember having seen them playing in the streets:

> We used to play ball on the corner of the apartment building where Os and Cas—two boys who, although one year older than I, were in my class. I wasn't very good at it, always in the goal or one of the last ones to be chosen, but I always did get chosen. There were no girls playing with us. We also jumped over walls and played button soccer.[1] How I played button soccer! I learned to play with my father; we used to play in the evenings,

> when he came home from work. I had a watch-lid team I painted with the colors of the S.C. Bahia, and I still have it. . . . I won all neighborhood championships, participated in championships organized by the toy manufacturer Estrela, I even won a button soccer table, trophies, and prizes. I remember that in fifth grade, when I changed schools, I participated in the school team for many years, we won the Children's Games sponsored by the city council several times. . . . Funny, why is it that the girls never even played button soccer? I never played against any girl...

All this happened about 30 years ago. You do not have to be a genius to know or realize that football in Brazil, as in many other places around the world, is still a game associated overwhelmingly with the masculine universe (Knijnik, 2011). It is not even a physical question (an issue always brought up to impede females from partaking in football and to highlight their supposed fragility, or assumptions about men's exceptional strength compared to women) because in button soccer there is no physical confrontation between athletes, only between the buttons. Even so, according to our subject's account, here girls or women were also absent.

Confirming this social perception of women's absence from soccer events, a number of studies have emphasized this continued link to the masculine domain and discrimination against females. There has recently been extensive Brazilian and international literature describing such a situation, of which two examples will suffice.[2] In England, Meân (2001), studying the discursive practice and production of gender identities among teenagers in the soccer fields, has argued that the buildup of the masculine identity, both at regional or national levels, is related to soccer—and that the construction of this identity is threatened by the increasing female presence in the sport. In Brazil, Altmann (2003) conducted ethnographic studies in schools, showing that boys occupied more and wider spaces in those environments, especially through sports. Girls, by contrast, were constrained and limited in school and sports.

If nowadays, however, masculine predominance is still strong, imagine what it was like in the 1970s, when Lukas was growing up on Brazilian streets. Girls were virtually invisible on the street or in games like soccer, especially in middle-class neighborhoods in the city of São Paulo. Lukas, however, remembers a remarkable experience involving girls. He recalled that dodgeball, which he played alongside girls, helped him later develop the ability in and liking for handball. But, to a certain extent, this experience with girls was traumatic:

## I Am Dancing on the Courts: Masculinities in Brazilian Sports

In second grade, I was eight years old, and we started to play dodgeball in school. I was good, much better than in soccer. I won medals in the school championships. I wasn't chosen, I chose. And we played with the girls! One year later, we organized a group that used to play every afternoon at school . . . And there were several girls. We played almost until nightfall and we had such fun! One afternoon, one of those girls, already 10 (I was nine), threw the ball hard in my direction; I didn't dodge, tried to catch the ball, which hit my finger and I fell to the ground. In great pain, I kept on playing and, at nightfall, I went home. My mother took me to the doctor, who diagnosed a broken bone. The next day, with a bandaged finger, I had to go to school, but the feeling of humiliation was strong and was confirmed by the teasing from the whole school: Word had already spread that a girl had broken my finger!

In the context of a patriarchal society, losing or taking a beating from a girl is something that can really mortify a boy, who is subject to huge cultural pressures to do better than girls; especially in this particular physical sense, the hierarchy of gender places higher expectations on boys. They must be stronger than girls, even if the girls are older than them; a true man does not cry, he does not even think of getting injured by or losing a competition to a girl (Cavaleiro & Vianna, 2010; Romero, 2010).

In sports, this humiliation is an even heavier burden, since this is a space increasingly valued for the buildup of masculine identity—oftentimes no matter what. It is in the playing fields, courts, and tracks that one finds a fertile soil to strengthen a masculine role model that Connell (1995) calls *hegemonic masculinity,* the symbols and violent practices that seek to rank man as a superior being and always dominant in relation to the woman, and to other types of configurations of masculine identity.

Terret (2004) points out that leaders of the YMCA—an association where, in the 19th and 20th centuries, a number of sports modalities practiced today originated—noticed that as the urbanization of society and mechanization made life easier, people needed to work lesser hours and with lower levels of physical ardor. In terms of young males, that raised fears that masculine youth would become feminized through sedentary occupations and lower levels of physical activity in the workplace. Partly in response to these fears, competitive sports were emphasized, aiming to educate young boys about the physical attributes of "being men" and building their masculine character.

The roles that sports have played in inculcating hegemonic masculinity, which is expected to be dominant in gender relations, has serious consequences at several levels. Perhaps one of the strongest impacts is the difficulty that men and women, or even boys and girls, have in finding opportunities to compete in sports together. Indeed, despite women's social, political, and cultural advancement, they are generally positioned as separate and distinct from men in sport. For centuries the sports field has been and continues to be an ideal space for men to reaffirm their sense of physical virility, for this is an environment where women have been positioned as *unequal* to men, and even within the genre of female sport, still have difficulty participating as respected athletes, as performers with sporting caliber (Struna, 1994; Votre & Mourão, 2003). Or, in Terret's (2004) words, "Sports, through its institutions, its practices, symbols, and discourses is an excellent example of an arena for the buildup of masculinity" (p. 213).

Lukas experienced those feelings himself: He was one of the best at dodgeball and his finger had been broken . . . by a girl! Even today, he seems to feel vexed at the humiliation and scorn he was subjected by his schoolmates . . . the *great* dodgeball player brought down by a little girl. This event in Lukas's life shows that, even in a recreational environment, the gender values that promote hegemonic masculinity (Connell, 1995) are heavily present in children's lives. The implications in children's lives left by sports sex segregation starts at the beginning of the adolescent years—if not beforehand—and can be seen in stages within sports education and school settings.

Darido (2002) investigated to what extent boys aged 9 to 11 saw the presence of girls playing soccer in school or with their male peers as a novelty or a challenge. Was it seen as a threat to the buildup of more accepted standards and shapes of masculinity in their communities? According to Darido, the traditional idea held by male students in Brazil was that, as boys, they should dominate sports, and girls would never be as good as them. Of course, if the girls proved otherwise, the boys would face vexing situations.

Botelho-Gomes et al. (2010), using extensive ethnographic research in schools in Portugal, demonstrated that teenagers of both sexes often feel inhibited to participate in school sports because of the gender stereotyping that is brought from outside the schools to many types of sports. The authors revealed that most of the students they interviewed and observed neither agreed nor liked the way that different sports received "masculine" or "feminine" labels, and that those labels repeatedly made them avoid sports, in order to escape from the risk of peer bullying.

By means of extensive interviews, Carvalho (2001) studied the way female teachers evaluate and issue opinions on their male and female students in Brazil. The author concluded that, while girls had difficulty in keeping their "feminine traits" appropriate in the eyes of their female teachers and be considered good students, boys too had great difficulty in building a masculine identity that would be considered adequate inside school boundaries, while being successful in their homework and school evaluations. In the author's opinion, boys found themselves on a tightrope, between "being perceived as [athletically] virile and at the same time a good student" (Carvalho 2001, p. 567). This would be evidenced, for instance, in the opinion teachers had of boys' notebooks: Neat, impeccable handwriting and drawings would immediately be assumed to be a notebook belonging to a girl, who'd therefore be expected to be an excellent student. Teachers would also make comments about contradictions and imbalances between some of the boys' behavior (agitation, inquisitiveness) and the style of their notebooks.

Based on these perceptions, female teachers eventually pigeonholed their male students into a specific type of masculine behavior and thus treated them accordingly, valuing one type of masculinity, as Carvalho has said, "with the right dosage": good at sports; playful without being aggressive; womanizer without crossing the line of what was socially acceptable; a good student without seeming to try too hard; poor handwriting and sloppy with school material, but would turn in homework on time. Those who were unable to meet this suite of expectations were either suspected of being homosexual or, if showing inadequate intellect and/or excessively violent behavior, were often suspended or expelled from the school environment (Carvalho, 2001).

Lukas grew up overwhelmed by that melting pot where gender values and hierarchies crashed, creating paradoxes that were difficult to understand and, even more, put into action. How do you restrain aggressiveness all the time? How do you conduct yourself in a relationship with girls? How can you be both disorganized and unsystematic at school, yet a good student? Apparently, the reflexes of such a culture on him left their marks and were revealed in a body that became tense just from thinking of being friendly with girls. Relationships with them could not be relaxed and easy, because there was the crucial need to show oneself to be in command, since a "true man" is always in control and in power. The hierarchy of genders is thus transported corporeally and builds an order of bodies: In this paradigm, someone has to be compliant so that the other may be in command. Unfortunately, in his case, the person in command suffers too, becomes tense, and does not use their body to its best advantage (i.e., relaxing, feeling confident, and relating to others spontaneously).

### Being a Real Man: The Symbol of a Hero
*Take a man, made of nothing, like us, life-size*
*soak the flesh, irrationally, hungrily, angrily,*
*then, close to the end, put up the banner and play the trumpet*

CHAPTER 6

*Serve it dead!*
(Anger! 'Recipe for building a hero' [IRA! Receita para se fazer um heroi])

This section discusses how, as a growing boy who was reaching his teenage years, sport and masculine concepts associated to sports practice (as discussed in chapter 1 of this anthology) were structuring and forming Lukas's life and personality. As a homosocial experience (Anderson, 2008) where girls were nearly absent, high-level sports practices were leading him to confront different types of gender pressures and unwritten gender policies (Anderson, 2008).

As affirmed, Lukas reached adolescence. Handball was an inexorable part of his life—practices, games, friends, school teams, weekends and contusions. A life in the sports arena, where he spent most of his time with all sorts of males—his teammates, older players, coaches, medical doctors, support staff, sports managers, and directors. Lukas was becoming an elite athlete in one of the best clubs in the city of São Paulo.

At fifteen, still in the first year of the under 16 level, Lukas was being called to practice with older players, U18 and U21, athletes whose physical potential was greater than his. He never missed one practice, which lasted for about two and half hours, and then he went on to training with the older ones. His parents complained that it was too much of a physical strain, but he was too thrilled and absorbed to be concerned. One Saturday afternoon, after playing a game in his own age level, Lukas was invited by the U21's coach, whose team was short of players, to play that night on the court of the Corinthians with the older team. He recalls:

> I was so excited. I persuaded my parents and off I went. It was freezing cold that August night in São Paulo. We were warmly clothed sitting on the bench of reserves, winning the game, when one of ours fell and badly injured his chin. The coach told me to step in, I didn't even have time to do my warm-up. . . . Throughout the game, I threw myself on the adversaries, defended a lot and, in a ball thrown at the corner, I threw myself in the area and scored a decisive goal, at the last minute deflecting from the foot of the goalkeeper, who had tried to kick me in the face. . . . Even the goalkeeper of our team, who was a 'myth' [legend] in the club, as he played in the Brazilian senior team since he was 16, complimented and applauded me on the court. . . . I remember that I was even able to get the phone number of a cute blond girl sitting in the audience. Next day, I could barely walk; my knee was swollen and hurt a lot. I was lucky that an uncle of mine who was a medical doctor was spending a few days with us and helped me with my injured knee.

## I Am Dancing on the Courts: Masculinities in Brazilian Sports

This is an example of the type of man that is valued in sports, a history of virility and public manifestations of pain that are not as demanded or expected in many women's sports, where often they are actually discouraged. According to Rial (2000), pain is a crucial element in the formation of masculinity: "Sacrificing the body in sports brings a symbolic capital to the player" (p. 248). A male sports hero absorbs pain and suffering and is a role model for a male-dominated society. Athletes have faith, they fight, make sacrifices, injure themselves, and are self-confident; fans believe them because sports heroes are brave; other men identify with them and "become men" with them. Women, so the narrative goes, observe and applaud.

Loland (1999), who studied attitudes about self in relation to the bodies of Norwegian athletes, concluded that it is not only sports that build an ideal of masculinity, which, transferred to the body, becomes a stage for demonstrations of heroism and sacrifice; the male athlete himself gets positive messages from his social world and from the media when he shows the marks of "battle" on his body, which for Loland, are signs of masculinity in Western culture, i.e., signs of "domination, power, and control" (Loland, 1999, p. 298).

Returning now to our narrative, Lukas says that this evolution did not come cheaply and it was his own body that paid for it. The older athletes, the "owners" of the places in the team, did not like to see a 15-year-old boy turn from a bibelot into a star in the team.

> Whenever the coach wasn't looking I got beaten up. I was kicked so hard in the groin that I ended up with massive distensions; I was elbowed in the belly, jerked around by the head. . . . I also went through a few rites of initiation, the "hazing": I stood naked in the locker room, everybody laughing at me, throwing deodorant over my body, slapping me with the bath towel. . . . They all said that this was what it would be like if I wanted to play with men not little boys, I'd have to get used to it. . . . But I didn't. Although playing very well, I ended up with a lot of contusions, which were mostly inflicted by my team "mates". . . . I was very naïve, went up for the same ball, and the older players—some of which were six years [more than] my age, which, in this phase makes quite a difference—took the opportunity to beat me. The next year, I didn't play for quite some time due to a contusion in the groin. Thus, I was cut off from the state team. I went into a crisis and almost stopped playing—but I've always enjoyed it so much! I only recovered technically two years later, but feeling out of place within the group.

## CHAPTER 6

Actually, he needed to adapt to that world with its own violent rules, but he was unable to do so. Unknowingly, his own body yearned for a pause; Lukas felt very uncomfortable in that context. He says that when he was 18, he took a trip with some teammates, but they got involved in fights with other boys for futile reasons, and since he did not feel like fighting, he fell apart from the group and saw his leadership—which for technical reasons had always been unquestioned—on the court become undermined.

This picture is symptomatic of what Connell (1995) said about the production of varied masculinities in a same social context. According to the author, men are not identical or unique, nor do they manifest their masculinity in a consistent manner. On the contrary, Connell's focus was on showing that gender involves much more than just role dichotomies of anatomically diverse bodies, and that men's way of being—masculinity—is variable and subject to change: "Gender relations include relations between men, relations of domination, marginalization, and complicity. A specific hegemonic form of masculinity has other masculinities grouped around it" (Connell, 1995, p. 189).

Unaware of these theoretical conceptualizations, Lukas plunged into a deep crisis of identity, which could be translated into a masculine identity crisis. He was no longer able to play with that group of players, yet he was unable to stop playing handball, something that was ingrained within him. Without expressing nor agreeing with the manifestations of hegemonic masculinity present in his sport, manifestations that were becoming increasingly visible (and he believed that they should diminish as people were growing into mature adults), Lukas didn't see his own masculinity as different from what he saw all his friends "wearing" or being valued in the social environment, even by the girls. He began challenging his own sexuality—was he gay? By the time things became too confused, he went to college and received a new invitation to play in a club.

### I Am Dancing on the Court

At his new university, Lukas experimented with other forms of physical and body activity. He kept playing handball, which was his passion, but he also danced ballet, practiced martial arts, and participated in a number of diverse body experiences. He recalls:

> At the time Wilhelm Reich´s bodily therapy was in fashion, so were yoga and shiatsu, hence there was a lot in the way of body politics going on. Therefore, without stopping to play handball, I got involved in other

## I Am Dancing on the Courts: Masculinities in Brazilian Sports

activities: I looked hilarious in tights, everybody watching me making pliés and pointes. . . . But I'll tell you something, it helped me a lot to improve my thrust and rhythm, and that's when I got my nickname and I was playing so well. They only didn't call me a fag because I dated girls and played handball, but while the ballet dancers accepted me—which was good for me, even sexually—lots of girls turned their faces on me. But my body loosened up, I became more comfortable with it, my back pains were gone, and I became more flexible. I found myself again, body-wise, and a friend from college invited me to play and work at another, smaller, startup club. It was great, I stayed with them for ten years.

From this testimonial, it becomes evident that masculinity is not something that should be looked at only from its negative side. Terret (2004) himself has questioned the motives of several studies on this subject, which focus in a pathological sense on the pain, contusions, homophobia, sexism, blood, and tears that masculinity brings. He concluded that because the subject of sport and masculinity has been scorned by a profoundly powerful feminist critique, "studies on sports and masculine fraternity are extremely rare" (Terret, 2004, p. 212).

At college, Lukas was beginning to know himself better and to experience his own sense of masculinity with pleasure and assertiveness. At the new handball club, since it was a startup, the space had yet to be built and defined by the managers and players. A fraternity was being built, one concerned with mutual respect and shared progress. They were just young men, coached and led by a young man, himself fresh out of a handball course for coaches. Yet, there was no intention of subduing or humiliating others. At least, that was his perception, and still is: "My closest handball friends are from that phase." New concepts of masculinity, even within sports, were being shaped. Everybody enjoyed playing well; they bonded around shared objectives, but they took pleasure in the game itself, in scoring goals and beating other teams, rather than in creating enemies or taking on a dominant position. This demanded a new definition of the body: competitive, but not excessively muscular; swift rather than strong; dancing bodies, flexible and harmonious rather than heavy and combative. Reflecting on the issue of the body in the gender debate, Connell (1995) has stated that often the body is considered as the limit, i.e., it would be out of the question to discuss cultural differences and constructions, since the body is supposed to be a biologically constructed entity and its differences would be seen as physically obvious and visible.

It is Connell (1995) himself, however, who refuted those statements when he wrote that there are "many possibilities of *re-embodiment* for men. There are different forms of using, feeling, and showing masculine bodies" (p. 200). But new *re-embodiments*, different uses, feelings, and perceptions of the body undoubtedly go through the view that the "re-signified bodily me" is seen by the world. Merleau-Ponty (1992a)—one of the philosophers who has reflected most on the issue of the new meanings that the body can take on—thought that body image is foremost intercorporeal; "the corporeal self" only exists when it is seen and is tangible to the other. The body is a "being" that sees itself and others while it is seen and gazed upon. Thus, the athletic image and the body image of a sportsman are only defined to the extent that it relates to others, to the players in his team or other teams, and to the public in general. Therefore, masculinity itself, which is promoted, reconceptualized and reinterpreted in and by the body, can afford to take on new meanings and re-embodiments.

Lukas's statements confirm that, even in sports where physical contact and confrontation are critical to success and do occur all the time, it is possible to invest in forms of embodiment—ergo, of masculinity—in which the pleasure of the experience is essential. These new embodiment practices would treat the body as an ally, not a worn-out being that expresses suffering and pain; not just another yield machine, but rather a sensitive body. According to Merleau-Ponty's (1992b) interpretation, a body that takes responsibility for itself as a subject agent but also an object of ongoing changes is no longer an "information machine but this present body of mine, the sentinel that silently surrenders to my words and acts" (p. 276).

## Breathing Body and Soul

Philosophy and psychology followed the path opened by Merleau-Ponty (1992a, b) in the discussion of the phenomenological body as opposed to the body-machine. Those reflections sought to find correspondence between the psychic activity and the feelings and movements of the body, especially when the state of reflection on the body is "absent."

Many athletes report how much their most satisfying movement experiences, as well as they best results, occurred at times when they were able to be "just" their bodies, without the act of thinking. Moragues (1998), a French psychologist specializing in sports who follows the Merleau-Ponty's (1992b) phenomenological philosophy, has reported that high-level athletes—both men and women—who already have stood on the podium often describe a "clinical and phenomenal" experience about their state of performance, i.e., a unique body expression at the peak of sports performance (p. 57). He contends that this expression can be distinguished by four permanent characteristics, among which two are pertinent here. The first is the *deactivation of thought*—according to the author, athletes believe that "it is necessary to not think and, especially, not think about what the body should or should not do" (Moragues, 1998, p. 58). Second, Moragues (1998) asserted that the experience of the body while in movement described by athletes is opposed to the psychic effort of thinking, as if the "body while in movement has some kind of 'knowledge' that makes it move by itself" (p. 57).

Casey (1999), a philosopher and psychologist who worked on the connections between unconscious and the prereflexive body actions, has insisted that it is impossible to separate mind and body, that at no time is there a body and mind in a pure separate state, because we are both—what happens within the human being is a "a constant mixture of body and mind, flesh and psyche" (p. 54). That is, the perception in the human being simply happens, not with the help from the body; rather, it is made *in the body*. My informant's perceptions go toward this direction. Almost at the end of the story, Lukas says this:

> When I heard that nickname, it was as if I had discovered myself—I began accepting myself and to feel accepted, like a dancer on and outside the court. I noticed that the players in my team moved to my rhythm—or better still, we established a rhythm, our own dance, which caused them to receive from me several balls at the front of the goal—I was assisting very well! I didn't even have to look to know where they were. Even backwards, I was able to throw the ball. A bulky guy, who, at first, used to get annoyed with the way I played, became a good friend of mine, we made quite a few good moves together. I got lighter; the dance on the court was getting increasingly more enjoyable. One day, in the locker room, my presence unbeknownst to them, I overheard a teammate who had played in the Brazilian national team and was the son of a famous coach, make complimentary comments on my play, saying that despite my 'singularity,' I led the team forward and made moves that enabled all my team fellows to score many goals. And he was right. Were it at the time sports statistics were valued as they are today, I'd have surely won a few prizes for largest assists.

On the one hand, one can clearly see a bodily reconfiguration toward the perception of a more sensitive body, not heroic and suffering, but content with itself. It is a body that, as Knijnik (2003) has reflected, is created and recreated by itself but also by who is in contact with it; it is constantly re-embodied by whoever notices it and feels perceived, in a constant dialogue between the world and the body itself. On the other hand, there seems to exist a "manner" by which this body shows that it is put in check by others who help to define it. What is this manner, which Lukas says others would object to, but end up accepting? Certainly, it is a manner that does not correspond to the standard masculine world, even more so in sports. This manner unquestionably translates into body, which, according to Loland (1999), is modeled on a sports culture that is hegemonic, since it can be found in many parts of the world. In the author's opinion, the masculine athlete body forms what he calls the ideal body of a man in Western societies—"youth, strength, power, heterosexuality and high performance" (p. 292). Amidst this masculine hegemony, though, it is possible to envision several bodily subjectivities present in the world of sports, subjectivities that, consciously or not, question this model.

As Lukas has shown, becoming disengaged from this patriarchal, hegemonic, and dominant model is a task that requires strength, which requires an individual path of reflection, trial, and error. Lukas's story shows—yet also demands—a political effort from whoever wishes to oppose the hegemonic standard. According to Connell (1995), rather than an organized and massive struggle, the deconstruction of patriarchy is a historical process that will unfold at several points through all kinds of struggle: "It is more likely that men disengage from the defense of the patriarchate in small numbers at a time in a wide variety of circumstances" (p. 202).

This reminds us that sport, itself being a hegemonic culture in Brazil and many other places, can also be a space of resistance to the gender order. Hence, this bodily pattern may be denounced and athletes can try other models of embodied masculinities that are more inclusive (Anderson, 2010). Lukas did it, through a painful path, which, as he himself says, is in constant development.

> Today, at 45, what kind of body has sport helped me to have? I have changed so much but I never forget the pleasure of jumping and throwing at a different rhythm from that people expected…I'll always try and regain my rhythm.

Bodily rhythm and sensitivity. Lightness of movement in a man and former athlete who had to be "tough" in every sense. Those images have an unquestionable symbolic potential that strengthen Connell's (1995) thesis, which states that it is the small or big symbols that should be built so as to change aspects of society that, even though deeply rooted, still remain historical constructs and, therefore, subject to change.

As we saw with the central character in our story, Lukas faced the joys and challenges of being his own body. Those were his small steps to confront hegemonic embodiment in the masculine world of sport. However, as stated at the beginning of this story, as Brazil will necessarily be in the center of the international sports arena during the next years, all sorts of social issues that surround sports will also be highlighted in the daily sports lives of Brazilians—and gender clearly is one amongst the most preeminent social themes within that context. Stories such as Lukas's are already showing how Brazilian men in sports are continuously being challenged to conform or to try to break the social-historical patterns that have been shaping their embodied masculinities.

## REFERENCES

Anderson, E. (2008). "I used to think women were weak": Orthodox masculinity, gender segregation, and sport. *Sociological Forum, 23,* 257–280.

Anderson, E. (2010). *Inclusive masculinity: The changing nature of masculinities.* New York, NY: Routledge.

Altmann, H. (2003). Maria(s) e homens nas quadras: Sobre a ocupação do espaço físico escolar. [Maria(s) and men on courts: About the possession of the physical space at school.] *Revista digital educação física, esporte e escola, 1,* 67–92. Retrieved from http://www.gtte.rg3.net

Botelho-Gomes, P., Silva, P, Graca, P, & Queiros, P. (2010). Em busca de indicadores promotores ou inibidores do desenvolvimento da pratica desportiva em jovens. In J. Knijnik (Ed.), *Genero e esporte: Masculinidades e feminilidades* (pp. 213–29). Rio de Janeiro, Brazil: Apicuri.

Burt, R. (1995). *The male dancer.* London, England: Routledge.

Butler, J. (2002). Como os corpos se tornam matéria. Entrevista a Baukje Prins e Irene Costera Meijer. [How bodies became substance. Interview with Bajkje Prins and Irene Costera Meije.] *Estudos Feministas, 10,* 155–167.

Butler, J. (2006). *Gender trouble. Feminism and the subversion of identity.* New York, NY: Routledge.

Carvalho, M. P. (2001). Mau aluno, boa aluna? Como as professoras avaliam meninos e meninas. [Bad student, good student? How women teachers evaluate boys and girls.] *Estudos Feministas, 9,* 554–574.

Cavaleiro, M. C., & Vianna, C. (2010). Chutar é preciso? Masculinidades e educação física escolar. In J. Knijnik & R. Zuzzi (Eds.), *Meninos e meninas na educação física: Genero e corporeidade no seculo 21* (pp. 137–154). Jundiai, Spain: Fontoura.

Casey, E. S. (1999). The unconscious mind and the prereflective body. In D. Olkowsky & J. Morley (Eds.), *Merleau-Ponty, interiority and exteriority: Psychic life and the word* (pp. 47–56). Albany, NY: New York Press.

Connell, R.W. (1995). Políticas da masculinidade. [Manhood policies]. *Educação e Realidade, 20,* 185–206.
Connell, R. W., & Messerschmidt, J. W. (2005). Hegemonic masculinity: Rethinking the concept. *Gender & Society, 19,* 829–859.
Cox, B.; Thompson, S. (2000). Multiple bodies: Sportswomen, soccer and sexuality. *International Review for the Sociology of Sport, 35,* 5–20.
Darido, S. C. (2002). Futebol feminino no Brasil: Do seu início à prática pedagógica. [Female soccer in Brazil: From beginning to the pedagogical practice]. *Motriz, 8,* 43–49.
Gard, M. (2008). When a boy's gotta dance: New masculinities, old pleasures. *Sport, Education and Society, 13,* 181–193.
Goellner, S. V. (2005). Mulheres e futebol no Brasil: entre sombras e visibilidades. [Women and soccer in Brazil: Between shadows and visibility]. *Revista Brasileira de Educação Física e Esporte, 19,* 143–51.
Gomes, P., Silva, P., & Queirós, P. (2004). Para uma estrutura pedagógica renovada, promotora da co-educação no desporto. [Developing a renewed pedagogical structure, which promotes co-education in sport]. In A. C. Simões & J. D. Knijnik (Eds.), *O mundo psicossocial da mulher no esporte: Comportamento, gênero, desempenho* (pp. 173–189). São Paulo, Brazil: Aleph.
Henry, J. M., & Comeaux, H. P. (1999). Gender egalitarianism in coed sport: A case study of American soccer. *International Review for the Sociology of Sport, 34,* 277–290.
Knijnik, J. (2011). From the cradle to Athens: The silver-coated story of a warrior in Brazilian soccer. *Sporting Traditions, 28,* 20.
Knijnik, J., & Vasconcellos, E. G. (2005). Les femmes en crampons à coeur ouvert au Brésil. In T. Terret (Ed.), *Sport et genre: v1—La conquête d'une citadelle masculine* (pp. 295–308). Paris, France: L' Harmattan.
Knijnik, J. (2009). *Handebol.* São Paulo, Brazil: Odysseus Editora.
Knijnik, J. D. (2003). *A mulher brasileira e o esporte: seu corpo, sua história.* [Brazilian woman and sport: Her body, her history]. São Paulo, Brazil: Editora Mackenzie.
Loland, N. W. (1999). Some contradictions and tensions in elite sportsmen's attitudes towards their bodies. *International Review for the Sociology of Sport, 34,* 291–302.
Meân, L. (2001). Identity and discursive practice: Doing gender on the football pitch. *Discourse & Society, 12,* 789–815.
Melo, V., & Lacerda, C. (2010). Masculinidade e danca, masculinidade e esporte: relações. In J. Knijnik (Ed.), *Genero e esporte: masculinidades e feminilidades* (pp. 111–136). Rio de Janeiro, Brazil: Apicuri.
Mennesson, C., & Clément, J. P. (2003). Homosociability and homosexuality: The case of soccer played by women. *International Review for the Sociology of Sport, 38,* 311-330.
Merleau-Ponty, M. (1992a). *Le Visible et l'invisble.* Paris, France: Gallimard.
Merleau-Ponty, M. (1992b). *Phénomélogie de la perception.* Paris, France: Gallimard.
Moragues, J. L. (1998). Le motionnel: Hypothèse d'une organization pulsionnelle originaire dans le mouvement. *Cliniques meditéranéennes, 57–58,* 259–271.

Rial, C. S. M. (2000). Rúgbi e judô: Esporte e masculinidade. [Rugby and judô: Sport and masculinity]. In J. M. Pedro & M. P. Grossi (Eds.), *Masculino, feminino, plural: Gênero na interdisciplinaridade* (pp. 229–258). Florianópolis, Brasil: Editora Mulheres.

Romero, E. (2010). As meninas babam o jogo e os meninos são mandões. In J. Knijnik & R. Zuzzi (Eds), *Meninos e meninas na educação física: Genero e corporeidade no seculo 21* (pp. 107–136). Jundiai, Spain: Fontoura.

Scraton, S., Fasting, K., Pfister, G., & Bunuel, A. (1999). It's still a man's game? The experiences of top-level European women footballers. *International Review for the Sociology of Sport, 34,* 99–111.

Struna, N. L. (1994). The recreational experiences of early American women. In M. Costa & S. Guthrie (Eds.), *Women and sport: Interdisciplinary perspectives* (pp. 45–62). Champaign, IL: Human Kinetics.

Terret, T. (2004). Sport et masculinité: Une revue de questions. *Revue International des sciences du sport et de l'éducation physique, 66,* 209–225.

Votre, S., & Mourão, L. (2003). Women's football in Brazil: Progress and problems. *Soccer and Society, 4,* 254–267.

## ENDNOTES

[1] Button soccer is a board game that simulates a real soccer game played on a table-top using concave 'disks' or 'caps clocks' as the players. It was very popular in Brazil until recently, played by boys as well as adults and old men.

[2] Menesson & Clément, 2003; Knijnik & Vasconcellos, 2005; Darido, 2002; Straton et al., 1999; Gomes, Silva, & Queirós, 2004; Cox & Thompson; Henry & Comeaux, 2000; Goellner, 2005—to mention only a few examples and enrich a potential reader's interest in this subject.

# Dance, Masculinity, and Physical Education: An International Perspective

Michael Gard

## INTRODUCTION

There have been a number of ethnographic, anthropological, and sociological studies that cast at least some light on the intersections between dance and masculinity. Internationally, a small literature exists, including works specific to particular countries and regions. In various ways, these works show how different cultures produce different answers to this question: *Who or what is a male dancer?* However, at present there have been no systematic attempts to offer an international perspective on masculinity and dance.

There are at least two reasons for attempting to bring this disparate literature together. First, a comparative approach can cast the findings from a specific context in a different light than if they were considered in isolation. For example, attitudes in one context might look more or less liberal when compared with attitudes in another context. Second, an international perspective allows us to consider the significance or otherwise of wider social forces such as colonization, de-colonization, and globalization.

CHAPTER 7

Cultural shifts can then be linked and compared to similar shifts in other parts of the world. For example, can we draw conclusions about the way the processes of globalization have changed and are changing ideas about men who dance?

But there is, perhaps, an even more intriguing set of questions that relate to dance and masculinity. For some time there has been a generally assumed notion that anxiety about men who dance—particularly men who participate in theatrical forms of dance like ballet and modern dance—has been a White, Western anxiety. To what extent is this true? In the first section of this chapter I attempt not so much to dispel this idea as to complicate it. I do this by drawing together scholarship from a range of fields to describe an intercultural dialogue across time and space in which the meanings ascribed to dancing men have shifted and migrated.

The second section of the chapter shifts the focus to schools, physical education, and the teaching of dance. Here I discuss the way cultural politics shape the reasons why we might teach dance, as well as how teachers do and might dare to teach dance in schools.

## DANCE, MASCULINITY, AND BELONGING

Is there anything that can be sensibly generalized about the interconnections between the practice of dance (any kind of dance) and the construction of masculinity around the world? My answer to this question is signaled by my attempt to write this chapter in the first place; if there were nothing to say then there would be nothing to write. And yet, my feeling is that it is essential to be clear about the limitations of this undertaking in order to minimize the danger of arriving at what may look like naively grandiose conclusions.

My primary focus in this chapter is what many dance scholars call "theatrical dance": ballet and other predominantly Western forms of artistic dance (such as modern dance) that are normally performed by professional dancers in front of paying audiences. Immediately, there are problems for the international perspective I am trying to take in this chapter. Ballet and other forms of theatrical dance have their historical roots in European countries and, in many respects, have little in common with the traditional and artistic dance forms found in non-European countries. This is important because the guiding curiosity in all my research into dance and masculinity has been the widespread ambivalence toward male theatrical dancers in Anglophone countries over the last 150 years or so. Given this focus, it is probably fair to ask whether non-Western forms of dance shed any light on the gender politics of Western theatrical dance at all. We should also remember that theatrical dance is only one amongst many other forms that Europeans and other Westerners do.

## Dance, Masculinity, and Physical Education: An International Perspective

A second and more fundamental point is that the sheer global diversity of dance forms, on the one hand, and culturally specific masculinities, on the other, probably renders most attempts to generalize not so much speculative as essentially meaningless. What follows, then, is not an attempt to make generalizations about the world, but rather to summarize a body of scholarship in order to provoke thought. To this end, I have included a number of studies of non-theatrical dance in non-Western countries. In essence, I am suggesting that we look at research into the genres of dance in which men participate around the world in order to draw potentially useful insights about Western theatrical dance.

Dance scholarship teaches us that all forms of dance are a means through which group membership is expressed. All dances have rules or conventions and, notwithstanding ideas about "freedom" and "self-expression" that are emphasized by some practitioners, these practices or styles are a fundamental precondition for calling something a dance in the first place. The ancestry of these rules is always a complex matter. For example, although it is commonly associated with Buenos Aires, the tango—like Argentina itself—is a hybrid creation with its roots in Africa and Europe. In the 19th century, the tango became influenced by both urban and rural Argentina (Taylor, 1998). In turn, the tango's hybrid past has led to a hybrid future, with different versions of the tango springing up in far-off places like Finland and Japan (Savigliano, 1995). Because dances have rules, and different cultures produce different kinds of dance, the ways in which people dance is probably always, at least in part, a matter of cultural politics. Anthropology is perhaps as good as any other place to begin to explore the cultural politics of dance, particularly as they relate to constructions of masculinity.

There is a strong tendency amongst scholars who research dance in specific cultural contexts to see dance as a kind of human universal. The most well-known of these is probably Hanna, with her two landmark publications *To Dance Is Human: A Theory of Nonverbal Communication* (1979) and *Dance, Sex, and Gender: Signs of Identity, Dominance, Defiance and Desire* (1988). It is difficult to know how useful or robust an observation this is, since one is struck by the regularity with which almost any area of human endeavor—sport, music, science, and the accumulation of wealth, to name only a few—is described as an expression of some innate human drive. If anything, the temptation to essentialize dance makes it more difficult to understand its cultural specificity or the significance of differences between cultures.

For example, although primarily ethnomusicology, Meintjes's (2004) field work with the Zulu in post-apartheid South Africa focuses on masculine display in Ngoma song and dance found in rural KwaZulu-Natal. These are complex matters, and yet

# CHAPTER 7

Meintjes (2004) argues that modern Ngoma embodies aspects of the political, social, and cultural struggles faced by Zulu men during the 20th century. In particular, she suggests that the various attacks on Zulu male authority have engendered a strident harking back to warrior narratives and ever more hyperbolic displays of physical power and boasts of sexual prowess through song and dance (Meintjes, 2004). That is, Ngoma singing and dancing have changed over time partly because of the changing position of men within Zulu and wider society. In this case it is at least possible to argue that dance forms take shape not in response to some essential quality possessed by a group of people, but rather as a way of preserving or defending the social and cultural forms that groups of people have created over time (Meintjes, 2004).

Many other similar examples could be offered, particularly if we turn to the cultural politics of nation states. Van Zile's (1998) research into the *Chinju kommu* sword dance of South Korea explores the struggles over whether the dance was originally for men or for women, and how and by whom it should be danced in the present. What needs to be stressed here is that because the dance is seen as a cultural institution, emblematic of the modern South Korean nation, local gender politics find their national expression in the struggles over, in some cases, the minutest detail of movement and costume. The quality of a gesture, the position of the legs, and the posture of the body all have the potential to be read as celebrating or undermining dominant ideas about the nation. We see similar issues at stake in Karayanni's (2006) extensive work in Cyprus, where dance forms with lengthy folk traditions are layered by ethnic tensions between Greek and Turkish Cypriots. While there is compelling evidence to show that Greek and Turkish cultures share interwoven histories, an enormous amount of energy on both sides of this divide has gone into dichotomizing Greek and Turkish music and dance so that, for example, music and dance forms that had clear Turkish flavors have been excised from mainstream Greek Cypriot cultural life. The struggle over Cypriot identity on the Greek side has created considerable cultural pressure for male dancers to move in particular ways and not others in order to avoid any association with the despised, "feminized" Turks (Karayanni, 2006).

The Cypriot example is suggestive on a number of levels because, as Karayanni (2006) argues, state laws against homosexuality are primarily a legacy of British colonial rule, and this legacy has subsequently been fiercely defended by church leaders and politicians. Homosexuality, like insufficiently "masculine" ways of dancing, is seen by some as a sign of national decay and likely to undermine the resolve and physical strength needed to defeat the Turkish threat. A reviewer of his work argues that Karayanni shows how "Middle Eastern dance was transformed through the European gaze and its underlying values into an art form acceptable to Western audiences as well as native élites who aligned themselves with the Western canon" (Kudsieh, 2006, p. 1). In particular, Karayanni shows how travelers and writers transformed belly dancing according to their Western, colonial, heterosexual tastes. And yet there is also the issue of

> the relationship between the status of belly dance in colonial discourse, the establishment of a Westernized Greek and Greek-Cypriot national identity, and the excision of Oriental Greek and Cypriot dances such as the Rebetika from national folklore. Modern national Greek identity is presented as masculine, dignified, and refined; it is an identity that completely dissociates itself from the (homo)erotic Oriental identity. (Kudsieh, 2006, p. 1)

There is clear historical evidence that sexually ambiguous male youths danced *chifteteli* (belly dancing) for the pleasure of Cypriot rulers as late as the 19th century, and that *chifteteli* has both Greek and Turkish origins (Karayanni, 2006). However, the *chifteteli* has been actively erased from Greek Cypriot history, as well as its classrooms, where the dual political projects of nation building and gender construction are enacted:

> Nationalist ideology prescribed the parameters of acceptable kinesthetic expression and in the process defined its alluring other: aberrant movement with its potential for spectacle and, therefore, excitement in sexual terms. This discourse also distils the principles that affected the pedagogy of my elementary school years as a Greek Cypriot in the early 1970s. During our physical education class we were taught some of those dances that had been established as "panhellenic": the kalamatianos, syrtos, and tsamikos (although the onus for learning the dances in my school was on the girls rather than the boys since dancing was deemed more fitting for girls). (Karayanni, 2006, p. 254)

Dunne's (1998) discussion of power and gender/sexual politics in the Middle East more generally makes a number of related points. For example, he argues that Islamic views about prostitution and homosexuality have waxed and waned throughout history in a similar way to that in Western history. However,

> Violence directed against male homosexuals appears to be on the rise. Effeminate male dancers known as *khawals* were popular public

performers in the 19th-century Egypt; today that term is an insult, equivalent to "faggot." The 19th-century *khawals* may not have enjoyed respect as "men," but there is little evidence that they were subjected to violence. Hostility to homosexual practices has been part of the political and cultural legacy of European colonialism. (Dunne, 1998, p. 11)

At the risk of obscuring important national differences, there are strikingly similar accounts in other countries. Hayashi (1998) argues that prior to the 1870s, Japanese traditional dances had been performed exclusively by men, while women had only been allowed to dance on special occasions. These traditional dances were not taught in schools. After 1870, the Japanese government imported a European-style physical education system that mandated martial arts and sports for boys and gymnastics and folk dance for girls. Hayashi claims that the government was clear about its desire to produce men ready for army service and beautiful, subservient women who would devote themselves to the support of men. Partly as a result of these changes, a strong prejudice against males' dancing developed. However, in 1994 dance became co-educational in Japanese high schools, a move that, perhaps not surprisingly, was strongly resisted by senior male physical education teachers.

A host of other anthropological work could be cited here to reinforce the point that nontheatrical forms of dance have operated across Indigenous (e.g., Tiwi Islands [Grau, 1993, 1994] and Africa [Oyorty, 1993]), migrant (e.g., Mexicans in the United States [Sanchez, 2004]) and modern urban cultures (e.g., northern Greece in Cowan, 1990) in order to define cultural groups to themselves and to symbolize the status, roles, and responsibilities of both men and women. And yet all of the literature cited above acknowledges the fluidity of dance—the ways in which dance reflects both changing social and cultural circumstances, as well as being a vehicle for resistance to norms. It is precisely because dance is a rule-bound activity that it harbors the potential for confrontation and disruption.

## BALLET BOYS

Ramsay Burt's (1995) foundational text, *The Male Dancer: Bodies, Spectacle, Sexualities*, makes the important point that Western suspicion of male theatrical dancers was not always a matter of homophobia. Broadly put, the decline of the male dancer during the Romantic period of the 19th century was as much a product of emerging class distinctions as anything else. Middle-class sensibilities, fueled by a range of social movements such as industrialization, muscular Christianity, and organized sport, began to see ballet as both a remnant of decadent, effete nobility as well as, in the specific case of the male dancer, ugly, rustic buffoonery. In one sense, then, we could actually link initial changes to Western European attitudes toward the male theatrical dancer in the 19th century to some of the non-Western research cited above. That is, while we are talking about very different kinds of dance, in all of these cases the moving male body is policed and/or transformed according to shifting cultural and national narratives, and the importance of men within these narratives.

One surprising aspect of Burt's work is its relative quietness about the influence of religion. In particular, it is at least worth noting that European Christianity had for centuries harbored serious misgivings about dancing bodies (for an example of the Church of England's opprobrium against dancing during the mid-1500s, see Haddon, 2004). In European countries such as the Republic of Ireland and Northern Ireland where the Catholic Church still plays an important role in public affairs, denunciations of modern artistic dance continued until relatively recently (Wulff, 2003). Of course, fear of dancing as a sinful entrée into sexual misconduct is not the same thing as homophobic suspicion of male dancers. In fact, given that the former sees dancing as leading to straight sex and the latter links dancing with gay sex, we could actually think of them as contradictory. However, the important link here is surely the association of dancing bodies with sex *per se*. After all, ballet dancers are, amongst other things, artists, and yet there are few, if any, other forms of artistic expression that immediately mark the artist with a sexual identity in quite the same way dance can. In other words, I am rehearsing an argument here about the flesh-despising currents that run through the history of Judeo-Christian cultures (and not just Protestantism), a point that takes us back to Burt.

As well as macrolevel economic and social forces, Burt also stresses the role of individual desire. During the latter half of the 19th century, the idea of individual sexual identities was emerging and the seeds of modern homophobia were beginning to sprout. While Burt claims that the male dancer/homosexual stereotype did not flower until Nijinsky and the Ballet Russes in the first decade of the 20th century, his argument is that the latter 19th century is a period in which it was simply becoming more difficult for Western men to take pleasure in looking at the bodies of other men. New codes of masculinity were reshaping desire such that men no longer simply had to prove that they were superior to women, as in the past; they now had to prove that masculinity was the opposite of femininity. Just like the hardening of Islamic ideas about homosexuality and gender ambiguity over the last 200 years, social life in modernizing Western European countries and their scattered colonies called for stricter and clearer rules about how men and women thought, looked, and moved.

CHAPTER 7

Space does not allow for a more complete summary of scholarship concerning the historical emergence of the male dancer/homosexual stereotype (for a book-length account, readers should consult Burt [1995] or for an excellent journal article version, Adams [2005].) What we can do here is to draw on historical accounts that show that many forms of dance, not just ballet, became potentially suspect terrain for boys and men in Western countries during the 20th century. For example, in the field of physical education, the 20th century began and continued to see folk and creative forms of dance as potentially harmful to young men, preferring to see organized sports as the proper proving ground for male bodies (Lloyd & West, 1988; Winter, 1999). Even where dance was encouraged, educators feared that "inappropriately" feminine movements could be "caught" by unsuspecting boys, much like the common cold, thus turning them into less-convincing males (see Adams; 2005 for examples). Winter's (1999) study of the career of the early 20th century physical educator Luther Hasley Gulick is instructive here. Gulick was a prominent New York educational progressive who believed in the power of folk dance to reinvigorate the American nation in the face of mass migration and what he took to be the subsequent threat to national identity. For Gulick, folk dances were an ideal vehicle for preparing America's girls—and only its girls—for the nation-building that lay ahead. Boys, by contrast, needed to develop the bravery, toughness, and teamwork that only sports and athletics could provide. Winter (1999) argues that for Gulick and his contemporaries, "national identity functioned as a performative practice, compelled through a gendered and racialized discourse of national identity" (p. 33). In other words, we see here the continuation of the way dancing bodies were understood as constitutive of collective identity, and the way that dance was invested with the power to both enhance and (in the case of a dancing male) undermine collective identity and cohesion. It is almost as if the dancing or moving body was credited with magical powers to save or corrupt societies and the individuals who composed them.

For more artistic forms of dance, the late 19th century and first decades of the 20th century are notable for the high number of prominent female, as opposed to male, dancers who earned international fame. It is during this period that solo dancers such as Isadora Duncan, Loie Fuller, Ruth St. Denis, Maud Allan, and Gertrude Hoffman rose to prominence, many of them, such as St. Denis and Allan, specializing in dance performances that drew from exotic representations of the "East" (for discussions of these dancers, see Thomas [1995] and Banes [1998]).

One of the insights we might take from this period of Western dance is the way in which stage dancers raided the imagery of the Orient in order to construct ideas about the West and the East in the context of imperialism and growing international mass migration. For example, Koritz's (1994) study of Maud Allan's popularity in England around 1908 argues that Allan presented audiences with exotic forms of movement that both disturbed and reassured the English about their place in the world and the existing gender order. Allan's vision of the East was considered "authentic" by many of her newspaper reviewers, but it was a comfortable authenticity that glossed the East as an undifferentiated mass—titillating rather than shocking or confronting. Allan's East was generalized, from no country in particular, and fitted comfortably with an imperialist ideology that saw Eastern peoples as both exciting and dangerous, but essentially in need of British imperial order.

The pioneering female modern dancers of the late 19th/early 20th centuries are instructive on a number of levels. They remind us that the male theatrical dancer is much less visible during this period of history, a point some scholars attribute to the generally low status of dancing as a profession at this time (Thomas, 1995). Taking a line from Burt's general thesis, there are grounds for attributing this invisibility not only to changing codes of personal masculinity but also new forms of nationalism and the place of men within new, robust, and often militaristic narratives of national identity. It is also worth remembering that the prominence of female dancers was explicable at this time through the various feminist movements across Europe and North America. In other words, this was a time when understandings of what makes a man were being narrowed down while the roles and status of women were opening up.

This is not to say there were no male theatrical dancers during this period. Besides the Ballet Russes stars, notably Nijinsky, other European-based artists emerged although these, like the Swedish-born Jean Börlin, had connections with Scandinavia where ballet enjoyed greater support than in southern and western Europe. Börlin gave a number of somewhat controversial recitals in Paris in the early 1920s, some of which were reported (probably incorrectly, according to Batson [1999]) to have been performed naked. Börlin's performances elicited a range of reactions, but on the whole he seems to have been ridiculed and cast as a disgrace to the recent memory of the Great War's fallen. One French reviewer of Börlin's *L'Homme et son désir* wrote,

> M. Jean Borlin, bastard son of the king of Sweden, has come to Paris to show us his thighs and his navel. . . . In one of his latest choreographic manifestations [*L'Homme et son désir*], he appears completely naked. Naked women, on stage, that finally can be understood. It is permissible for a daughter of Eve to believe herself well enough made to show her nakedness to all passersby; and besides, women have no shame, everyone knows that. . . . The naked man is permissible only as a gladiator. . . . In

any case, leave us alone with all these polar choreographies! Or, at least, please show us only female dancers. Enough male dancers! And I'm surprised that a poilu [French World War I soldier] has not yet protested against these exhibitions of hairless bodies. (Batson, 1999, p. 239)

Batson (1999) reminds us that this performance came after Nijinsky's debut in Paris more than ten years before. Male dancers had been somewhat rehabilitated by the Ballets Russes, but Batson's view is that Nijinsky's performance reflected a hypermasculinity that attempted to obscure an anxiety about being "manly enough." Drawing on Freud via the cultural theorist Judith Butler, Batson interprets this as a "melancholia" for what is lost:

> One might then argue that Nijinsky's supercharged "masculine" performances point not only to a discomforting (perceived) femininity, but also to his grasping for and incorporating that which he, at least discursively, was not allowed to have: a conventionally understood masculinity. Similarly, then, insistent calls for a specularized "true" masculinity after the devastation of World War I may point to the ungrieved loss of that very masculinity not only for the artists themselves, but also, at least allegorically, for the nation. (Batson, 1999, p. 242)

As I stressed at the beginning of this chapter, there have been no scholarly attempts to evaluate the status of the male dancer from a historically or sociologically comparative point of view. However, what I have presented above suggests there is a potentially fruitful but as yet unexplored line of research that connects both "Eastern" and the "Western" ideas about the male dancer. This research would be concerned with the ways in which the East and the West used and were used by the other to arrive at rather similar ideas about whether and how a man should dance. The late 19th and early 20th centuries seem to be pivotal here because this is a period in which the global circulation of people, capital, systems of government, commodities, art, and even tastes were undergoing unprecedented change. It is also a time when the idea of the nation state was finding strident expression across Europe and many of its colonies, and new nationalistic narratives about who belongs and who does not were taking shape (for a detailed account of these developments see Hobsbawm [1990]). My point is that, although globally complex, the scholarship discussed here suggests that the male dancer became suspect (or at least potentially suspect) because of the ways in which he came to be seen as both a symbol of national identity and, later, symptomatic of sexual, social and national decay. However, returning to my question about dance as an innate expression of human desires, I would add that the change in status of the male dancer never appears to be something that is simply "home grown." While it is clearly a matter of internal group cohesion and local cultural politics, it seems just as fair to say that the male dancer, like masculinity itself, is a matter of boundary patrol and the definition of self—be it a person or a nation—in relation to others.

Although it seems likely that Burt's (1995) history of the male dancer will remain the definitive version for some time to come, this work leaves open questions about the extent to which we must see the male dancer/homosexual stereotype as a phenomenon with its origins in Western Judeo-Christian cultures, leaving to one side the tricky problem of how we would go about defining which are Western Judeo-Christian cultures and which are not. For example, what exactly would we want to say about ballet in countries like Russia? While some English-speaking ballet writers have been inclined to romanticize the status of ballet in Russia (for example, Clark & Crisp, 1984) and, in particular, its male ballet stars, it is surely not too glib to say that Russia was and still is a big place. Historical and fictionalized accounts of the life of Rudolph Nureyev suggest that, as in the West, ballet has been celebrated more by the moneyed than the unmoneyed (for example, see Kavanagh's [2007] definitive biography *Rudolf Nureyev: The Life,* or Colum McCann's [2003] fictionalized account, *Dancer*). In a similar vein, a number of ballet histories (for example, Au [1988]) have contrasted the relatively high status of male ballet dancers in 19th-century Denmark with their virtual disappearance in other Western European countries. Throughout this period, Danish ballet retained its royal patronage and, no doubt, was therefore celebrated by the upper echelons of society. However, this says nothing about the attitudes of the vast majority of people, and there is no obvious reason to suspect that the male dancer/homosexual stereotype was or is any less prevalent in Denmark. Wulff's (1998) ethnography of some of the world's leading ballet schools, including the Royal Swedish Ballet, gives no indication that homophobic suspicion of male dancers has been absent in supposedly liberal Scandinavian countries.

A 2001 edition of *Dance Magazine* included an article featuring testimonies from male dancers about the prejudices they had faced as they pursued their career as boys and young men. While anecdotal, what these brief accounts suggest is that these boys—who grew up in the second half of the 20th century in either the U.S., Italy, Belgium, France, or Argentina—all faced considerable harassment from friends and family members for choosing dance as a career. In stark contrast, two Chinese-born men wrote that there was no prejudice directed towards male ballet dancers in China and that they were respected, first and foremost, as artists.

Where does this leave us? In my view, there are no simple grounds on which to base definitive conclusions about the origins or modes of proliferation of anti-male dancer sentiment. What the study of folk and other nontheatrical dance forms around the world suggests is that, via its colonial activities, industrializing 19th-century Europe exported some of its emerging prejudices about homosexuality and its developing discomfort with the dancing male body to other parts of the world. For example, as we saw above, there exists evidence that certain forms of male dancing have simply been erased from the cultural landscapes of some Middle Eastern countries. However, this leaves unanswered questions about the extent to which homophobic suspicion of male dancers originated in the West or, perhaps, found already receptive and fertile ground in other places. In other words, to what extent should we accept the view, popularized during the 20th century, that romanticizes non-Western cultures for their celebration of male dancers while singling out the West as an island of prejudice?

## DANCE, MASCULINITY, AND PHYSICAL EDUCATION

In the final section of this chapter, I turn to the physical education classroom and the status of dance within it. This may seem a large departure from the preceding discussions. However, it is fairly clear that the marginalization of dance within physical education in Western classrooms over the last 100 years is a product of similar social forces that brought about the decline of the male dancer. A long list of physical education scholars (e.g., Brennan, 1996; Flintoff, 1991; Gard, 2003; Paechter, 2000; Talbot, 1997; Wright, 1996) have argued that it was primarily via gendered ideologies and constructions of gendered bodies that physical education as an institution historically aligned itself with the predominantly masculine world of games and sports playing. Of course, times change and there are clear signs that some physical educators want to use dance, both in the preparation of teachers and in the school classroom. Physical education scholars from outside the native English-speaking West have also identified the effect of gender ideologies on physical education in general and dance in particular. For example, Ravé, Pérez, and Poyatos (2007) have shown that a high percentage of Spanish school students hold narrowly stereotypical views about gender-appropriate physical activity and body shape. Larsson, Fagrell, and Redelius (2009) make a similar point in the context of Swedish physical education. They also stress the ways in which physical education content is skewed toward what they call a "tribute to masculinity," a situation in which male students are simply assumed to be disinterested in activities like gymnastics and dance.

Keeping in mind the historical and social background that I have sketched in this chapter, how then do we rescue dance in the physical education classroom, particularly where boys are concerned? A number of academics, dancers, dance writers, and dance educators have answered this question by suggesting that we need to make dance "boy friendly" (e.g., Clarke & Crisp, 1984; Crawford, 1994; Dymoke, 1998; Villella, 1992). At its most straightforward, this position rests on the idea of boys having an essential nature that is at odds with artistic dance's general aesthetic. Dance, they argue, should be presented to boys in ways that emphasize its athletic qualities and affinities with competitive sports. Fisher (2007) calls this the "make it macho" strategy and she, Keefe (2006), and Adams (2005) provide excellent historical accounts of this strategy in both artistic and educational circles.

Against this strategy, Fisher and others (e.g., Adams, 2005; Gard, 2001; Keefe, 2006; Risner, 2002, 2007) have rejected the idea of pandering to masculine stereotypes in dance education. Taken together, these authors argue that, as an educational medium, one of dance's most important attributes is its difference from the forms of masculinity embodied in games and competitive sports. We should not forget that the birth of modern sports in 19th-century Western Europe was explicitly linked with a desire to produce tough, athletic, competitive boys and men. Put another way, sports were invented to breed certain kinds of males (Mangan, 1981). Seen this way, it would be ironic and misguided if we now assumed that stereotypical ideas about masculinity are an unchangeable essence that competitive sports simply and naturally reflect. Critics of the "make it macho" strategy point out that dance's value is partly in embodying alternative masculinities. Fisher (2007) goes further by arguing that we need to accept that dance is not sport, and that ballet and other forms of dance call for a different set of movement skills and qualities. Fisher (2007) is probably mistaken in drawing such a sharp qualitative distinction between dance and sport; there is surely considerable overlap between the physical and psychological demands of sport and artistic dance. However, from an educational point of view, any field's claim to a place in the curriculum would seem to rest partly on its distinctiveness from, rather than similarity to, other fields of study.

One alternative to being trapped in what amounts to an ideological deadlock about the kinds of movements boys should or should not do in dance is to consider the kinds of concepts I have considered in this chapter. In particular, what I have in mind here is a focus on the power of dance to articulate group identities, boundaries, and the insiders and outsiders created in this process. That is, rather than arriving at firm conclusions about which movements create what kind of identities (an idea that, as we have seen in this chapter, has a long history), physical educators might involve students in the process of decoding and recoding movement. For example, what do movements signify and why? Here I am reminded of David Gere's (2001) analysis of the choreographer Joe Goode's work *29 Effeminate Gestures,* in which the choreographer works to make explicit the bodily workings of male effeminacy, precisely which movements signify effeminacy in a Western man and which do not. What are the rules?

All rational approaches to dance education have their drawbacks since they each tend to overlook the fact that dancing can be fun and even exhilarating, and that this is probably the best reason to teach it. However, one advantage of trying to explore identity, group membership, and otherness through dance education is that it offers a virtually endless supply of source material. What the study of dance history and culture tells us is that any identity—be it gendered, classed, ethnic, or anything else—can be embodied. In fact, identities are often embodied, for it is through recognition of the physical that they have the power to include or exclude. It is true, of course, that group identities are manifest in sound, word, touch, and taste. And yet, movement is a simple and immediate vehicle for articulating identity and otherness.

An identity-focused approach to dance education has many risks. Some children might take this as an invitation to ridicule or even vilify certain groups of people. This means that dance education, like any dance genre, must have its ground-rules—its rules for insider status, as it were. Certain kinds of dance will be unacceptable according to culture and context. But this, too, is an interesting educational puzzle for students to consider: How and in what circumstances might dance offend people?

I would also want to stress that, although they may not describe it in the same way as I have done here, dancing about identity and otherness is something that physical educators do all the time. By asking small children to move "like robots" or "like they are walking quicksand" or "like they are floating on air," they invite students to inhabit a new identity, if only for a few seconds. Folk, social, and theatrical dances make a similar demand on the imagination, although physical educators often simply stress the mechanics of the dances they teach rather than making explicit the group that this or that dance invites dancers to join. This is a shame because it fails to engage the pleasure of fantasy and identity play. For many or most children and young people, group membership will be something that they consciously enact, resist, or at least think about every day.

One final point: Creating pedagogical rules for movement is a potentially productive, stimulating, and sometimes hilarious way of stimulating the dance-making process. In other words, what kind of dance would emerge if particular rules applied such as "wrists must never flex" or "bodies must never lose contact" or "no movement can ever be done twice"? My experience of using these kinds of stimuli is that strange new beings appear with strange new identities. In other words, students create new groups of insiders that they will be able to differentiate from outsiders, and the power of movement to include or exclude will be making its presence clear. This does not mean that we should design dance education experiences that set out to generate unnecessary divisions between students or reinforce harmful social divisions that exist in the world. Teachers need to remain alert to these possibilities and be prepared to challenge them if they arise. However, being someone or something, and not someone or something else, is an inherent part of dance experience. Part of the educational potential of dance is to allow students space to depersonalize inclusion and exclusion—at least to some extent—through performance, and thus to make the practices of inclusion and exclusion more visible and open to scrutiny and disruption.

## CONCLUSION: USING DANCE IN PHYSICAL EDUCATION

Sussman (1990) is just one of many dance scholars who remind us that physical education once had a tradition that linked it firmly to artistically minded modern dance. This was particularly so in U.S. liberal arts colleges during the first half of the 20th century, where women's physical education was virtually synonymous with modern dance. My 15 years as a physical educator have taught me that Western physical education has all but erased this tradition from its memory. This process of forgetting has left physical education poorer and without a sense of its own creative possibilities. The history of dance is a treasure trove of ideas, waiting to be raided by physical educators. It is physical education's squandered inheritance. Not only does the history and anthropology of dance teach us how fluid and flexible ideas about group membership (including masculinity) are, they also hint at the ways in which we have derived our group identities from other groups. Above all, the history and anthropology of dance makes clear that group identity is, amongst other things, a performance with rules.

More broadly, there are some encouraging signs of life for dance education. Recent years have brought more dance—both social and artistic—to television screens in most Western countries. This apparent spike in interest is open to multiple interpretations, including increasing general acceptance of male dancing. Perhaps not coincidentally, this has happened at the same time as the importance of the creative arts in education is being revisited, most notably thanks to the work of high-profile educational commentators such as Ken Robinson, who has been particularly enthusiastic about the educational value of dance. Of course, these two developments are not necessarily symbiotic; much of reality television dance seems more preoccupied with celebrity and physical beauty and less with dance as a collective, cultural, or artistic endeavor. Nonetheless, we are perhaps in a historical moment in which there is more interest in (or at least less resistance to) dance, particularly amongst boys and men. In educational settings, this potential can only be exploited if teachers have compelling reasons and methods for teaching dance. In this chapter I have argued that one seam of possibility is to link dance experiences to embodied identities. This means seeing dance not simply as one more way in which calories can be burned and a physically active life pursued. Rather, my suggestion here is that dance is a vehicle through which we can learn more about ourselves and the social groupings to which we do and do not belong.

## REFERENCES

Adams, M. L. (2005). Death to the prancing prince: Effeminacy, sport discourses and the salvation of men's dancing. *Body and Society, 11*, 63–86.

Au, S. (1988). *Ballet and modern dance*. London, England: Thames and Hudson.

Banes, S. (1998). *Dancing women: Female bodies on stage*. London, England: Routledge.

Batson, C. R. (1999). Borlin, masculinity, and "L'Homme et son desir." *Dance Chronicle, 22*, 239–249.

Brennan, D. (1996). Dance in the Northern Ireland physical education curriculum: A farsighted policy or an unrealistic innovation? *Women's Studies International Forum, 19*, 493–503.

Burt, R. (1995). *The male dancer: Bodies, spectacle, sexualities*. London, England: Routledge.

Clarke, M., & Crisp, C. (1984). *Dancer: Men in dance*. London, England: British Broadcasting Corporation.

Cowan, J. K. (1990). *Dance and the body politic in northern Greece*. Princeton, NJ: Princeton University Press.

Crawford, J. R. (1994). Encouraging male participation in dance. Journal of Physical Education, *Recreation and Dance, 65*, 40–43.

Speaking out: More male dancers tell it like it is. (2001, November). Dance Magazine. Retrieved from http://www.thefreelibrary.com/Speaking+out%3A+more+male+dancers+tell+it+like+it+is.+%28Cover+Story%29.-a080116504

Dunne, B. (1998). Power and sexuality in the Middle East. *Middle East Report, 206*, 8–11, 37.

Dymoke, K. (1998). Premier league. *Animated*, pp. 28–29.

Fisher, J. (2007). Make it maverick: Rethinking the "make it macho" strategy for men in ballet. *Dance Chronicle, 30*, 45–66.

Flintoff, A. (1991). Dance, masculinity and teacher education. The *British Journal of Physical Education, 22*(4), 31–35.

Gard, M. (2001). Dancing around the 'problem' of boys and dance. *Discourse: Studies in the Cultural Politics of Education, 22*, 213–225.

Gard, M. (2003). Moving and belonging: Dance, sport and sexuality. *Sex Education 3*, 105–118.

Gere, D. (2001). 29 effeminate gestures: Choreographer Joe Goode and the heroism of effeminacy. In J. C. Desmond (Ed.), *Dancing desires: Choreographing sexualities on and off the stage* (pp. 349–382). Madison, WI: The University of Wisconsin Press.

Grau, A. (1993). Gender interchangeability among the Tiwi. In H. Thomas (Ed.), *Dance, gender and culture* (pp. 94–111). London, England: MacMillan Press.

Grau, A. (1994). Dancers' bodies as the repository of conceptualisations of the body, with special reference to the Tiwi of Northern Australia. Paper presented at *Semiotics around the world: Synthesis in diversity*. Proceedings of the Fifth Congress of the International Association for Semiotic Studies. New York, NY: Mouton de Gruyter.

Haddon, C. (2004). *The first ever English Olimpick Games*. London, England: Hodder & Stoughton.

Hanna, J. L. (1979). *To dance is human: A theory of nonverbal communication*. Austin, TX: University of Texas Press.

Hanna, J. L. (1988). *Dance, sex, and gender: Signs of identity, dominance, defiance and desire*. Chicago, IL: University of Chicago Press.

Hayashi, M. (1998). Dance education and gender in Japan. *Choreography and Dance, 5*, 87–102.

Hobsbawm, E. J. (1990). *Nations and nationalism since 1780: Programme, myth, reality*. Cambridge, England: Cambridge University Press.

Karayanni, S. S. (2006). Moving identity: Dance in the negotiation of sexuality and ethnicity in Cyprus. *Postcolonial Studies, 9*, 251–266.

Kavanagh, J. (2007). *Nureyev: The life*. London, England: Penguin.

Keefe, M. (2006, November/December). Men dancing athletically. *The Gay and Lesbian Review*. Retrieved from http://www.glreview.org/article/article-932/

Koritz, A. (1994). Dancing the Orient for England: Maud Allan's "The vision of Salome." *Theatre Journal, 46*, 63–78.

Kudsieh, S. (2006). Review of Dancing fear and desire: Race, sexuality, and imperial politics in Middle Eastern dance. *Postcolonial Text, 2*, 1–4.

Larsson, H., Fagrell, B., & Redelius, K. (2009). Queering physical education: Between benevolence towards girls and a tribute to masculinity. *Physical Education and Sport Pedagogy, 14*, 1–17.

Lloyd, M. L., & West, B. H. (1988). Where are the boys in dance? *Journal of Physical Education, Recreation and Dance, 59*, 47–51.

Mangan, J. A. (1981). *Athleticism in the Victorian and Edwardian public school: The emergence and consolidation of an educational ideology*. Cambridge, England: Cambridge University Press.

McCann, C. (2003). *Dancer*. London, England: Phoenix.

Meintjes, L. (2004). Shoot the sergeant, shatter the mountain: The production of masculinity in Zulu Ngoma song and dance in post-apartheid South Africa. *Ethnomusicology Forum, 13*, 173–201.

Oyortey, Z. (1993). Still dancing downwards and talking back. In H. Thomas (Ed.), *Dance, gender and culture* (pp.184–199). London, England: MacMillan Press.

Paechter, C. (2000). *Changing school subjects: Power, gender and curriculum*. Buckingham, England: Open University Press.

Ravé, J. M. G., Pérez, L. M. R., & Poyatos, M. C. (2007). The social construction of gender in Spanish physical education students. *Sport, Education and Society, 12*, 141–158.

Risner, D. (2002). Re-educating dance education to its homosexuality: An invitation for critical analysis and professional unification. *Research in Dance Education, 3*, 181–187.

Risner, D. (2007). Rehearsing masculinity: Challenging the 'boy code' in dance education. *Research in Dance Education, 8*, 139–153.

Sánchez, M. I. C. (2004). El Diablo en una botella norteña: Music and the construction of Mexican masculinity. *Third Text, 18*, 483–495.

Savigliano, M. E. (1995). *Tango and the political economy of passion*. Boulder, CO: Westview Press.

Sussmann, L. (1990). Recruitment patterns: Their impact on ballet and modern dance. *Dance Research Journal, 22*, 21–28.

Talbot, M. & McFee, G. (1997). Physical education and the national curriculum: Some political issues. In G. McFee & A. Tomlinson (Eds.), *Education, sport and leisure: Connections and controversies* (pp. 34–64). Aachen, Germany: Meyer & Meyer Verlag.

Taylor, J. (1998). *Paper tangos*. Durham, NC: Duke University Press.

Thomas, H. (1995). *Dance, modernity, and culture: Explorations in the sociology of dance*. London, England: Routledge.

Van Zile, J. (1998). For men or women? The case of Chinju kommu, a sword dance from Korea. *Choreography and Dance, 5*, 53–70.

Villella, E. (1992). *Prodigal son*. New York, NY: Simon & Schuster.

Winter, T. (1999). "The healthful art of dancing": Luther Halsey Gulick, gender, the body, and the performativity of national identity. *Journal of American Culture, 22*, 33–38.

Wright, J. (1996). Mapping the discourses of physical education: Articulating a female tradition. *Journal of Curriculum Studies, 28*, 331–351.

Wulff, H. (1998). *Ballet across borders: Career and culture in the world of dancers*. Oxford, England: Berg.

Wulff, H. (2003). The Irish body in motion: Moral politics, national identity and dance. In N. Dyck & E. P. Archetti (Eds.), *Sport, dance and embodied identities* (pp. 179–196). Oxford, England: Berg.

# Sport, Masculinities, and Pain: An Australian Rules Football Perspective

Deborah Agnew and Murray Drummond

## INTRODUCTION

Australian Rules football is the indigenous football code of Australia and its most popular spectator sport. It dates back to the mid-1850s and is one of the oldest forms of football in the world. It is played with an oval leather ball—thereby heightening the unpredictability of the bounce upon hitting the ground—on a large, oval-shaped grass field. The concept is based on one team defeating an opposing team by scoring more points. Six points are awarded for a goal (the ball is kicked through two large posts set 6.4 meters apart), and one point is awarded for a ball that passes through two designated posts outside the goal. The playing field is much larger than for other codes of football, and the duration of games is lengthier too—normally in excess of 120 minutes. There is no off-side rule and players can move the ball in any direction; this also means that they can be physically tackled from any angle. Australian Rules football is thus a contact sport and physically demanding from an athletic point of view; midfielders are known to run up to 20km during a match.

# CHAPTER 8

Since the early 1980s, the elite-level sport of Australian Rules football, run as the Australian Football League (AFL), has changed significantly. Commercial income from television, advertising, and sponsorship enabled the sport to become fully professional, with several of the best players now earning one million dollars a year. The majority of the players earn in excess of $100,000-$200,000 per year. These salaries are modest by the standards of professional football codes in Europe and the United States, but the players are just as committed to their sport career. Indeed, this emergent professionalism in the AFL has meant that full-time players are expected to train harder and play with more intensity. An important, albeit unintended, consequence of this physical regimen is that overuse injuries have increased significantly. Moreover, now that the players' bodies are bigger and stronger, and many can run faster, collision injuries have become more pronounced. That said, the expectation of players to play in pain and with an injury has long been part of football culture, and remains a commonplace marker of athletic masculinity. Arguably, elite-level AFL players set the benchmark in terms of the expectations of footballers in lower levels of competition to also play in pain and with an injury. This can have serious implications for men engaging in lower grades, such as the pre-elite level, particularly the many younger males aspiring to be AFL footballers.

This chapter will outline the way in which a group of men playing in a pre-elite Australian Rules football competition express their notions of football and pain within the context of their sense of masculinity. These men are all involved in a club with the South Australian National Football League (SANFL), which is arguably the premier state-based competition in Australia and from which many footballers are drafted into AFL teams.

Australian Rules football is one of the most popular sports in Australia. However, with regard to long-term health and acute injuries, it is also one of the most dangerous sports—arguably because players seldom wear any protective clothing. Norton, Schwerdt, and Lange (2001) found that the high risk of collision in contact sports such as Australian Rules football can lead to chronic injuries and incapacitation in retired players later in life. In addition, retired Australian Football League (AFL) footballers have a higher incidence and severity of osteoarthritis in the knee than those not participating in contact sports (Deacon, Bennell, Kiss, Crossley, & Brukner, 1997). Despite advances in medical rehabilitation and conditioning there has been an increase in the number of games missed due to injury (Orchard et al., 1997, cited in Norton, Craig, & Olds, 1999).

Playing with pain and injury, while common in football, can jeopardize the long-term health of players. Yet within football culture, a player who is prepared to play in pain is widely thought to not only have courage, but an exemplary attitude toward his club and the game itself. There are many factors that influence a decision to play in pain or with an injury (Waddington, 2001). Among the more significant are the performance pressures placed on players by coaches, team managers, supporters, and the media. This pressure can be extended to club doctors, who may be coerced into challenging medical ethics to return a player to the field before their rehabilitation is complete (Howe, 2004; Waddington, Roderick, & Naik, 2001). Peer and cultural acclaim is also associated with playing in pain, one of the many reasons players tolerate such discomfort (Messner, 1992, cited in Gard & Meyenn, 2000). Little or no reaction to pain is seen as a good example to other players, as well as placing the best interests of the team above those of the individual. It is often perceived as more surprising when a player chooses not to compete while injured than when they do (Messner, 2002).

Masculinities are a social construction defined by many factors, including culture, family ethnicity, and history (Connell, 2000). The many factors leading to the construction of masculine ideals means there is not just one form of masculinity, but a variety of masculinities. It is often argued that masculinity exists in contrast to femininity (Connell, 1995). An idealized form of masculinity, hegemonic masculinity, is a concept that refers to the dominant position of men over women in particular, and also other subordinate and marginalized masculinities such as homosexuality (Connell, 1995). Characteristics that are seen as masculine are those that promote violence, toughness, and an interest in heterosexual sexual conquest. Australian Rules football is among the sports with the highest injuries because it is a high-collision sport, and as such footballers have been described as fitting the model of hegemonic masculinity (Norton, Schwerdt, & Lange, 2001). It is argued that masculinity is learned through the tolerance and normalization of violence as well as willingness to risk joint surgery to extend their playing careers (Donaldson, 1993, cited in Pringle, 2005; Fitzclarence & Hickey, 1998; Keddie, 2002). Aggressiveness is also associated with hegemonic masculinity and is a trait widely idolized within contact sports. Footballers who are willing to annihilate opponents are branded heroes, while those who do not are marginalized (Burgess et al., 2003). In an effort to minimize the risk of injury, particularly head injuries, rule changes have been brought into effect, making deliberate head contact illegal. However, the speed and intensity of the game has also increased significantly, which raises the risk of sustaining an injury (Norton, Craig, & Olds, 1999).

Finch, Donohue, and Garnham (2002) found that junior Australian Rules footballers thought it was unsafe to continue to play with an injury. Table 8.1 summarizes the findings from this study. Responses show that while junior footballers have the opinion that injuries should be fully rehabilitated before the player returns to play, almost half of those surveyed stated they would continue to play in pain. The reasons for this included the desire to be selected in the national AFL draft and the belief that this chance would be affected if they were unable to play. Other reasons for playing with an injury included feelings of isolation and lack of support from the club while injured. This same study found that players thought the media had a role in influencing footballers to play with an injury due to the glorification of those who play while hurt. Finch et al. (2002) stated that these attitudes toward playing with an injury could increase the incidence and seriousness of injury.

Hegemonic masculinity is also promoted through the media. Physically aggressive behavior is rewarded through dominant messages (Messner, Hunt, & Dunbar, 1999). For example, commentators are often heard saying players have been "out muscled," "buried," or "wholloped" by their opponents (Messner, Hunt, & Dunbar, 1999, p. 3). In addition, male sporting commentaries reinforce the notion of a "real" sportsman by urging footballers to not give in to pain, but to stand up to the challenge by being physically courageous, which in turn encourages male athletes to overconform to the sporting ethic. Aspects of this include making sacrifices for the team and also accepting risks to play through pain. Above all, a "real" sportsman does not give in—not to pressure, pain, or fear. Challenges are not backed away from; those who stand up them are seen as morally and physically courageous (Hughes & Coakley, 1991). These elements are perceived as fundamental aspects of the sporting

**TABLE 8.1: The attitudes and beliefs of junior Australian Rules footballers with regard to injuries (n=103)**
(Finch, Donohue, & Garnham, 2002, p. 152)

| Attitudes of junior Australian Rules footballers | % |
|---|---|
| It is safe to play with injuries | 5.8 |
| Willingness to play football with injuries | 58.3 |
| Would play with injuries if chances of being drafted in the national AFL draft would be affected | 76.6 |
| Playing with injuries would lead to long-term health problems | 64 |
| Belief that footballers should be fully rehabilitated before returning to play football | 69.9 |
| Admire AFL footballers who play in pain | 40.7 |
| The media/commentators glorify those who play in pain | 50.5 |

culture. The media also reinforces hegemonic masculinity through the domination of male sports shown on television (McKay, 1991). In order to change the traditional stereotypical gender discourse, as well as the discourse used by the media with regard to men and masculinities in particular, more research is needed into the attitudes of elite male sportsmen with regard to sport, masculinity, and pain. The present study is a contribution toward that goal.

The authors adopted a qualitative framework using a social constructionist perspective. Social constructionism is a sociological theory based on the view that ideas and practices—past and present—need not exist as they currently do. They are human inventions (Hacking, 1999). Indeed, Hacking argues that much of our life experience is socially constructed. This claim challenges the notion that identity is naturally occurring and is the result of individual will (Calhourn, 1995). Interviews are a widely used method in qualitative inquiries, and they proved particularly valuable for the present inquiry. Some 23 footballers and two medical professionals were recruited as interview subjects. The aims of the study were to identify the attitudes of SANFL footballers toward playing in pain and with an injury, and to identify the ways in which they constructed masculinity and how that in turn influenced their decision to play with pain and injury. The research questions addressed: How does the social construction of masculinity impact the way in which footballers play in pain and with an injury? What are the major factors influencing a footballer's decision to play in pain and with an injury? What are the perceived consequences of playing in pain and with an injury?

Participation in the study was voluntary, with participants recruited through personal and professional acquaintances through the lead author's role as a sports trainer at the club. All of the footballers were 18–33 years of age and within the senior training squad; as such, these players received financial remuneration from their club. Four of the footballers who participated had previously been part of an Australian Football League (AFL) club but, at the time of this study, were playing SANFL football.

Two focus groups, one comprising five participants and the other comprising seven participants, were conducted at the outset; participants were asked to reflect on the key topics of sport, pain, masculinity, and media constructions of masculinities. The findings from the focus groups were used to refine the semistructured interview guide utilized in the 13 individual interviews with 11 footballers, the head sports trainer, and the club physician. The main topics covered in the interviews were masculinity, sport, pain and injury, and the media. Topics were expanded upon in relation to particular responses from participants; however, the use of the interview guide allowed consistency throughout all of the interviews, thereby ensuring that all relevant topics were covered (Damon & Holloway, 2002).

The data was analyzed using an inductive thematic approach, in which common themes were identified and analyzed in relation to sport, pain, and the construction of masculinities. An inductive approach attempts to make sense of the situation without bringing pre-existing expectations to the study. It begins with a specific situation and draws upon direct program experience instead of a priori theories or hypotheses (Patton, 1990). An inductive analysis approach involves beginning with the individual experiences and searching for patterns that emerge across cases. Throughout the analysis, the data was grouped according to similarities and differences based on the researcher's understanding, experiences, and judgment.

## FINDINGS

### Masculinity

While the authors acknowledge that there are varying forms of masculinities, participants were invited to discuss the concept of masculinity within the context of their football subculture. As Drummond (2005) has argued, given the difficulty for young males to define masculinity, discussing *masculinities* with these men would likely complicate the interviews. Therefore, masculinity was an umbrella term used within the interview context, with participants invited to make their own sense and interpretation of the concept. Intriguingly, masculinity proved to be a difficult notion for most of the participants. The majority of those interviewed admitted they had not previously considered the concept of masculinity and many did not perceive themselves necessarily as masculine. This is an interesting ideological construct given that the very nature of playing Australian Rules football provides a means through which masculine identity is developed, maintained, and perpetuated. However, the players claimed not to perceive themselves as masculine. Most of the footballers indicated that masculinity was inherently physical, while attributing big muscles to being "manly." One footballer stated that masculinity is "the amount of muscle on your body and how well you can see it." On further reflection, participants contended that personality traits were associated with being masculine, such as mental and physical strength, having good leadership skills, not worrying about being physically hurt or feeling down emotionally, having self-confidence, not being overly sensitive, and being responsible.

A number of participants claimed that being masculine meant being the Australian stereotypical male, as one footballer commented:

## Sport, Masculinities, and Pain: An Australian Rules Football Perspective

> I guess what I first thought of would be almost like a stereotypical Australian opinion of masculinity, you know, that bloke's bloke, that stuff from back in 1970 where you know a man's man. It's almost like clichés I'm saying now but it's almost that old traditional thing where you know . . . it's the bloke at the pub who holds all his emotions in check and all that sort of stuff.

Generally, most participants claimed that masculinity is shaped through the way in which young boys are raised and influenced by their surroundings, whether by family and friends or in particular the school yard. One of the greatest influences in shaping this group's sense of masculine identity was their fathers. Participants stated their fathers taught them morals such as honesty and attributes like standing up for themselves, as well as toughness:

> When you're young and you get upset about things your old man would always be like "don't cry" and "don't be a pussy" and those kind of stuff, so I dunno about yours but yeah, your old man teaches you a fair bit about it.

Role models in sport were also mentioned as being an important influence on learning what it is to be masculine. Several participants recalled looking up to prominent AFL footballers when they were young and wanting to emulate them when they grew up. This is important, particularly for young males who aspire to be like AFL footballers and possibly attempt to copy the actions of their favorite players. If footballers are seen to be physically courageous, therefore befitting the team's performance, and lifting heavy weights to achieve a muscular physique, young males are likely to try to copy these actions, further reinforcing these types of masculine ideals. The media also has an important role in the portrayal of these actions. What they choose to present and represent can help to reiterate what is culturally constructed masculine behavior and what is not, thus influencing how society portrays masculinity.

## Sport and Masculinity

Respondents argued that football in particular is one of the primary sports that reinforces masculine ideals. The competitive nature of football was seen as a way to prove manhood. One participant claimed that

> in terms of two men, or a group of men versus another group of men competing and one defeating the other, there is almost nothing more

masculine really. In a physical game something mentally is not really masculine but physically [the more physical the game, the more masculine it is]. You know you've beaten them, definitely.

It was also contended that success was the predetermining factor in proving masculinity through sport. They argued that a highly successful team would be seen as more masculine, and that losers are forgotten and winners remembered. Some participants stated that masculinity meant how much one could withstand pressure when tested. Sports like football involve frequent heavy tackles that require courage and strength from the players to respond to the test. When a player passes this test by continuing to play after an extremely hard tackle, this particular ideal is reinforced.

> I definitely think that it can shape your manhood, you know, if you're seen as the strong one or the one that's always got their head over the ball or doing courageous acts in a game. I guess then people would be looked upon as being manly.

## Masculine and Feminine Sports

The notion of sports being gendered was discussed heavily by participants. They suggested that what is seen to be a masculine sport and what is considered a feminine sport is largely dependent upon the amount of physical contact within the sport. Not only were sports classified as being either masculine or feminine, the level of masculinity required for particular sports was also discussed. Seemingly, the more physically aggressive the game, the more masculine the characteristics required by its players. To not have such characteristics, and even to portray perceived feminine attributes such as avoiding collisions and withdrawing from a heavy physical contest, was linked with being unsuccessful in physically combative sports:

> The more physical the game is, I think, the more manly you might have to be to be at a high level of it. You can't be more feminine, otherwise you won't get anywhere. You have to be manly and stick up for yourself and go in hard at the ball.

Further, team sports such as Australian Rules football and the rugby codes were seen to be more masculine than individual sports such as floor exercises in gymnastics and diving. While these latter sports were appreciated for masculinized characteristics such as strong mental focus and discipline, their lack of interpersonal physical contact led to them being perceived as less masculine than team sports that offered opportunities to display one's masculinity through combative physicality.

## The Media and Masculinity

Almost all of the participants considered that the media promoted masculinity, mostly through the images presented in the newspapers of muscular male athletes. They claimed that the media portrayed the construct of a "typical footballer" who, with well-defined muscles, appeared aesthetically strong and robust:

> It's what a stereotypical footballer would look like I think, muscly [sic], big, I think intimidation comes into play on the field.

Another footballer spoke of the desire to improve one's muscle mass when seeing such images:

> Yes because he's a good player, but I don't look at a bodybuilder and want to be like him because we're not in the same sort of sport.

This suggests that body size is important in relation to function in their sporting discipline, but not as crucial to their appearance.

In addition to promoting masculinity in the print media, most participants stated that television also promotes masculinity though the replaying of big tackles in sports such as Australian Rules football and the rugby codes, thereby emphasizing the culturally embraced elements associated with the physicality of these sports:

> The sports like footy or Rugby or whatever, you see the big hits on telly and they would replay those and promote them now and then. So I guess through that kind of way and through sort of being physical and you know showing the emotion of sport, I think that portrays or helps to promote masculinity.

While most of the footballers in this research argued that the media did not impact their personal feelings of masculinity, they conceded that because the media is a powerful entity, it could have an impact on footballers' masculine identities through articles on performance. One participant claimed,

> I mean if they say that such and such hasn't been performing, his masculinity to others will be viewed in a different light because the media's such a powerful thing.

CHAPTER 8

**Identity**
Almost all of the participants confirmed that being a footballer was a key part of their identities: Football had great significance in their lives and helped to shape their own sense of masculinity. Many concluded that due to the number of hours required to play football at a high level with training and game days, it was difficult for football not to have prime significance in their lives. Most footballers were unsure about how their identity would change once their football career had finished, although they did expect that it would. Many thought that the change in their sense of identity would be gradual, over the few years following the end of their playing career. Others did not believe people would view them much differently once they stop playing football, but conceded that they would certainly spend their time differently. Some indicated that not playing football would have a benefit in terms of enabling them to spend more time with friends and family.

> Probably at the end of the day it's going to be a good thing because it'll open up so many other doors for our family and friends and everything else which you just, you put on the shelf for the last period of time, so it's probably going to be a good thing when I do finish up.

However, others felt that not playing football would lead to a loss of friends and contacts.

> I don't think I'd have, in a social sort of context, as many friends or contacts, I guess, because once you're not round a club anymore you sort of lose track of people so I guess if I didn't have footy I wouldn't have those friends—you'd definitely keep a few, but you'd lose a fair few people along the way.

**Playing with Pain and Injury**
The majority of participants admitted that they rarely go out onto the football field 100% fit. While they claimed they did not often play with serious ailments, most would have niggling concerns or feelings of stiffness and soreness for most games during the year. One of the more senior players in the squad, when asked how often he plays with pain, stated,

> Quite a bit these days. It would obviously vary in degrees of pain. There's general soreness and all those type of things, it's pretty commonplace, especially when you're my age you know, 33. I can't remember the last

time I've walked out there and felt 100%, like I did when I was 20, so basically pretty much constantly these days.

As a result of playing with some degree of discomfort, many players admitted to making attempts to either mask their pain (through the use of painkilling drugs) or to lie about the amount of pain they are experiencing.

One reason for masking pain was to avoid being labeled "soft" by other teammates, or specifically by the coaches:

> I don't want to look soft [laughs], yeah something like that. Oh, you don't want the coaches to think you're soft and that sort of thing and that kind of viewpoint comes as much from the coaches as it does from the players so yeah I think it's probably the expectations of the people around you. I want people to think of me as someone they'd go to war with and all that sort of jazz so definitely, it's a motivating factor.

Various justifications for playing with pain and injury were offered, although several consistencies emerged. Among the strongest reasons given for attempting to push through "pain barriers" to continue playing was purely the enjoyment of playing football, as epitomized by this statement:

> It's just the enjoyment. It's everything we touched on before. I still enjoy it, I still contribute, it's part of me. It's something I've done and I will probably continue to do until I can't do it anymore. It's again you go back to a cliché, but everybody says you're a long time retired . . . but it's pretty accurate because once we finish up and stop playing, the next 30, 40, 50 years of my life I won't be playing again, and I enjoy it so much so I'll play it as long as I can until my body basically says you shouldn't be playing anymore.

The interviewees acknowledged that they were more likely to continue playing in pain in cases where it was "vital" that a game must be won. This type of commitment to play despite pain also occurred when there were talent scouts in the crowd; the impressions of these observers were likely to impact players' chances of being drafted into the AFL.

> I would play with two broken legs, I would do anything because that's a massive opportunity and that's something that would set you up for the

rest of your life, it's not just one game, you're talking about a whole career in another league with a lot of money, so I'd cover anything up.

One participant viewed a decision to not play in pain when a talent scout was in the crowd as relinquishing a potential AFL career. He was motivated by a need to feel he had given his all in such circumstances; the pain could be forgotten after the game, but the memory of trying to realize a dream to be drafted would always linger.

> I suppose something Lance Armstrong said, pain is temporary but quitting is forever so I dunno if you can push through it, you can never remember pain afterwards so looking back preseason now I can't remember how much it hurt. I knew it did hurt, but I can't remember how much it did hurt. And so if you quit while you're in pain, my feeling is that when you look back on it, you don't remember the pain so you feel as if you've given up. So any motivating factor, however small, could probably convince me to play through pain.

However, participants were not unanimous in their desire to do *anything* to push through the pain to play in important games. Some claimed they would rather be 100% fit, as playing with pain or injury could affect their bodily function, which could lead to a poor on-field performance and may also affect their potential AFL career. Indeed, one former AFL player stated that he would not play with pain if scouts were in the crowd, but many others would.

> To me, no, I would not play because, I mean, I know how scouts are; if I went out and played and I'm in discomfort and I played poorly, they're not going to know, they're going to record "[his name]: too slow"; they'll do it just like that, bang, you're labelled too slow, just from one game. I've seen it happen a hundred times. You know, "can't turn, blah, blah," whatever your problem is, so no way, I'd rather miss it.

Performance in football was another of the more prominent reasons for withdrawing from the game rather than attempting to play with pain or injury. As football is a team game, playing with serious pain might not only compromise individual performance but also let the team down—in short, detrimental to the chances of the group actually winning.

### Sport, Masculinities, and Pain: An Australian Rules Football Perspective

## Painkillers in Football

The use of painkilling injections such as cortisone and local anaesthetics brought mixed reactions from participants. Some stated that they thought it was acceptable to take painkillers or have injections for important games, such as the grand finale while others admitted they would have an injection for any game, not just those that were especially important. One participant proclaimed, "Just because players play with pain doesn't mean you want to, so if you can avoid it you will, but you'll still play, so if you can take painkillers to help, then you do it."

Players argued that if they were given appropriate information about the side effects of a painkilling injection then they would be in a better position to consider risk—such as the possibility that anaesthetic would not only mask the pain but have the consequence of making the pain-causing injury worse. However, many interviewees revealed that they were basically unaware of the associated health risks. This indicates that players either do not have accurate information on the risks of having regular pain killing injections in order to play, or they do not have adequate levels of health literacy to understand the ramifications of injections or other painkilling measures.

From a medical perspective, the club medic's opinion was that if players were counseled enough about the risks and benefits of having injections they would be capable of giving informed consent.

> In terms of informed consent, I think you know if you counsel them enough then the answer is yes, they do have the knowledge, but then it's probably the overlay of pressure from other players and coaching staff to play and the whole expectation to play, so it's a bit of the meshing of the those two.

From this physician's experience, the availability and application of local anaesthetics was more common at the AFL level than at the SANFL level. The amount of money involved at the higher level was offered as a reason for the more frequent use of injections. The base salary for one player at the AFL level is typically more than the entire salary cap for a whole club at SANFL level. With this amount of money being paid to AFL footballers, it is essential that they play as much as is reasonably possible.

## Support While Injured

When players sustain an injury, the amount of available support can often provide additional motivation to overcome injury and return to the field. In the present study, players claimed that much support came from sources external to the club, such as family and friends.

> Yeah, you need it 'cause you get fairly grumpy and frustrated and shitty with life and I know I do. I guess you might make it difficult for people around you, but then generally they . . . will help you out.

As the injured player himself knows how he feels, often he will rely on substantial internal motivation more than external sympathy. Interviewees suggested that if someone sustained a long-term injury, it was up to the player to display the correct attitude toward recovery, such as by still attending training and participating regularly in physical rehabilitation.

Ironically, competition for positions on the team was given as a reason why some teammates do not show support to each other when injured. Interviewees also thought that when players were unable to actively participate in training sessions with the main group because of injury, they were at risk of being unintentionally ostracized from the team. A few respondents argued that, when out of the team because of injury, having someone take their position provided extra motivation to recover from the ailment quickly.

> The main thing that probably does motivate you is yourself. You just want to get back out there and take that guy who took your spot and take his spot again because you know you were there first so you just want to get back up there and prove it to yourself.

Unfortunately, this can lead to a paradoxical situation. Players worry about losing their place in the team when injured, so they push through the pain to retain their spot. By pushing through the pain, however, they may exacerbate the injury or underperform, and find themselves omitted from the team, which was precisely what they were trying to avoid, thereby experiencing further feelings of ostracism.

Generally, players claimed a lack of support from the coaching staff when injured, but did not begrudge them for it. It was generally accepted that the coach should only be concerned with the players who are fit and available, as injured players are of no immediate value to the team. It was suggested that the focus of the coach should be week-to-week and not on the rehabilitation of the long-term injured. However, some participants contended that this was one area where procedure could improve. Indeed, the lack of support from the coaches was suggested as being a motivating factor for trying to "push through pain."

### Sport, Masculinities, and Pain: An Australian Rules Football Perspective

Oh, to a certain degree you know they're going to support you, but no player ever wants to go up to a coach and tell them he's injured, and when you're injured you feel like you're just forgotten so no one wants to be injured, and I don't think you can count on too much from the coaching staff when you are injured.

## Long-term Health

The footballers held little regard for their long-term health. This seemed to be due for the most part to their ignorance of specific consequences of both sustaining major injuries while playing football and of receiving regular injections of local anaesthetic in order to play while injured. With regard to having regular painkilling injections, the club physician alluded to the types of problems that could arise:

> If you've an arthritic knee and every time you're having to play football you're injecting local in the knee then that's probably going to accelerate the underlying arthritis . . . Whereas if you're having regular injections say for a painful finger it doesn't really say if it's just a sprain so it's probably not going to give you too much problems, or another one, AC joints get pretty regularly injected when they get injured and the likelihood of people having long-term problems from that is probably pretty remote. So it's a case by case, I tend not to use local painkilling injections too much before a game so players need to use pain. Pain is useful feedback about how they're going.

The long-term effects from regular painkilling injections were not a concern for most of the participants in this study. While they were aware that negative consequences could result, they were largely unaware of what those might include, aside from their knowledge about arthritis. However, knowledge about long-term injury did not necessarily translate into action to prevent it:

> I mean just by playing sport I'm sure I'm getting impact or I'm having issues I know for sure that in 10–15 years' time I'll get out of bed and I won't be able to move because my knees will be seized up from arthritis and all that sort of stuff, but in the back of my mind I know that and I will still play, you know what I mean? So at the end of the day I know there's some sort of repercussions coming from playing sport because of the surgeries and everything else I've had. So, [if I were to have an

## CHAPTER 8

injection] you'd want it to be something pretty compelling from an injury stand point.

Many participants declared they would rather enjoy life now, rather than worry about what would happen to them once their playing days were over. The friendships they formed and their love of football were given as reasons to play now and suffer the consequences later.

> Yeah, that's just sort of the nature of how we think, I think. Just enjoy what you're doing because it's fun. It's quality of life now.

This notion of quality of life during youth was a compelling part of the interviewees' perspective. The risks of injury impacting quality of life later on was a concern for some; however, none were prepared to argue for dramatic change. They did not seek to have the rules of contact sports changed in order to minimize injury, nor did they want to prevent young boys from taking part in football because of concerns about long-term injury. Quality of life in the younger years was of paramount concern.

With regard to some of the long-term health risks that could result from playing contact sports, the club physician stated,

> It depends on the type of injury . . . just playing competitive contact sports as an adult is a risk factor for osteoarthritis for knees and hips, and that's pretty well proven. Especially if you have a major ligament disruption of a knee, that seems to increase your risk of arthritis. Other things, adult footballers if you follow them through they generally get disc degeneration of lower 2 lumbar disc as a consequence of playing adult level football. Dislocated shoulder increases your risk of arthritis of shoulder joint, obviously they're the sort of main long-term implications of those injuries. And your joints that get injured, probably increases your risk of getting arthritis there.

For those who had considered their long-term health, functionality was the main concern. Particularly those who were nearer the end of their football careers, with families, pain that prevented them from everyday functions such as playing with their children was something they had thought about. The key factor influencing their decision to continue to play or otherwise was the severity of the injury:

Unless it was your neck I wouldn't think of it. If I can't walk because my knee gets dodgy I'm not really going to care now, especially on the field. It's the last you have, but if you're hit in the neck or something, that's the only thing.

## DISCUSSION

The concept of masculinity proved to be difficult and elusive for the men in this research project. Multiple masculinities were not considered by participants; rather, to be masculine was simply to have a muscular physique, therefore attributing masculine identity to body image, and in particular muscle bulk. Many of the footballers in this study did not see themselves as being particularly masculine, most often due to what they perceived as a lack of muscularity on their part compared to other players (such as in the AFL). This suggests that in the realm of professional football, muscle bulk is one of the predetermining factors associated with masculinity. That perception is consistent with the research of Glassner (1992, cited in Loland, 1999) and much of Drummond's (2001, 2005) work, which argue that muscles are a dominant sign of masculinity in sport and that the ideal male body— in respect to hegemonic masculinity—is highly muscular.

Welland (2002) has argued that many sports provide opportunities to demonstrate perceived masculine characteristics, such as toughness and physical strength. This is particularly pertinent for aggressive sports like Australian Rules football, in which physical body contact is common. According to the footballers in the present research project, the more contact in a sport, then the more masculine the sport is perceived to be. Further, sports that require strength and toughness—though devoid of physical contact—were also linked with being masculine. According to the interviewees, characteristics such as strength and courage were thought to lead to success in sports that are perceived as manly. The opinions of footballers in this research support those in Koivula's research (2001), with physical contact thought to be the key component separating masculine-appropriate and feminine-appropriate sports.

Current research shows that footballers are hesitant to request medical assistance, and even go so far as to lie or conceal their pain. Williams and Best (1990, cited in Courtenay, 2000) stated that the way in which masculinity is constructed leads to the attitude that men are tough and strong as well as self-reliant. For footballers, to admit pain is to show vulnerability, which does not fit with the archetypal notion that men are strong and can withstand pain. Medical assistance detracts from their self-reliance and therefore, as this research has identified, pain is dismissed unless the men cannot perform physically. Health risks taken by footballers can be linked to hegemonic masculine ideals such as the suppression of pain to either establish power or maintain position. From this research it was suggested that those who can withstand the pain longer are more likely—all else being equal—to remain on the team. This supports the work of Iso-Ahola and Hatfield (1986, cited in Straub & Williams, 2003), who argued that in sport the successful and the unsuccessful may be separated by their tolerance of pain. The risk of sustaining further damage while playing with pain was seen as an acceptable risk for many footballers, which again reinforces hegemonic masculine ideals.

It has been established in this research that footballers feel a sense of isolation when injured. This is one of the more significant reasons for trying to continue playing in pain. It is necessary to acknowledge that when injured, players are unable to complete training sessions with the main group, causing an almost inevitable separation from the team on the field. However, as shown by this research, the idea of an injury report policy, which brings the injured players into the group to share their rehabilitation progress, was well received and thought likely to help to alleviate feelings of isolation. Given that many men construct their sense of identity through doing rather than being, and that sport provides an avenue for this to occur, the partial involvement of injured players with the main training group allows their membership to be maintained and, in addition, does not compromise their sense of masculinity (Morgan, 1990, cited in Robertson, 2003). Even with physical impairments, involvement in sports allows men to gain some sense of control over their lives (Robertson, 2003); it is therefore important to minimize the exclusion of injured players from the team, for it is then that they feel a loss of control and a distance from teammates.

The footballers in this research gave little consideration to their long-term health. Admittedly, players expressed a lack of knowledge of the consequences of playing with pain and injury, other than for arthritis. This lack of knowledge extended to the long-term implications of painkilling injections such as cortisone and local anaesthetics. Their views support previous research by Finch et al. (2002), who found that junior footballers understood that playing while injured would lead to health complications later in life, but continued to do so regardless. The present study assessed the attitudes of senior SANFL footballers, but could equally be applied to the carrying of junior-level attitudes through to senior levels of the game.

This research posed pertinent questions about the responsibility for informed consent. The team physician argued that with appropriate counseling, players would have the knowledge to make informed decisions regarding playing in pain and with an injury, as well as informed consent to painkilling injections. However, Waddington et al. (2001) have argued that the culture of the football club determines the standard of health care given to the players, and that problems of power and influence arise when coaches or managers become involved in the treatment process. Given the current perceptions about playing in pain as an appropriate attitude toward one's sport, it is important for medical staff to remove the coach and managers from the treatment process. The team physician in this research alluded to limiting the decision to administer painkilling injections to himself and the player, and possibly the head trainer. This allows the physician to appropriately counsel the player with regard to the risks of their decision to have a painkilling injection without pressure from outside influences. This research therefore recommends the establishment of occupational health and safety policies with regard to medical treatment in football.

One of the more influential reasons for playing with pain for the footballers in this research project was the prospect of being selected in the national AFL draft. This is consistent with research conducted by Finch et al. (2002), who found that the chance of being drafted dramatically increased the likelihood that junior footballers would play with pain. For men in this research, the prospect of being drafted also increased the likelihood of their agreeing to have painkilling injections to enable them to play important games, such as when talent scouts were present. From this research, it is evident that the current AFL draft system leads to poor health-related decisions by footballers. It is therefore necessary to conduct a review of the AFL draft and the trade systems in order to promote better health-related behaviours in young male athletes.

With regard to the media, the views of the men in this research support research by Finch et al. (2002) that the media lionize players who play with pain or injury. Finch et al. (2002) argued that the glorification by the media of playing when hurt is irresponsible given that, as previously mentioned, aspiring footballers hope to emulate their AFL role models. Many of the footballers in this research admitted to wanting to be just like their AFL idols. This supports Finch et al.'s study (2002) stating that role models such as AFL footballers have the potential to influence the attitudes of younger players. This could include unhealthy behaviors such as playing in pain or with an injury. It is necessary to assess the media's role in influencing a footballer's decision to play with pain or injury in order to address the promotion of unhealthy practices. Footballers in this research argued that the media had little impact on their decision to play in pain in the SANFL, but that it was more likely that the media could have an impact on the decisions of AFL footballers due to greater exposure at the national level. Therefore, further research into the influence of the media at the AFL level is needed, including guidelines for the broadcast of Australian Rules football to limit the perception that playing with an injury and in pain is heroic, or even acceptable.

## CONCLUSIONS

The primary recommendations that emerge from these findings include promoting the inclusion of injured teammates in the main training group to lessen feelings of ostracism, encouraging outside interests other than football in order to minimize the loss of football identity following retirement from sport, excluding coaches and team managers from the treatment decision-making process to minimize external pressures on the athlete to consent to painkilling injections, acknowledging the inevitability of pain and injury within a sporting context and focusing on injury prevention to reduce the risk of long-term consequences from being involved in sport, and working towards changing cultural and subcultural attitudes towards pain and injury in men and boys.

Further research is required at all levels of Australian Rules football to develop a more comprehensive understanding of the issues confronting young men in terms of playing football and the decision to play in pain and with an injury. Moreover, research among elite football groups such as the AFL is crucial given the cultural status of the men involved and the influence they hold over male footballers within community-based leagues, including young males in junior football. This is required to create changes in cultural and subcultural attitudes toward masculinity, football, and pain in the hope of altering broader societal attitudes among men toward their health.

## REFERENCES

Burgess, I., Edwards, A., & Skinner, J. (2003). Football culture in an Australian school setting: The construction of masculine identity. *Sport, Education & Society, 8*, 199–212.

Calhourn, C. (1995). *Critical social theory*. Oxford, England: Blackwell Publishers.

Connell, B. (1995). *Masculinities*. Los Angeles, CA: University of California Press.

Connell, R. (2000). *The men and the boys*. Maryborough, Australia: Allen & Unwin.

Courtenay, W. (2000). Constructions of masculinity and their influence on men's well-being: A theory of gender and health. *Social Science & Medicine, 50*, 1385–1401.

Damon, C., & Holloway, I. (2002). *Qualitative research methods in public relation and marketing communications*. New York, NY: Routledge.

Deacon, A., Bennell, K., Kiss, Z., Crossley, K., & Brukner, P. (1997). Osteoarthritis of the knee in retired, elite Australian Rules footballers. *Medical Journal of Australia, 166*(4), 187–190.

Drummond, M. (2001). Boys' bodies in the context of sport and physical activity: Implications for health. *Journal of Physical Education New Zealand, 34*, 53-64.

Drummond, M. (2005). Men's bodies: Listening to the voices of young gay men. *Men and Masculinities, 7,* 270–290.

Finch, C., Donohue, S., & Garnham, A. (2002). Safety attitudes and beliefs of junior Australian football players. *Injury Prevention, 8,* 151–154.

Fitzclarence, L., Hickey, C., & Matthews, R. (1998). *Where the boys are, masculinity, sport and education.* Victoria, Australia: Deakin Centre for Education and Change.

Gard, M., & Meyenn, R. (2000). Boys, bodies, pleasure and pain: Interrogating contact sports in schools. *Sport, Education and Society, 5,* 19–34.

Hacking, I. (1999). *The social construction of what?* Harvard, CN: Harvard University Press.

Hughes, R., & Coakley, J. (1991). Positive deviance among athletes: The implications of overconformity to the sport ethic. *Sociology of Sport Journal, 8,* 307–325.

Keddie, A. (2002). *It's more than a game: Little boys, masculinities and football culture.* Retrieved from http://www.aare.edu.au

Koivula, N. (2001). Perceived characteristics of sports categorized as gender-neutral, feminine and masculine. *Journal of Sport Behaviour, 24,* 377–393.

Loland, N. (1999). Some contradictions and tensions in elite sportsmen's attitudes towards their bodies. *International Review for the Sociology of Sport, 34,* 291–302.

McKay, J. (1991). *No pain, no gain? Sport and the Australian culture.* Victoria, Australia: Prentice Hill.

Messner, M. (2002). *Taking the field: Women, men and sports.* Minneapolis, MN: University of Minnesota Press.

Messner, M., Hunt, D., & Dunbar, M. (1999). Boys to men: Sports media messages about masculinity, 1999. *Children Now.* Retrieved from http://www.childrennow.org/index.php/learn/reports_and_research/article_search/boys_to_men_sports_1999/

Norton, K., Schwerdt, S., & Lange, K. (2001). Evidence for the aetiology of injuries in Australian football. *British Journal of Sports Medicine, 35,* 418–423.

Norton, K., Craig, N., & Olds, T. (1999). The evolution of Australian football. *Journal of Science & Medicine in Sport, 2,* 389–404.

Patton, M. (1990). *Qualitative evaluation and research methods* (3rd ed.). Thousand Oaks, CA: SAGE Publications.

Pringle, R. (2005). Masculinities, sport and power. *Journal of Sport & Social Issues, 29,* 256–278.

Robertson, S. (2003). 'If I let a goal in, I'll get beat up': Contradictions in masculinity, sport and health. *Health Education Research, 18,* 706–716.

Straub, W., & Williams, D. (2003). Pain apperception of contact and non-contact sport athletes. *The Sport Journal, 6.*

Waddington, I., Roderick, M., & Naik, R. (2001). Methods of appointment and qualifications of club doctors and physiotherapists in English professional football: Some problems and issues. *British Journal of Sports Medicine, 35,* 48–53.

Welland, I. (2002). Men, sport, body performance and the maintenance of 'exclusive masculinity.' *Leisure Studies, 21,* 235–247.

# Steroids, Male Body Image, and the Intimate Self

Daryl Adair

## INTRODUCTION

Struggles for social distinction, status, and identity are fundamental dimensions of societies the world over (Bourdieu, 1987). Within that milieu, two facets of interest here are conceptions of gender and norms of physical appearance. In keeping with the theme of this book, the focus is with male embodiment and notions of masculinity—in this case, the body as a locus for the physical expression of manliness. For some men, an enhanced muscular form is highly valued; the assumption is that muscularity enhances masculinity (Klein, 1993). There are, of course, numerous cultural variations associated with the "ideal" male body (Monaghan, 1999). Moreover, some observers would object to muscularity being presented as a *sine qua non* for masculinity (Lorber & Martin, 1998). I have no intention here of arguing a case either way. Instead, my goal is to try to understand interest in the muscularity of male bodies and, more particularly, men who use illicit anabolic androgenic steroids (AASs) to try to modify their physical form (Kanayama, Barry, Hudson, & Pope, 2006; Iriart,

Chaves, & Orleans, 2009; Hakansson, Mickelsson, Wallin, & Berglund, 2012.). This might be done to please themselves, female partners, male partners, or both (Halkitis, Moeller, & DeRaleau, 2008; Filiault & Drummond, 2010; Blashill & Safren, 2014).

For many years, AASs have been drugs of choice among men who seek a support mechanism (in combination with exercise) to create or accentuate a demonstrably muscular frame (Cohen, Collins, Darkes, & Gwartney, 2007; Ip, Barnett, Tenerowicz, & Perry, 2011). There are, of course, a range of supplements and drugs—some legal, others illicit—that constitute what has been labelled "appearance and performance enhancing drugs (APEDs)"; AASs are but one substance under that rubric (Hildebrandt, Harty, & Langenbucher, 2012). From a scientific perspective, "AASs are cholesterol derivatives of testosterone with effects that are both anabolic and androgenic to build lean muscle." The associated social purpose has been described as an effort to "enhance masculinization" (Fronczak, Kim, & Barqawi, 2012). This relates to conceptions of manliness in which physical attributes like size, strength, physique and power are coveted (Brown, 1999; Denham, 2008). The use of illicit (nonprescription) AASs to pursue and achieve such body image goals has been the subject of a significant body of research (Monaghan, 2002; Olrich, 1999; Kanayama, Hudson, & Pope, 2010; Dodge & Hoagland, 2011; Smith & Stewart, 2012a, 2012b).[1] There have also been reams of scholarship devoted to health risks associated with illicit AAS use/misuse/abuse (Monaghan, 2001; Samaha et al, 2008; Quaglio et al, 2009; van Amsterdam, Opperhuizen, & Hartgens, 2010). Less well known, but also part of the debate, are the voices of scholars who question what they see as unnecessarily alarmist and histrionic depictions of AAS. Instead of a "don't do drugs" message, these advocates take a realist perspective, advocating education and knowledge-broking in order to foster the capacity for informed choices and better prospects for harm minimization among users (Keane, 2005; Kraska, Bussard & Brent, 2009; Proszenko, 2012; Coomber, 2013). Indeed, among a survey of health professionals who responded to questions about the relative risk to health of 19 different types of illicit drugs, AAS were rated as "relatively low harm" (van Amsterdam, 2010).

In the present chapter, the research angle is very narrow and thus much more limited than what has been covered by the vast body of literature mentioned previously. Of interest in this chapter is how AASs users try to mitigate or manage side effects associated with this family of drug. That is indeed a harm minimization philosophy.[2] Here again, though, the focus is very specific. Of concern are four reported side effects of AAS use among males: testicular atrophy (shrinkage of testicles), hypogonadism (diminished functionality of the gonads), gynecomastia (increase in breast tissue), and acne (a skin disease). The chapter explores how such impacts are understood and characterized and how AAS users "afflicted" by these side effects (physical and social) seek to remediate their bodies. In many cases, of course, they also attempt to preserve the muscular frame they sought by deploying a steroid regime.

There are key caveats in all of this: Side effects of AAS use vary depending on factors like the type of drug used (the range is significant), frequency of supplementation, management of steroid cycles (periods of use), steroid stacks (combinations of steroids and/or related drugs), and individual responses to doses. There is, as the online forum Steroid.com has put it, a risk-reward process of experimentation: "As the dosing increases, so do the [muscular] rewards, but so do the potential side-effects" ("Anabolic Steroids Cycles and Stacks," 2000). If, as research has indicated, a key aim of AAS use by men is to optimize their physical appearance (alongside other factors like muscularity and power), then excessive or poorly managed supplementation risks compromise that ideal.

## TESTICULAR ATROPHY, HYPOGONADISM, AND AZOOSPERMIA

It would be alarmist to suggest that AAS use necessarily brings about long-term impacts on testicular size or gonadal function. However, for the inexperienced or naive, awareness of risk and mitigation thereof is important. The same holds true, albeit for different reasons, for AAS aficionados: while they have the benefit of familiarity with this diverse family of drug, both dosage and duration are considerations in order to avoid or minimize negative health impacts. In terms of the male testicles, which are routinely concealed from public display, shrinkage has implications for intimacy and sex appeal in private contexts. Moreover, some AAS users experience azoospermia, which in lay terms is the lack of any sperm in the testes. In addition to the appearance and functionality of testicles, there can be social dimensions to physical changes stemming from AASs. In many cultural environments having "balls" (i.e., balls that function) is a metaphor for men possessing the courage and fortitude to show leadership, make tough decisions, and so on. Having "big balls" is a euphemism for being exceptionally brave. Small gonads, dysfunctional gonads, or even no gonads imply the reverse: someone who is weak, cowardly, and unfit to lead—in short, not a "real" man (Morgan, 1993; Martin, 2013b; Mott & Roberts, 2014).

The *actual* size, shape and performance of male testicles is typically a private matter and thus not a subject of public discussion. Indeed, if males experience shrunken or deficient gonads this is typically a cause of embarrassment for them, not pride. However, there are rare occasions when a partner provides insights into the impact of testicular atrophy on an individual and their relationship. For example, in a perjury court case, Kimberly Bell, the so-called "mistress" of Major League baseball slugger Barry Bonds, was called to the witness stand. Bonds was accused of using AASs; he was on trial for allegedly lying to the grand jury during its investigation of the BALCO performance-enhancing drug investigation. Of interest here is Bell's depiction of Bonds' physical condition in the wake of his steroid use. She claimed that "his testicles changed shape and shrank." Bell also testified that Bonds "grew—and shaved—chest hair and developed acne on his back." She also announced that his sexual performance declined ("Barry Bonds' testicles," 2011). This was hardly an endorsement of AASs from the perspective of a female partner. It is reasonable to assume that Bell's characterization of Bonds's compromised physicality caused the latter some embarrassment.

Another MLB star, Jose Canseco, suffered a similar public humiliation. On the American television show "Hollywood Exes," Canseco's former partner, Jessica, announced that she was considering reconciliation: "I would feel bad as a person if I turned my back on him. . . . He is family. And he's the father of my kid" (*The Huffington Post*, 2012). According to a news report, though, "after hearing what Jessica went on to say about his testicles, Jose may not *want* to move in with her" (emphasis in the original; Huffington Post, 2012). She told the television program "Hollywood Exes," "Jose doesn't have saggy balls . . . cuz he took steroids and it was like, shrinked 'em up. They were so tight!" As Nicole (the presenter) laughed, Jessica went on, "I was like, 'Your walnuts have turned into one peanut, okay?'" (*Huffington Post*, 2012). To baseball devotees, this was not new information. In his 2005 autobiography *Juiced: Wild times, Rampant 'Roids, Smash Hits and How Baseball Got Big*, Canseco had already admitted as much. Nevertheless, he offered a consolational caveat to that story. As a reviewer of *Juiced* recounted, Canseco "wrote that rampant steroid use had shrunken his testicles, but that his abuse of human growth hormone had counteracted the effects by making his penis grow larger" (Movie Fan, 2007). Without dwelling on the veracity of such claims, the overarching point is that the appearance and functionality of male genitals is variously a source of pride, curiosity, amusement, fulfilment, disappointment, and so on. This suggests that for users of AASs, managing cycles and monitoring health impacts are to be taken seriously.

In a landmark survey of illicit AAS users in the United States, 51% of respondents indicated that they had experienced the adverse effect of testicular atrophy (Ip et al., 2011). Moot therefore, is how users cope with this issue, and what they do to remediate that situation. Because nonprescription AASs are illicit in many countries, there is an understandable reticence to overtly seek or trust advice from registered medical practitioners (Cohen et al., 2007). One important source of information, therefore, is web forums (with anonymous users) devoted to the dissemination of advice about how to use AAS responsibly while trying to convey an understanding that there are risks associated with naive or excessive use of this family of drug. Even a cursory glance at these sites (e.g., www.steroid-forums.com, http://forums.steroid.com/, http://anabolicsteroidforums.com/, and http://www.steroidology.com/forum) indicates an intense interest among subscribers about how best to manage their bodies and indeed utilize meds. This is also an environment in which AAS users describe to other like-minded individuals their experiences of muscle enhancement.

Typically, testicular atrophy eventually reverses after discontinuation of AAS (van Amsterdam, 2010), though long-term users can have persistent symptoms. Boregowda, Joels, Stephens, & Price (2011) acknowledge that AAS devotees are generally "aware of the risk of testicular atrophy" and often take measures to mitigate against it; however, the process is not simple. There are suggested pharmaceutical 'antidotes,' but access to some of them is confounded by their illicit status. For example, Boregowda et al. (2011) report that many AAS users "take illegally acquired hCG [human chorionic gonadotropin] to try and prevent [testicular atrophy] happening." Steroid forums discuss that type of issue. The pharmaceutical complexity of their efforts to self-manage is immediately apparent:

> I have some slight testicular atrophy from a previous cycle that I didnt use hcg [human chorionic gonadotropin] on for not researching enough, its really not that bad but anyway (it still bugs me). I wanted to do a 6 wk prop cycle @ 600mg/wk but I will put hcg in it for sure this time at 1000ius every 3 days during cycle and at 2000 ius eod [every other day] after my last shot for 12 days then start the SERM [selective estrogen receptor modulators] therapy. Anybody think that I will be able to regain some testicular volume that I lost from a previous cycle? (Edzilla, 2010)

By way of response, Edzilla was provided with this advice:

> At that volume, you could really cause some downgrade and cause more harm then good. Why such high dosages? I wouldn't even run it during cycle at only 6 weeks, just hit it for a week after the cycle. Actually, I'd run a 4 week PCT [post-cycle therapy] now and get yourself back before you start again. Fix the problem first where you have no inhibitory substances in you. If you don't, it could be even harder to get back after the cycle. Remember HCG is only tricking the system, it's not actually bringing you back, and too much can make it even harder to come back. (D_rson, 2010)

# CHAPTER 9

A similar request for information was submitted to a different forum by Stev7667 (2011):

> I did a 16 or 17 week Test/Tren cycle about 5 years ago. I ran some tamoxifen afterward for abiut [sic] 20 days but my testicles have failed to return to their full size years later. My question is, is there any hope of recovering size after this long or should I just give up? I could get more HMG (its expensive thou [sic]) and I could easily keep running HcG for up to 6 months if necessary. Note: my balls are 26.5 ML. . . . I believe they were close to twice there [sic] current size previously.

By way of response, Stev7667 was provided with this advice by MR10X (2011):

> HCG directly stimulates your balls to produce test, if it doesnt [sic] get you back to normal none of those other things like Clomid, Nolvadex, or drugs like that will do anything. The HCG will stimulate your balls to produce test and Clomid and Nolvadex will help you deal with the estrogen to prevent gyno, when your balls are back to size stop the HCG and continue the clomid and nolvadex to get your other hormones back like they should be.

It is difficult to see how a novice reader could make much sense of this "pharmo-language." Online users of steroid forums therefore need to do their homework.

For some AAS users, the functionality of testicles, not merely their size and appearance, is of prime concern. AASs have the effect of suppressing biological antecedents to full testicular function, though this is typically a temporary impact. Barceloux and Palmer (2013) report, "Although chronic AAS abuse produces hypogonadism, decreased serum testosterone, and impaired spermatogenesis, these changes are reversible within a few months to 1 year following cessation of AAS use." Where this anticipated reversal has not occurred, there are drug treatments for AAS users to overcome azoospermia (Menon, 2003). However, in the case of chronic steroid users "gonad failure and infertility . . . can be prolonged and irreversible" (Boregowda et al., 2011). What is again apparent is AAS users' efforts to self-manage the unwanted impacts of steroids notwithstanding their pharmaceutical complexities:

> can someone please set my girl at ease, she want[s] to get pregnant but is worried my steroid use will effect my sperm and our unborn child will come out lookin [sic] like a pro bodybuilder with two heads and four

arms, I know my sperm count will be reduced and therefor [sic] will not produce as many swimmers, is there a doc or someone with a medical degree in here that can vouch that the swimers [sic] I do produce will not be effected from the steroids or influenced by them at all, any feed back would be great. (Aussiemuscle, 2008)

By way of response, Aussiemuscle received this advice from Machola (2008):

Babies will be fine. Steroids won't effect [sic] the babies' health unless your wife is taking them while pregnant. As for raising sperm count there's two routes you can go. The best way is get off gear and take your pct. Clomid and Nolva will raise sperm count. It may take a few months depending on how long you've been shut down. 2nd way is to take hmg [Human Menopausal Gonadotropin] for a few months. They use this for some guys on trt [Testosterone Replacement Therapy] and guys with naturally low sperm counts because you will produce sperm even when you're shutdown. Good luck.

Why is there such an emphasis on steroid community advice and self-diagnosis via specialized online forums? Tan and Scally (2009), in a review of anabolic steroid-induced hypogonadism, point to an explanation:

A medical quandary for physicians presented with hypogonadal patients secondary to AAS administration is there is currently no FDA approved drug to restore HPTA function. Standard treatment to this point has been testosterone replacement therapy (TRT), human chorionic gonadotropin (hCG), conservative therapy ("watchful waiting" or "do nothing"), or off-label prescribing of aromatase inhibitors or selective estrogen receptor modulators (SERM).

The pharmaceutical nuances of both problem and treatment are beyond the scope of this chapter. Rather, the key point is that the management of AAS use and its impacts are extremely technical and complex areas of knowledge even for those with medical expertise (Coward et al., 2013). Thus, it is no surprise that AAS users face difficulties mapping out a steroid cycle and supporting treatments to try to reduce the impact of testicular atrophy and/or hypogonadism and, for long-term or high dose users, any associated azoospermia. Smith and Stewart (2012a) have labeled this online sharing of medical information among AAS users as "virtual ethnopharmacology." Yet, as these authors acknowledge in a related paper, this is also about trying to understand one's body in light of the risk-reward tension outlined previously (Smith & Stewart, 2012b).

That search for credible information seems all the more important in light of a survey by Ip et al. (2011) in which they discovered "an apparent disconnect between AAS users and healthcare providers." While a majority of respondents reported visiting a physician regularly, only 33% of them disclosed their AAS use. Doubtless this stems from the illicit nature of AASs, which they are using sans prescription. However, Ip et al. (2011) ascertained a deeper problem of perception: "Only 8.8% of respondents believed that physicians and pharmacists were knowledgeable regarding AAS." These researchers concluded that there is a palpable communication gap between AAS users and healthcare providers, with patients either wary of admitting drug use to physicians or not having sufficient confidence in them to advise about the appropriate use of steroids. This again helps to explain the tendency towards online learning from the steroid community and self-diagnosis. However, doing so becomes even more complex when, according to researchers, up to 80% of AAS users practice polypharmacy, the self-administration of combinations of various drugs to either enhance the impact of steroids or mitigate against their side effects (Evans, 1997; Perry, 2005).

## GYNECOMASTIA

Enlargement of the male breasts, jokingly referred to as "man boobs" or "bitch tits," is typically the subject of ridicule ("Man boobs," n.d.; "Bitch tits," n.d.). Men who prize the appearance of their chest and torso exercise to reach a tight muscular frame. One of their goals, it seems, is to avoid the prospect of "boobs" or "tits." With age and weight gain, some enlargement and sagging of the male breasts is to be expected, though the subject is a cause of mirth, not titillation. In an episode of the American situational comedy show *Seinfeld,* two of the characters, Cosmo Kramer and Frank Costanza, conspire to develop what they describe as a "male support undergarment," which they label either as the "Mansier" or as the "The Bro" (Sony Pictures, 1995). This episode pokes fun at the insecurity of men who exhibit what is technically known as "pseudogynecomastia," a very common but nonetheless embarrassing condition associated with a combination of ageing and weight gain. There are, however, two very different types of breast conditions for males. Pseudogynecomastia is the accumulation of fat in the breast region, while gynecomastia involves the growth of breast tissue in males ("Pseudogynecomastia," n.d.). Neither, it must be said, does much for the self-confidence or sexual allure of men who exhibit these symptoms (Wassersug & Oliffe, 2009). However, gynecomastia (GM) is of interest to this chapter because it is a possible side effect of the use of AASs and, in some cases, may require medical treatment.

According to de Barros and Sampaio (2012), "GM is a multifactorial disease and many conditions may be associated with it." There are physiological causes—such as low testosterone production, endocrine abnormalities, thyroid and liver problems—each of which impact on the ratio of estrogen vs. testosterone in males, a secondary effect of which may be atypical breast development. However, physiological GM can be temporary and transitory. It may occur as a routine developmental stage in infant and prepubescent boys, resolving as the child becomes a teenager. This transformation stems from the changing hormonal status of males as they move into adolescence. As compared to men, boys tend to exhibit a relatively high level of estrogen; this changes during puberty when new androgens such as testosterone are produced that alter this balance. The hormonal evolution of boy into man routinely affects various parts of the body, including the breasts, which typically become muscular and taut, especially when combined with physical activity ("Gynecomastia," 2014).

In this chapter, the focus is on nonphysiological GM. This stems from either the medical or the illicit use of a range of drugs, a side effect of which can be enlargement of breast tissue. Nonphysiological GM has, for example, been identified as an impact from prescribed drug treatments for serious ailments, such as HIV and prostate cancer, especially where androgen deprivation therapy is utilized (Dickson, 2012; Deepinder & Braunstein, 2012). Patients with major illnesses may well view GM as a minor side effect when considering the wider health challenges they face. However, for users of AASs, nonphysiological GM is an unwelcome physiological outcome given that their aim is, by and large, to look and feel more muscular and masculine (Orlandi, Venegoni, & Pagani, 2010). "Man boobs" compromise that aim.

No surprise, then, that GM is a point of discussion on steroid forums. In a post entitled "WTF man boobs can you help?", Vincor (2008) wrote:

> So I am on my 9th week of my Sus [Sustanon] 500mg wk and Deca [nandrolone decanoate] 400mg wk and I have had gyno since week 5 or so and I have been taking .25 ai [aromatase inhibitor] every day and I can't get rid of it. I am embarressed to wear tight shirts cuase [sic] it's very noticable. Can you guys help me and let me know what else I should do? . . . I am taking BD [British Dragon] Arimidex right now.

## CHAPTER 9

In response, Redz (2008) commented:

> Bitch tits is scary stuff I would stop [the cycle] right away and get some letro [Letrozole] asap and for now up the dose of arimidex until you get the letro and start pct [post-cycle therapy] asap.

Vincor (2008) replied: "What side should I expect from Letro?"
Emilio Rebenga (2008) responded: "The reversal of gyno if it isnt [sic] too late."
This caused Vincor (2008) some anxiety:

> Isn't too late? What does that mean [?]. If I can't get rid of it will I have to get them removed. I have a buddy who [had] gyno surgery but, he is overseas right now so can['t] get advise [sic] from him at the moment.

Emilio Rebenga (2008): "Run the Letro . . . it should reverse it . . . if it dosent [sic] then its [sic] too late". Big Dubya (2008) was more empathetic:

> Yah I'd stop the cycle and go straight to pct. Gyno sucks. Agree try Cbino's letro protocol and see if it helps if it hasn't gone away. I tried for about 3 months while off cycle and it didn't seem to be helping so I decided to come off and wait for surgery. Letro alone is tough - kills your sex drvie [sic], energy, and makes your joints sore. I hated it. But worth a shot if it's new gyno. Surgery is not going to be fun either. LOL I actually just put a small piece of waterproof skin-colored tape across each nip when I wear a tight t-shirt or polo just to keep the nips from protruding . . . makes it completely unoticeable [sic] . . . Also got my body fat close to 10% which has helped a lot. Still gonna [sic] get the surgery later this year when I find a surgeon I'm comfortable with. Good luck bro. I know gyno sucks...

The physiological and pharmaceutical complexities of all this are beyond the scope of this chapter; the key point, as stressed previously, is the struggle by AAS users to elicit relevant medical information. As indicated by the above exchange, which is a familiar type of discussion in steroid forums, users are indeed concerned about minimizing side effects and health risks associated with AAS. What they appear to lack and indeed are in need of is advice with the appropriate level of medical expertise. This would, however, require a cultural shift on the part of both doctors and AAS users. Information seeking and knowledge broking is often problematic in contexts where the substances under discussion are illicit (Cohen et al., 2007).[3]

However, if there is an acceptance that harm minimization is a virtuous approach, then AAS users both require and deserve medical guidance given the custom and practice of doctor-patient confidentiality. Until then, both steroid forums and feature articles within such sites, as with "Gynecomastia: A Dude Grows Breasts—Estrogen Side Effects of Male Anabolic Steroid Use" (Spellwin, 2014), provide users with some basic guidance. Mitigating against major side effects is important, for in the case of significant GM, interventions such as liposuction or excision are invasive and expensive responses (Babigian & Silverman, 2001).

## ACNE

The human propensity to experience acne, which comes in many forms and different levels of severity, varies considerably; its etiology is not well-understood (Cunliffe, 1999). Our interest here is with what has been labelled acne medicamentosa, otherwise known as drug-induced acne. In short, this is a skin disorder that emerges as a side effect of taking a drug, prescribed or illicit. Drilling down further there is the notion of "steroid" acne, an adverse response to a range of corticosteroids or AASs (Plewig & Jansen, 1998). Our focus here is with the latter in their illicit (nonprescribed) form. According to Melnik, Jansen, and Grabbe (2007), AAS "leads to stimulation of the sebaceous glands"; this provides the conditions under which inflammation and scarring become more likely (Williams, Dellavalle, & Garner, 2012). For AAS users who have previously had acne, the risk of it recurring increases as a consequence of adopting this drug regimen (Melnik, Jansen, & Grabbe, 2007). Whatever the case, acne is common: According to a major survey of AAS users in the United States, 52.4% of respondents reported adverse effects in the form of some kind of acne (Ip et al., 2011). In extreme cases, the very severe skin conditions acne conglobata and acne fulminans can develop, most often "induced by AAS abuse" (Melnik, Jansen, & Grabbe, 2007).

In terms of side effects from AASs, acne might be considered a minor impact. After all, many teenagers experience some form of acne, whether mild or severe; this condition is not specific to users of AASs. However, there appear to be three factors that confound an assumption that the experiences of those with acne are necessarily innocuous. First, researchers have ascertained that youth with acne tend to have "significantly more depressive symptoms, lower self-attitude, more feelings of uselessness, fewer feelings of pride, lower self-worth, and lower body satisfaction than those without acne" (Dalgard, Gieler, Holm, Bjertness, & Hauser, 2008). Moreover, acne "is also associated with an increased risk of anxiety, depression and suicidal ideation" (Bhate & Williams, 2014). This means that *anyone* with acne, whether an AAS user or otherwise, faces the prospect of poor self-image stemming from a skin disorder that, while irritating, also presents social concerns in terms of physical appearance. Indeed, research by Williams and Garner (2012) suggests that "facial scarring due to acne affects up to 20% of teenagers" and that "acne can persist into adulthood, with detrimental effects on self-esteem."

Second, one of the purposes of AAS use, as an APED, is to "promote physical changes to muscle or body fat to improve athletic performance, physical appearance, and perceived social opportunity or self-esteem" (Hildebrandt, Harty, & Langenbucher, 2012). Muscle is surrounded by skin; indeed, skin is the visible canvas over which muscularity and other features of physical appearance are drawn. And skin is, to some degree, a canvas that is alterable. For example, practices of body art (tattooing and piercing) are socioculturally located self-expressions through color, shape, and meaning (Martin, 2013a). In a sense, therefore, AAS users are concerned—at least in part—with the appearance of their skin as the canvas upon which their muscularity is made visible. Therefore, skin "matters." Acne, particularly that which is observable in areas that AAS users focus upon (such as the neck, back and arms), has the capacity to confound the aesthetic capital achieved by muscularity. Mitigating against or responding to acne as a side effect of AAS is therefore a concern for many users. Kraus, Emmert, Schön, and Haenssle (2012), who have conducted research with bodybuilders, have described this as the "dark side of beauty."

Third, acne may be deemed problematic as a signal of AAS use, especially among adults (acne is normally associated with puberty and adolescence). As a widely experienced medical condition, AAS users might be expected to consult with their physicians about treatment. However, there may be a strategic reason for avoiding diagnosis by a doctor, particularly in severe or late onset cases of acne. Some medical practitioners have demanded that adults who present with acne (especially in the absence of a previous condition) be screened for the use of AASs. For example, a report in the *Dermatology Times* commented, "Since many of the side effects of anabolic steroids are manifested in the skin, dermatologists are in a unique and favorable position to detect their use, if they are aware of such clinical signs" (Petrou, 2011). Similarly, Melnik et al. (2007), in an article condemning AAS, recommend that physicians be alert to acne as a sign of illicit steroid use. Their solution is unlikely to be what AAS advocates want to hear: "The most important measure in doping acne is the immediate cessation of exogenous administration of AAS" (Melnik et al., 2007).

There is, as we have seen, a propensity for information seeking within the online "steroid community." Acne is no exception. In an online forum, PrinceDianobol (2013) commented, "Acne has been a big problem for me since my last cycle over

6months ago!"; hence he was seeking advice how to address it. In response, Filthyy (2013) recommended a course of natural supplements:

> Vitamin B5: 14 grams (7 gr in the morning, and 7 gr before bed)
> Zinc: 100 mg daily (50mg in the morning, and 50mg before bed)
> Pycnogenol [antioxidant from Pine bark]: 240 mg (120mg in the morning, and 120mg before bed)

Black Bear (2013) contributed to the discussion: "Zinc really works. I believe it works as a mild aromatase and 5-alpha reductase inhibitor." PrinceDianobol (2013) was pleased with that response, but curious: "Thank you! Very very much appreciated! Quick question, are all these dosed orally? Or need to be injected?" Black Bear (2013) wrote back: "Lmao [laughing my ass off], if you injected zinc I think you would die." PrinceDianobol (2013) responded: "Hahaha well shit thats [sic] good to know. Thanks mate." Black Bear (2013) concluded,

> All oral baby. Good luck with the acne prince Dball. That shit sucks, and can permanently wreck your face if you don't take care of it. Just a common side effect of androgenic hormones. I'm fortunate and inherited my mom's skin (and not my dads). So acne is pretty tame. I know zinc works. My girlfriend cleared up her acne with zinc picolinate. It's the most bioavailable form of zinc, or at least the most accesible [sic] one. It's cheap. . . . Don't take zinc with calcium or iron. They compete for absorption. So preferably on an empty stomach, but if you are sensitive it could cause nausea.

In summary, then, although acne seems relatively innocuous by comparison to other known side effects of AAS use, it has an aesthetic stigma that confounds efforts to improve appearance; the experience of acne may produce negative psychosocial impacts; and acne may be a trigger to suspicion of AAS use. For men concerned about their appearance, acne compromises their sense of bodily pride.

## CONCLUSION

This chapter examined how men have made sense of their bodies in light of possible side effects associated with the use of AASs. This exploration of the intimate self revolved around the aesthetic and/or functional attributes of three key areas of the male body: the testicles, the breasts, and the skin. The shrunken size and altered shape of the male gonads were a concern for some AAS users; for others, the key issue was regaining a sperm count sufficient to allow for reproduction. The growth of breast tissue was certainly a cause of consternation among steroid users, particularly those for whom the condition persisted well after the cessation of a cycle. The appearance of acne was a cause of frustration, though remedial prospects appeared more likely than for the aforementioned impacts of AASs.

This chapter reveals men who are particularly interested in the shape, size, and texture of their bodies. The masculinization of the male form is optimized by the deployment of AASs to mold a muscular frame (along with the associated exercise needed to produce what is commonly understood to be an androgenic body). However, there is—as emphasized by a Steroid.com advisory—both reward and risk in such a process. This chapter has focused on the risk associated with AAS use and how AAS users have sought to anticipate or manage key side effects. The focus was deliberately with impacts on the intimate self. AASs are associated, at least in part, with aspirations of improving appearance, being more sexually attractive, and raising self-esteem via changes to body image. Anything that confounds or compromises those goals must surely be a source of anxiety. The reported side effects of steroids can indeed be problematic to a man's intimate sense of self. This is particularly so, it must be said, if AAS users are not appropriately informed and educated about such risks; the reliance of so many on steroid forums is, in that respect, unfortunate. For harm minimization to function adequately, users of illicit substances like AASs need trustworthy and confidential medical advice. There are plenty of campaigns encouraging men to visit their doctor for a prostate examination. For some AAS users, there are other parts of the intimate self that also require empathetic medical scrutiny.

## **REFERENCES**

Anabolic Steroids Cycles and Stacks. (2000). *Steroid.com*. Retrieved from http://www.steroid.com/steroid_cycles.php

Aussiemuscle. (2008). "Do steroids effect sperm[?]" [Forum comment]. Retrieved from http://www.aboard.in/showthread.php?t=16207

Babigian, A., & Silverman, R. T. (2001). Management of gynecomastia due to use of anabolic steroids in bodybuilders. *Plastic and Reconstructive Surgery, 107*, 240–242.

Barry Bonds' testicles shrunk, he blamed steroids for elbow injury, ex-mistress testifies. (2011). *SILive.com*. Retrieved from http://www.silive.com/sports/index.ssf/2011/03/barry_bonds_testicles_shrunk_h.html

Bhate, K., & Williams, H. C. (2014). What's new in acne? An analysis of systematic reviews published in 2011–2012. *Clinical and Experimental Dermatology, 39*, 273–278.

Big Dubya. (2008). WTF man boobs can you help? [Forum comment]. Retrieved from http://forums.steroid.com/anabolic-steroids-questions-answers/346355-wtf-man-boobs-can-you-help.html

Bitch tits. (n.d.). In *Urban Dictionary*. Retrieved from http://www.urbandictionary.com/define.php?term=bitch+tits

Black Bear. (2013). Austinites acne stack?? Anyone help me out here [Forum comment]. *Steroidology.com*. Retrieved from http://www.steroidology.com/forum/anabolic-steroid-forum/662033-austinites-acne-stack-anyone-help-me-out-here.html

Blashill, A. J., & Safren, S. A. (2014). Sexual orientation and anabolic-androgenic steroids in US adolescent boys. *Pediatrics, 133*, 469–475.

Boregowda, K., Joels, L., Stephens, J. W., & Price, D. E. (2011). Persistent primary hypogonadism associated with anabolic steroid abuse. *Fertility and Sterility, 96*, e7–e8.

Bourdieu, P. (1987). *Distinction: A social critique of the judgement of taste*. Cambridge, MA: Harvard University Press.

Brown, D. (1999). Male bodybuilders and the social meaning of muscle. *Auto/biography, 7*, 83–90.

Canseco, J. (2005). *Juiced: Wild times, rampant 'roids, smash hits and how baseball got big*. New York, NY: HarperCollins.

Cohen, J., Collins, R., Darkes, J., & Gwartney, D. (2007). A league of their own: Demographics, motivations and patterns of use of 1,955 male adult non-medical anabolic steroid users in the United States. *Journal of the International Society of Sports Nutrition, 4*, 1–14.

Coomber, R. (2013). How social fear of drugs in the non-sporting world creates a framework for doping policy in the sporting world. *International Journal of Sport Policy and Politics*, 1–23.

Coward, R. M., Rajanahally, S., Kovac, J. R., Smith, R. P., Pastuszak, A. W., & Lipshultz, L. I. (2013). Anabolic steroid induced hypogonadism in young men. *The Journal of Urology, 190*, 2200–2205.

Cunliffe, W. J. (1999). *Acne*. London, England: Taylor & Francis.

D_rson. (2010). Re: Slight testicular atrophy [Forum comment]. Retrieved from http://www.elitefitness.com/forum/anabolic-steroids/slight-testicular-atrophy-702593.html

Dalgard, F., Gieler, U., Holm, J. Ø., Bjertness, E., & Hauser, S. (2008). Self-esteem and body satisfaction among late adolescents with acne: Results from a population survey. *Journal of the American Academy matology, 59*, 746–751.

De Barros, A. C. S. D., & Sampaio, M. C. M. (2012). Gynecomastia: Physiopathology, evaluation and treatment. *Sao Paulo Medical Journal, 130*, 187–197.

Deepinder, F., & Braunstein, G. D. (2012). Drug-induced gynecomastia: An evidence-based review. *Expert Opinion on Drug Safety, 11*, 779–795.

Denham, B. E. (2008). Masculinities in hardcore bodybuilding. *Men and Masculinities, 11*, 234–242.

Dickson, G. (2012). Gynecomastia. *American Family Physician, 85*, 716–722.

Dodge, T., & Hoagland, M. F. (2011). The use of anabolic androgenic steroids and polypharmacy: A review of the literature. *Drug and Alcohol Dependence, 114*, 100–109.

Edzilla. (2010). Slight testicular atrophy [Forum comment]. Retrieved from http://www.elitefitness.com/forum/anabolic-steroids/slight-testicular-atrophy-702593.html

Evans, N. A. (1997). Gym and tonic: A profile of 100 male steroid users. *British Journal of Sports Medicine, 31*, 54–58.

Filiault, S. M., & Drummond, M. J. N. (2010). Muscular, but not "roided out": Gay male athletes and performance-enhancing substances. *International Journal of Men's Health, 9,* 62–81.

Filthyy. (2013). Austinites acne stack?? Anyone help me out here [Forum comment]. *Steroidology.com.* Retrieved from http://www.steroidology.com/forum/anabolic-steroid-forum/662033-austinites-acne-stack-anyone-help-me-out-here.html

Fronczak, C. M., Kim, E. D., & Barqawi, A. B. (2012). The insults of illicit drug use on male fertility. *Journal of Andrology, 33,* 515–528.

Gynecomastia. (2014). *MedicineNet.com.* Retrieved from http://www.medicinenet.com/gynecomastia/article.htm

Hakansson, A., Mickelsson, K., Wallin, C., & Berglund, M. (2012). Anabolic androgenic steroids in the general population: User characteristics and associations with substance use. *European Addiction Research, 18,* 83–90.

Halkitis, P. N., Moeller, R. W., & DeRaleau, L. B. (2008). Steroid use in gay, bisexual, and non-identified men-who-have-sex-with-men: Relations to masculinity, physical, and mental health. *Psychology of Men & Masculinity, 9,* 106–115.

Hildebrandt, T., Harty, S., & Langenbucher, J. W. (2012). Fitness supplements as a gateway substance for anabolic-androgenic steroid use. *Psychology of Addictive Behaviors, 26,* 955–62.

Huffington Post. (2012). Oh no she didn't! Jessica Canseco talks Jose's testicles. Retrieved from http://www.huffingtonpost.com/2012/06/28/hollywood-exes-jose-canseco-steroids-testicles-video_n_1633315.html

Ip, E. J., Barnett, M. J., Tenerowicz, M. J., & Perry, P. J. (2011). The anabolic 500 survey: Characteristics of male users versus non-users of Anabolic-Androgenic Steroids for strength training. *Pharmacotherapy: The Journal of Human Pharmacology and Drug Therapy, 31,* 757–766.

Iriart, J. A. B., Chaves, J. C., & Orleans, R. G. (2009). Body cult and use of anabolic steroids by bodybuilders. *Cadernos de Saúde Pública, 25,* 773–782.

Kanayama, G., Barry, S., Hudson, J., & Pope, H. (2006). Body image and attitudes toward male roles in anabolic-androgenic steroid users. *American Journal of Psychiatry, 163,* 697–703.

Kanayama, G., Hudson, J. I., & Pope, H. G. Jr. (2010). Illicit anabolic-androgenic steroid use. *Hormones and Behavior, 58,* 111–121.

Keane, H. (2005). Diagnosing the male steroid user: Drug use, body image and disordered masculinity. Health: *An Interdisciplinary Journal for the Social Study of Health, Illness, and Medicine, 9,* 189–208.

Klein, A. M. (1993). *Little big men: Bodybuilding subculture and gender construction.* New York, NY: State University of New York Press.

Kraska, P. B., Bussard, C. R., & Brent, J. J. (2009). Trafficking in bodily perfection: Examining the late-modern steroid marketplace and its criminalization. *Justice Quarterly, 27,* 159–185.

Kraus, S. L., Emmert, S., Schön, M. P., & Haenssle, H. A. (2012). The dark side of beauty: Acne fulminans induced by anabolic steroids in a male bodybuilder. *Archives of Dermatology, 148,* 1210–1212.

Lorber, J., & Martin, P. Y. (1998). The socially constructed body: Insights from feminist theory. In P. Kivisto (Ed.), *Illuminating Social Life* (pp. 279–300). Newbury Park, CA: Pine Forge Press.

Machola. (2008). Re: Do steroids effect sperm[?] [Forum comment]. Retrieved from http://www.aboard.in/showthread.php?t=16207

Man boobs. (n.d.). In *Urban Dictionary*. Retrieved from http://www.urbandictionary.com/define.php?term=man+boobs

Martin, C. W. (2013a). Tattoos as narratives: Skin and self. *Public Journal of Semiotics, 4*(2), 2–46.

Martin, L. (2013b). Why men don't have balls anymore. *Elite Daily*. Retrieved from http://elitedaily.com/dating/why-men-dont-have-balls-anymore/

Melnik, B., Jansen, T., & Grabbe, S. (2007). Abuse of anabolic-androgenic steroids and bodybuilding acne: An underestimated health problem. *JDDG: Journal der Deutschen Dermatologischen Gesellschaft, 5*, 110–117.

Menon, D. K. (2003). Successful treatment of anabolic steroid-induced azoospermia with human chorionic gonadotropin and human menopausal gonadotropin. *Fertility and Sterility, 79*, Supplement 3, 1659–1661.

Monaghan, L. (1999). Creating the "perfect body": A variable project. *Body & Society, 5*, 267–290.

Monaghan, L. (2002). Vocabularies of motive for illicit steroid use among bodybuilders. *Social Science & Medicine, 55*, 695–708.

Monaghan, L. F. (2001). *Bodybuilding, drugs, and risk*. Abingdon, Oxon: Psychology Press.

Morgan, D. (1993). You too can have a body like mine: Reflections on the male body and masculinities. In S. Scott & D. Morgan (Eds.), *Body matters: Essays on the sociology of the body* (pp. 69–88). London, England: Falmer Press.

Mott, C., & Roberts, S.M. (2014). Not everyone has (the) balls: Urban exploration and the persistence of masculinist geography. *Antipode, 46*, 229–245.

Movie Fan. (2007). Washed up Celebrities: Jose Canseco [Weblog post]. Retrieved from http://washedupcelebrities.blogspot.com.au/2007/08/jose-canseco.html

MR10X. (2011). Re: Testicular atrophy recovery years after cycle? [Forum comment]. Retrieved from http://thinksteroids.com/forum/steroid-forum/testicular-atrophy-recovery-years-134304110.html

Olrich, T.W. (1999). Perceptions of benefits and losses associated with the use and discontinuance of anabolic-androgenic steroids among male bodybuilders. *Journal of Personal and Interpersonal Loss, 4*, 231–242.

Orlandi, M.A., Venegoni, E., & Pagani, C. (2010). Gynecomastia in two young men with histories of prolonged use of anabolic androgenic steroids. *Journal of Ultrasound, 13*, 46–48.

Perry, P. J., Lund, B. C., Deninger, M. J., Kutscher, E. C., & Schneider, J. (2005). Anabolic steroid use in weightlifters and bodybuilders: An internet survey of drug utilization. *Clinical Journal of Sport Medicine, 15*, 326–330.

Petrou, I. (2011). Anabolic androgenic steroid use, abuse on the rise. *Dermatology Times*. Retrieved from http://dermatologytimes.modernmedicine.com/dermatology-times/news/clinical/clinical-pharmacology/anabolic-androgenic-steroid-use-abuse-rise

CHAPTER 9

Plewig, G., & Jansen, T. (1998). Acneiform dermatoses. *Dermatology, 196*, 102–107.
PrinceDianobol. (2013). Austinites acne stack?? Anyone help me out here[?] [Forum comment]. *Steroidology.com*. Retrieved from http://www.steroidology.com/forum/anabolic-steroid-forum/662033-austinites-acne-stack-anyone-help-me-out-here.html
Proszenko, A. (2012). Doctor sanctions steroids. *Sydney Morning Herald*. Retrieved from http://www.smh.com.au/sport/cycling/doctor-sanctions-steroids-20121027-28c9k.html
Pseudogynecomastia: How it differs from gynecomastia (n.d.). In *Web's Encyclopedia of Gynecomastia*. Retrieved from http://www.gynecoma.com/pseudogynecomastia-symptoms-diagnosis-treatment/
Quaglio, G., Fornasiero, A., Mezzelani, P., Moreschini, S., Lugoboni, F., & Lechi, A. (2009). Anabolic steroids: Dependence and complications of chronic use. *Internal and Emergency Medicine, 4*, 289–296.
Rebenga, Emilio. (2008). WTF man boobs can you help? [Forum comment]. Retrieved from http://forums.steroid.com/anabolic-steroids-questions-answers/346355-wtf-man-boobs-can-you-help.html
Redz. (2008). WTF man boobs can you help? [Forum comment]. Retrieved from http://forums.steroid.com/anabolic-steroids-questions-answers/346355-wtf-man-boobs-can-you-help.html
Samaha, A. A., Nasser-Eddine, W., Shatila, E., Haddad, J., Wazne, J., & Eid, A. H. (2008). Multi-organ damage induced by anabolic steroid supplements: A case report and literature review. *Journal of Medical Case Reports, 2*, 1–6.
Smith, A. C. T., & Stewart, B. (2012b). Body perceptions and health behaviors in an online bodybuilding community. *Qualitative Health Research, 22*, 971–985.
Smith, A. C., & Stewart, B. (2012a). Body conceptions and virtual ethnopharmacology in an online bodybuilding community. *Performance Enhancement & Health, 1*, 35–38.
Sony Pictures. (1995). The Doorman. Retrieved from http://www.sonypictures.com/tv/shows/seinfeld/episode_guide/?sl=episode&ep=616
Spellwin, G. (2014). Gynecomastia: A dude grows breasts—estrogen side effects of male anabolic steroid use. Retrieved from http://bodybuilding.elitefitness.com/gynecomastia-dude-grows-breasts-estrogen-side-effects-male-anabolic-steroid-use
Stev7667. (2011). Testicular atrophy recovery years after cycle? [Forum comment]. Retrieved from http://thinksteroids.com/forum/steroid-forum/testicular-atrophy-recovery-years-134304110.html
Tabachnick, D. E. (2010). Why safer steroids are dangerous. *The Mark News*. Retrieved from http://pioneers.themarknews.com/articles/2572-why-safer-steroids-are-dangerous/
Tan, R., & Scally, M. (2009). Anabolic steroid-induced hypogonadism—towards a unified hypothesis of anabolic steroid action. *Medical Hypotheses, 72*, 723–728.
van Amsterdam, J., Opperhuizen, A., & Hartgens, F. (2010). Adverse health effects of anabolic-androgenic steroids. *Regulatory Toxicology and Pharmacology, 57*, 117–123.
Vincor. (2008). WTF man boobs can you help? [Forum comment]. Retrieved from http://forums.steroid.com/anabolic-steroids-questions-answers/346355-wtf-man-boobs-can-you-help.html

Wassersug, R.J., & Oliffe, J.L. (2009). The social context for psychological distress from iatrogenic Gynecomastia with suggestions for its management. *The Journal of Sexual Medicine, 6*, 989–1000.

Williams, H.C., Dellavalle, R.P., & Garner, S. (2012). Acne vulgaris. *The Lancet, 379*, 361–372.

# ENDNOTES

1 Beyond the body image goals of AAS, Tan and Scally (2009) point out that they "are now a commonly prescribed drug" to address "disease-associated morbidity, decreased muscle mass and decreased muscle strength." Of course, AAS is "not treatment for the underlying disease cause."

2 Such a pragmatic approach is important because, as one survey of AAS users revealed, 88.5% of respondents reported adverse side-effects of steroids, 56% indicated concern about "possible negative effects of AAS on their long-term health," while "an overwhelming majority (93.3%) reported plans to continue AAS use in the future" (Ip et al., 2011).

3 A survey of physicians in Australia indicate that 2% of doctors had prescribed AAS for the purposes of body-building, with 77% indicating "interest in obtaining more information on effects and side effects of AAS" (Melnik et al., 2007). However, while this approach might be construed as knowledge-gathering in the interests of harm minimization, critics may see this type of medical involvement as problematic. Melnik et al. (2007), for example, perceive that the medical supply of "non-therapeutic" AAS by physicians suggests that they have an "uncritical and careless approach" to the health and well-being of their patients. From this perspective, the general practitioners are playing an "assisting role in AAS abuse" (Melnik et al., 2007). This assumes, of course, that doctors are overseeing AAS *abusers*, not simply users.

# Manliness and Mountaineering: Sir Edmund Hillary as New Zealand Adventurer and Male Icon

Toni Bruce and Richard Pringle

## INTRODUCTION

The death of a national icon invariably provokes a period of national reflection on the individual's contribution to the nation, if not to the world. In this chapter we analyze public discourses around the death of Sir Edmund Hillary, the New Zealander renowned as the first man to reach the summit of the world's highest mountain. Hillary died in 2008, more than half a century after he and Sherpa mountaineer Tenzing Norgay first stood on top of Mount Everest.

Hillary's place as a national icon, hero, legend, role model, and inspiration[1] is undeniable. For most of the second half of the twentieth century, he cast a large shadow, literally[2] and figuratively, over New Zealand's imaginings of itself. Such was his impact that even 18 months after his death he received by far the most votes in a national poll asking people to identify the greatest *living* New Zealander ("Who Takes," 2009). His passing was accompanied by national mourning; his body lay in state (an honor usually reserved for prime ministers and Governors General), and his funeral was broadcast on two national television stations, on the national radio station, and live via webcast.

In this chapter, we examine media representations for what they reveal about masculinities and the place of mountaineering within New Zealand. We will argue that Hillary's appeal emerged out of his international adventures, apparently modest refusal to buy into the fame and idolatry thrust upon him, and commitment to improving the lives of the Sherpa people in the Himalayas. Our overall analysis reveals three key themes—*the Adventurer, the Kiwi Bloke*[3] and the *Humanitarian*—and their articulation to masculinities and national identity. An editorial reflecting on Hillary's number 1 ranking in the inaugural *Readers Digest* "Most Trusted" survey several years before his death incorporates the themes quite explicitly: "He is the complete package: the *conqueror of Everest,* and a *man* renowned for his openness and honesty, *immense humility* and *utter selflessness* [emphasis added], as illustrated by his work building medical clinics and schools in Nepal" ("Sport, Trust," 2005, para 7). We will argue that these themes (as refracted through the words of journalists and the public) reflect key imaginings of a desired New Zealand identity while functioning to reinscribe men (and particular forms of masculinity) as central to a dominant sense of national self. Thus, while our focus is on discourses of masculinity, the significant intertwining of all three themes means that elements of each will be used to inform our prime argument. Overall, we propose that because Hillary was seen as successfully performing the dominant form of New Zealand masculinity, his engagement in behaviors, such as humanitarianism, that fall outside dominant understandings was not only accepted but valued. As a result, Hillary's popularity was associated with a form of cosmopolitan humanitarianism that is often overlooked in academic discussions of masculinities, and that suggests a need to more broadly consider the ways in which we understand intersections of gender and national identities.

Throughout, we weave together Hillary's biography, theory, empirical research, and our analysis as we attempt to make sense of media and public responses to the man described by one newspaper as "the epitome of New Zealand manhood" ("Antarctic Adventures," 2008, p. 9).

In order to contextualize the analysis, we first present a brief biography of Hillary's achievements, followed by a theoretical discussion of key concepts that inform our investigation. We note that the biography draws upon multiple sources of information, including media coverage, encyclopedia entries, Hillary's own writing, and biographies of him written by others. Like all representations, it is necessarily partial and functions as a launching pad for the ensuing analysis rather than as a detailed investigation of his life (for comprehensive narratives, see Booth, 1993; Hillary, 1999; Johnston, 2006).

## SIR EDMUND HILLARY: A BRIEF BIOGRAPHY

Edmund Percival Hillary was born in Auckland, New Zealand, in 1919 and died in the same city in 2008 at the age of 88. More than 50 years earlier, in an era when only one ascent on Mt. Everest was permitted each year, Hillary and Sherpa mountaineer Tenzing Norgay gained international renown by being the first to reach the summit of the world's highest mountain. They were members of a 1953 British expedition led by John Hunt (who was subsequently knighted along with Hillary). Hillary announced their Everest success in what is now accepted as his typically understated fashion, with the words "We knocked the bastard off" (a phrase widely celebrated in the media and public response to his death). Hillary and Tenzing Norgay initially shared the glory, resisting media, government, and public pressure to identify which of them had first stood on the world's highest point; instead, both stated that they reached the summit at almost the same time (Booth, 1993; Hansen, 2000; Johnston, 2006). After Everest, Hillary continued to engage in adventures in harsh climates. Five years later in 1958, using modified farm tractors, Hillary and his team became the first to reach the South Pole on motorized vehicles, a somewhat controversial achievement given that they were in a support role for another British expedition, this time led by Vivien Fuchs (also later knighted). In 1977, a Hillary-led team became the first to travel from the mouth of the Ganges to its source in the Himalayan Mountains, and in 1985, after flying to the North Pole with US astronaut Neil Armstrong, he became the first person to stand at both poles and on the summit of the world's tallest mountain.

The dominant cultural story of Hillary identifies him as a meticulous planner, independent thinker, and bold adventurer who remained humble and approachable, lending his name and support to outdoors and conservation organizations and projects worldwide (Booth, 1993; Hansen, 2000; Johnston, 2006). With the support of his family, Hillary devoted much of his life to humanitarian work in partnership with the Sherpa people of Nepal. Known there as the Burra Sahib (big in heart), he founded the Himalayan Trust in 1963, which built schools, bridges, health clinics, water supplies, a hospital, and an airstrip, and supported reforestation projects in response to the needs expressed by the local people. After the death of his first wife Louise Rose and younger daughter Belinda in a 1975 Kathmandu air crash, Hillary experienced a period of depression—an aspect of his life that has received little focus. Hillary was survived by his son Peter (who also climbed Everest), daughter Sarah, and second wife June Mulgrew (the widow of a longtime climbing friend) who he married in 1989. Hillary was a popular New Zealand High Commissioner to India with responsibilities for Nepal and Bangladesh from 1985–1988. He received many international accolades, including a knighthood that he reportedly would have turned down if it had not already been accepted by the then Prime Minister of New Zealand on his behalf. Additionally, Hillary was appointed a Knight of the Order of the Garter by Queen Elizabeth in 1995,[4] was granted honorary Nepalese citizenship, and posthumously, received India's second-highest civilian award, the Padma Vibhushan. He was the only living New Zealander to have his face appear on New Zealand currency (the $5 note) and has had numerous places named after him, as well as statues in Orewa and near New Zealand's highest mountain Mt Cook/Aorangi.

## ANALYZING MEDIA COVERAGE/DISCOURSES

Upon his death, Hillary's popularity and legendary status evoked a national outpouring of grief that was similar in intensity to that which followed the murder of New Zealand yachtsman and environmentalist Sir Peter Blake in 2001. As previous research has concluded, media coverage of Blake's death provided a barometer of the nation's insecurities around Whiteness, masculinity, and national identity (see Bruce & Wheaton, 2010, 2011; Cosgrove & Bruce, 2005). In a similar vein, we see media coverage of Hillary's death as providing another valuable discursive space in which to interrogate contemporary visions of masculinity and, more broadly, what it means to be a New Zealander.

We acknowledge, as Kane (2010) points out in a New Zealand context, that "the cultural foundations of any human practice as recognized in its social representations, images or narratives are not universal, uncontested or perfect reflections of culture" (p. 40). We also draw upon the work of theorists such as Stuart Hall, Michel Foucault, and Judith Butler to assist our investigation of the specific representations that surrounded Hillary's death. Foucault (1978), for example, identified his prime research objective as being "to sketch out a history of the different ways in our culture that humans develop knowledge about themselves" (pp. 17–18). He argued that this knowledge was important to examine, as it was constituted within and constitutive of power relations. In other words, he conceptualized that knowledge and power operate conjunctionally so that the knowledge humans develop of themselves is the result of the workings of power, *and* that this knowledge subsequently has effects in terms of the exercise of power and the negotiation of power relations. More specifically, Foucault (1978) theorized that "it is in discourse that power and knowledge are joined together" (p. 100); he argued that discourse shapes how humans make sense of our social world. Of importance here are discourses revealed in the narratives of the mainstream media, which actively create rather than merely reflect dominant cultural beliefs (Denzin, 1996; Hall, 1984; McRobbie, 1997). As Hall (1984) argues, media discourses construct "plausible frameworks" through which we tell ourselves and others "a certain story about the world" (p. 8). This theoretical position leads us away from a focus on whether or not the media are telling the "truth" about Hillary, and toward a consideration of what kind of story is being told about the place of mountaineering (with Hillary as its iconic representative) in New Zealand culture and about the state of Kiwi masculinity (and, indirectly, New Zealand character) in the media coverage of his death.

Our analysis of media and public discourses surrounding Hillary emerge from a textual analysis (see McKee, 2001; Turner, 1997) of hard copies of three North Island daily metropolitan newspapers (*New Zealand Herald, Waikato Times,* and *Dominion Post*) and the largest Sunday newspaper (*Sunday Star Times*), as well as retrospective analysis of articles from the major South Island newspaper (*Christchurch Press*) and smaller regional newspapers accessed via the Newztext database.[5]

Turner (1997) argues that "media texts offer especially rich opportunities to observe the cultural construction of meaning, locations where we can see the social production of ideas and values happening before our very eyes" (p. 326). Until recently, the method of textual analysis of newspapers was limited by the predominantly one-way nature of communication, which left researchers in the position of making educated guesses "at some of the most likely interpretations" that the pubic might make of what they read (McKee, 2001, p. 140). However, rapid developments in Internet access and technology mean that public interpretations are now much more accessible via the comments people post on news (and other) websites in reaction to media coverage. Thus, our analysis also extends beyond news reporting to include a much wider range of public voices that contribute to constructing the "plausible frameworks" through which we can understand Hillary's place in the world. In stark contrast to the past, when newspapers published only a small selection of reader comments in the "Letters to the Editor" section,[6] today's technology and global reach enables hundreds if not thousands of comments to be published online. As a result, our sample includes more than 700 public comments posted on two major media websites (the online edition of New Zealand's highest-circulation daily newspaper, nzherald.co.nz, and the Fairfax newspapers aggregator, stuff.co.nz, which includes most other major newspapers), as well as those published in the print editions of the analyzed metropolitan newspapers.[7] Thus, we were able to analyze both the "social production" by the mainstream media and the "interpretations" made by New Zealanders (at home and abroad); those from countries with significant links to

Hillary's life such as the UK, Nepal, and India; and others from a range of countries (the diversity indicates Hillary's global impact) including Australia, Fiji, Canada, the USA, Mexico, Brazil, the Philippines, Malaysia, Tibet, Germany, Austria, Spain, Italy, and France. We differentiate these public postings from the news coverage by using square brackets to identify the author, date and time of the post; many did not carry the author's name and are thus tagged as Anon (e.g., [Anon, 12 Jan, 11:35am]).

Through an interrogation of this expanded body of coverage using the concept of articulation, we consider what visions of masculinity are revealed in the images and stories about Sir Ed (a term he reportedly preferred over the more formal Sir Edmund). Cultural studies theorist Stuart Hall, in an interview with Lawrence Grossberg, explained that "a theory of articulation is both a way of understanding how ideological elements come, under certain conditions, to cohere together within a discourse, and a way of asking how they do or do not become articulated, at specific conjunctures" (as cited in Grossberg, 1996, pp. 141–142). Most important in terms of this analysis is the recognition that there is no necessary correspondence between elements that are articulated. While some elements may appear to be naturally linked, this connection is always ideological and discursive and its boundaries have to be patrolled and maintained. For example, our analysis reveals a public belief that the discursive strength of historically masculine characteristics (represented as being embodied by Hillary) is fading, along with an underlying angst about such shifts. As a result, we not only identify discourses that strongly articulate Hillary and masculinity, but also interrogate the coverage for what it reveals about contemporary insecurities about understandings of masculinity. Due to the nuances of New Zealand's history, these specific insecurities act simultaneously to highlight insecurities about the nation more broadly. We identify, for example, an underlying sadness that men of Hillary's type are far from common, an implicit recognition that New Zealand (and global) values and expectations of men have changed, and a sense that something important may have been lost along the way. At the same time, we highlight aspects of Hillary's life that were instrumental to his popularity, such as his humanitarian work, that have not, at least by academics, been identified as significant in terms of shaping understandings of New Zealand masculinities.

## THEORIZING MASCULINITIES

Our analysis begins from the theoretical position that discourses of masculinity are neither universal nor uncontested. Indeed, what it means to be masculine or manly changes over time and context. As Roper and Tosh (1991) have put it, "masculinity is always bound up with negotiations about power and is therefore often experienced as tenuous" (p. 18). In this sense, masculinities are widely understood by sociologists as multiple, sociohistorical constructions that exist not alone but in relation to femininities. There have been lengthy academic debates about defining, theorizing, and examining masculinities, particularly the concept of hegemonic masculinity (Flood, 2002; Mac an Ghaill, 1996; Pringle, Kay, & Jenkins, 2011; Whannel, 1999). However, gender theorists have typically acknowledged that masculinities are linked to male bodies in a symbolic or allegorical way (Connell, 2002) rather than in a biological or genetic sense. This symbolic linking has resulted in social theorists tending to discuss masculinities in relation to concepts such as narratives, images, myths, ideologies, discourses, articulations, and/or performances (e.g., Whannel, 1999).

Judith Butler's (1990) work informs our conception of masculinity as a "free-floating artifice" that is linked to how people *read* bodies as *performative texts* (p. 6). A respected form of masculinity, in this sense, is not an innate quality but something that requires effort in its performance; being masculine requires work (as does being feminine). A prime power effect of gendered discourses is that they enable people to read the performances of males and females as seemingly dissimilar or, as Mills (2003) suggests, they act in part to "characterize men and women as fundamentally different" (p. 65). While theorists such as Butler have focused more immediately upon masculinity as a gendered performance that shapes an individual's view of self and others, our interest is in how Hillary's bodily performances have been read by the media and the New Zealand public. We argue, following Giddens (1991), that identity is related to the "ability to keep a particular narrative going" (p. 52), which may result in the conscious or unconscious adoption of particular storylines that not only shape an individual's bodily performances but, more importantly in our case, how other people (e.g., journalists, the public) interpret those performances.

Kane (2010) points out that Hillary had "thrust on him the role of cultural icon" (p. 32), and our analysis reveals that even the news media recognized the constructed nature of the Hillary storyline. One newspaper highlighted a Hillary quote: "I was just an average bloke; it was the *media* [emphasis added] that transformed me into a heroic figure" ("Obituary," 2008, p. C8). Another took a similar approach, identifying Hillary as "a modest man who never lost the common touch even though *other people* [emphasis added] turned him into a hero" (Calder, 2008b, p. C20). The *Christchurch Press* remarked: "The most remarkable feature of the life of Sir Edmund Hillary was that he remained so unaffected by the adulation and clamour which surrounded him after the Everest feat. He persistently rejected what he described as the 'hoopla' or 'carry-on' surrounding his media image and the public hero-worship which went with it" ("The Values," 2008, p. 13).

In addition, several articles explicitly reflected on connections between the story told about Hillary and the *real* Hillary, while at the same time implying a direct correlation between the story and reality. For example: "Everyone admired him: for once the hyperbole must be almost true" ("Sir Ed," 2008, p. A11). Certainly, the public comments made it very clear that Hillary was admired by many people around the world, but especially New Zealanders. More than 10% of New Zealanders' posts (71 comments) on the nzherald.co.nz website explicitly identified how Hillary galvanized nationalistic feelings, making them feel proud to be New Zealanders. For example: "Sir Ed was the greatest New Zealander ever. I am proud to call myself a Kiwi because of him. It is a sad day for us all" [Richard, 11 Jan, 12:49pm]; "Ed. You made me proud to be a New Zealander. Thank you, thank you, thank you" [Maxie, 11 Jan, 1:10pm]; and "He was the one who made me proud to be a kiwi!" [Billy, 11 Jan, 1:37pm]. A letter in the *Nelson Mail* stated: "We loved him for being the genuine article, not a myth" ("End of an Era," 2008, p. 13).

In thinking about Hillary's conceptualization as a New Zealand hero and as an exemplar of an idealized form of masculinity, we understand that it is important to not only examine his accomplishments or public performances but the broader narratives circulated in Aotearoa/New Zealand that have enabled locals to read his performances in particular ways. Historians have critiqued and simultaneously promoted the idea of New Zealand as a pioneering or settler country dominated by Pakeha masculinist ideals (e.g., Belich, 1996; Phillips, 1987; Sinclair, 1986). We concur with Bannister (2005) that these masculinist ideals are socially constructed rather than emerging in some natural way from the past. Instead, New Zealand nationalism and ideals of masculinity were formed within power relations, and have survived by reinforcing notions of a white settler society and serving the interests of ruling groups (economically advantaged Pakeha males) at the expense of others such as women, gay men, Maori, and immigrants of other cultures, many of whom have been excluded at various times from being considered "real" New Zealanders (Bannister, 2005; Kite, 2002; Spoonley, 1997). These ideals stemmed, according to Phillips (1987), from a Pakeha population imbalance that favored men in a manner that constituted the pioneering nation as "a man's country." As a result, activities most strongly attributed to males, such as sport, war, and mountaineering, became mythologized in ways that produced patriotic stories of nationalism (Andrews & Kingsbury, 2008; Hansen, 2000; Pickles, 2002; Sinclair, 1986).

Representations of the success of the 1905 All Blacks over *mother* England (occurring shortly before New Zealand was granted Dominion status in 1907) and the tragedy at Gallipoli during World War I have, along with the *conquest* of Everest, become founding narratives of New Zealand identity. Men who can be articulated to narratives are described in terms that celebrate strength, courage, hard work, determination, mateship, discipline, and modesty, often accompanied by a marginalization of women or activities deemed as feminine (Cosgrove & Bruce, 2005; Duley, 1997; Hill, 2002; Phillips, 1996). Indeed, Hood (1997) argued that "the exclusion and denigration of women has been the necessary flipside of equating masculinity with national identity" (p. 21).

These nationalist narratives have, over time, become discursive resources drawn upon to forge an exemplary form of masculinity as well as understandings of New Zealand's national identity. Kane (2010), for example, argues that the prevailing mythology of New Zealand masculinity has "focused on pioneering male mateship, characterized by egalitarianism, courage, determination and adaptability" (p. 31). Hillary's representation includes many of these characteristics, as well as elements that Pickles (2002) regards as central to locally born heroes and heroines: First, he achieved his feats overseas as a New Zealander who proved his worth in relation to Britain, and received endorsement from Britain for doing so; and second, he embodied what Pickles has labeled "colonial egalitarianism" (p. 7).[8] Pickles explains further:

> Unlike individual, God-ordained icons from elsewhere, kiwi icons were represented as humble, ordinary, everyday men. . . . It was through such 'decency,' free of the hierarchies of the British class system, and "thriving in the fresh air" of "God's Own Country" that kiwi icons derived their strength. (p. 7)

Certainly, the public embraced the idea of Hillary's egalitarianism (also represented in terms such as modesty and humility), as the following public post demonstrates:

> I think it all comes down to his words "WE knocked the bastard off" to the rest of the team waiting below the summit. In a natural moment of triumph, with no pre-prepared speech, he just naturally shared the glory with others. (Ronen dorfan, 13 Jan, 7:24am)

Yet it is important to recognize that pivotal historical moments, such as New Zealand's successful 1905 rugby tour of England and Wales, involvement in World War I, and Hillary's ascent of Everest, which are central to the construction of New Zealand masculinities and gender relations, gained prominence via the workings of power. Indeed, all of these events were strategically used by politicians to help forge a national identity. The many victories of the 1905 All Blacks, at a time when Britain was dominant in world politics, provided political fodder for then-Premier Richard Seddon to laud the benefits of the healthy, rural, masculine New Zealand lifestyle (Phillips, 1996). Similarly, Hillary's success was "symbolically framed as a shared achievement warranting national pride; then-Prime Minister Sidney Holland called it 'an honour in which I feel all the people of New Zealand will share'" (Kane, 2010, p. 35).

Individuals whose storylines enable them to be taken up as heroes/heroines, stars, or celebrities are, according to Gilchrist (2007), constructed in particular social contexts and are by definition "public creatures" (p. 396). In other words, their performances are only judged heroic within specific contexts and in relation to existing narratives or cultural norms that circulate within them. These existing narratives are, however, subject to debate and modification in relation to changing cultural priorities, and can change over time. Thus, the hero/heroine can be conceptualized as a "mediated product of society" in two prime ways: "one according to an archetypal or historical construction of what it means to be a hero, informed by past examples; the other by a more relativist conception, informed by the current debates and priorities of culture and society" (Gilchrist, 2007, p. 397; Rojeck, 2001). Thus, we argue, drawing on Rojek (2001) that, as with other hero/heroines, the discourses about Hillary are "best explained by their deep, structural relationship with the ideological contexts of [his] time" (p. 12). Hillary's death generated such a wide response precisely because of the ways that his image has continuously "engage[d] social issues and dilemmas" and helped to "work over 'useful' questions" (Rojek, 2001, p. 12). Thus, as Andrews and Kingsbury (2008) argue, Hillary's "life and achievements constitute far more than a standard slice of colonial history" (p. 178).

In the remainder of the chapter, we consider how Hillary's death helped "work over" useful questions about two key aspects of New Zealand identity: the place of mountaineering and the state of masculinity in early 21st century New Zealand.

## IN THE RIGHT PLACE AT THE RIGHT TIME: MOUNTAINEERING AND NEW ZEALAND'S EMERGING MASCULINE NATIONALISM

Hillary rose to national prominence before television and the Internet at a time when New Zealand, and Hillary himself, arguably embraced an identity that saw both Britain and New Zealand as home (Andrews & Kingsbury, 2008; Hansen, 2000; Pearson, 2006; Spoonley, Bedford, & Macpherson, 2003; Wiles, 2008). Indeed, it was only in 1949, four years before the Everest summit was reached, that people living in New Zealand stopped being British subjects and legally became New Zealand citizens (Belich, 2007). The successful ascent as part of a British-run expedition was announced on the day of Queen Elizabeth II's coronation in 1953, and widely represented as a coronation gift. The young Queen then knighted Hillary, the first of the two major honors he would receive from Britain. Queen Elizabeth II came to power as discourses of Empire were coming to a close, replaced by an emerging discourse of Commonwealth.[9] As a result, the success of Hillary and Tenzing was woven into the evolving fabric of the British Empire, and the place of New Zealand and India within it (Andrews & Kingsbury, 2008; Hansen, 2000). Hansen (2000) argues:

> Hillary's antipodean accent and Tenzing's foreign language both suggested their marginality in Britain. . . . As part of the diaspora of British settler colonies, Hillary was white but not quite British . . . and his position exemplifies a particular type of colonial ambivalence in the metropolis. British representations of the ascent as a triumph of the "Commonwealth" attempted, in part, to contain this ambivalence by incorporating Hillary, Tenzing, and Hunt into Greater Britain. (p. 322)

For New Zealand and other *new* Commonwealth nations like India, "colonial rule had created states without citizenship [and] people who had never known what it meant to be a citizen" (Hansen, 2000, p. 329). As Anderson (1983) and Turner (1994) have argued about nationalism more generally, a specifically New Zealand masculine identity needed to be invented or imagined; as a result, the specific conjuncture of Hillary's success created space for him to be embraced as a national hero. Despite the fact that Hillary himself "vacillated between British and New Zealand identities" (Hansen, 2000, p. 329), he became "for many New Zealanders . . . the icon for a New Zealand identity that replaced the affinity they still felt for Britain" (Hansen, 2000, p. 326). Similarly, Andrews and Kingsbury (2008) argue that for many New Zealanders, "his achievements were central to their country's emerging identity as distinct from Britain. This latter way of thinking embraced Hillary and elevated him to the status of an icon for a new country" (p. 179).[10] In our analysis, this nationalistic differentiation was also evident: One journalist used Hillary's "we knocked the bastard off" phrase specifically to contrast egalitarian New Zealandness with class-based Britishness, calling the statement "a perfect Kiwi-ism unthinkable in the mouths of the British members of the 1953 Everest expedition," such as the "very posh John Hunt" (Hubbard, 2008, p. C3).

Media discourses at the time of Hillary's death functioned to cement the articulation of mountaineering and New Zealand nationalism, and connected directly with colonial narratives of conquest of the land. By *knocking the bastard off,* Hillary's

## CHAPTER 10

success could be articulated to a romanticized history of rugged, virtuous, hardworking men who *broke in* the land of Aotearoa/New Zealand. This articulation remains popular in contemporary television advertisements, especially for beer, and is aimed at a predominantly urban male population (e.g., Law, 1997).

Despite Hillary's involvement in a variety of adventures, it was the Everest ascent (and his ensuing humanitarian work with the Sherpa people in Nepal) that defined his cultural identity in the bulk of the coverage. As one public post said, "I've been reading tales of Everest and Sir Ed and how proud I felt to be a kiwi because of his achievements and success. . . ." [Rose, 11 Jan, 12:17pm]. The majority of large photographs of Hillary focused on his Everest days, such as full-page images of the mountaineer that led the *Dominion Post, Weekend Herald,* and *Sunday Star Times* news sections or commemorative editions (see Figures 10.1, 10.2, and 10.3). Even the *Herald*, which featured a recent large photo from Hillary's 2007 return to Scott Base on the front of its commemorative section, connected Hillary to Everest in the headline: "the man, the mountain, the life" (see Figure 10.4).

Only the *Waikato Times* (not pictured) took a slightly different approach, using an Everest photograph on its banner but highlighting a range of other images of Hillary on the front page. Over 60% of the more than 100 images in the *Herald* and *Sunday Star Times* immediately after Hillary's death focused on the Everest ascent or activities directly associated with it, such as his return to Nepal to help celebrate the 50th anniversary of the climb. Hillary's other adventures were virtually invisible: Between the two newspapers, less than 7% of images highlighted his Antarctic adventure and none of his other expeditions appeared to warrant photographic coverage.[11]

In public comments, the Everest ascent clearly impacted those who were old enough to remember the event. The selection of comments below show the worldwide impact of this event, with people from New Zealand, the UK, and Australia all addressing his direct impact on them.

> As a nine-year-old child living in the heat of tropical North Queensland I shared the excitement of my father (a kiwi) as we listened to the BBC (by means of crackling short wave radio) announcing that his countryman had reached the summit of Everest. (Jacqui, 22 Jan, 10:58am)

> I was 10 when Everest was conquered & lived in Taranaki. That day I was 10 feet tall, so delighted that Ed Hillary and cousin George were in that team & that a NZer actually "Knocked the bastard off." (Anon, 13 Jan, 1:31pm)

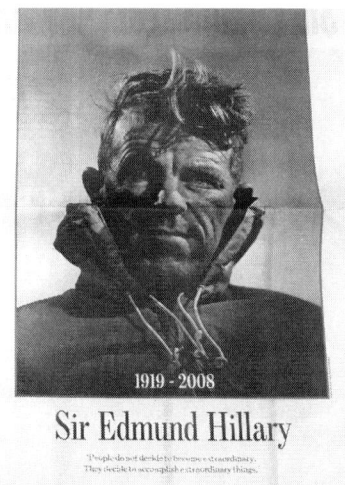

FIGURE 10-1. Front page,
*Sunday Star Times,* January 12

FIGURE 10-2. Front page, *Weekend Herald*
Commemorative edition, January 13

FIGURE 10-3. Front page, *Dominion Post*
January 12

FIGURE 10-4. Front page, *Weekend Herald*
Commemorative edition, January 13

As a five year old boy in England I remember being amazed by the news of Sir Edmund's feat of climbing Mount Everest, he became a boyhood hero and has remained so ever since. (Anon, 12 Jan, 11:35am)

Sitting here in Canada listening to talkzb (internet) people calling in to remember Sir Ed. My Canadian wife and son wondering why I am so emotional. I have lived in Canada for 40 years but the pull of home still makes me very emotional and proud. One of my earliest memories at home in Hawkes Bay was the day he climbed Mt Everest. Just the excitement and how proud we all were of him. They even composed a song. "Hilary we'r [sic] so Proud of You now you'v [sic] done it reached the summit. Won it for the red white and blue. Coronation celebrations cheers for you congratulations. Hilary we are proud of you." I wonder who wrote those lyrics. But as a 7 year old I knew all the words and have never forgotten them. (Jimpope, 11 Jan, 9:42pm)

The importance of the Everest achievement in Hillary's popularity was not limited to those who remembered the event itself. For example: "With Sir Ed's conquering of Mount Everest he gave me confidence to try anything. Though I was born long after his conquest, I look up to him" (Anon, 15 Jan, 10:53am); "Although I was born nearly twenty years after his historical ascent, Sir Edmund Hillary was one of the people I greatly admired" (Anon, 13 Jan, 7:21am); and "rip sir Ed. I had just turned one when you 'knocked the b@#S*^% off' but have grown up knowing about your achievements" (Nanakiwi, 12 Jan, 12:06pm).

In 1953, Hillary's international success at a critical moment of nation-building meant that mountaineering (like rugby union and war) cemented its place "as a crucial factor in the formation of a heroic and masculinised New Zealand national identity" (Morin, Longhurst, & Johnston, 2001, p. 134; see also Pickles, 2001). This nationalism was highly gendered (Bell, 2003; Hansen, 2000; Hill, 1997; Morin et al., 2001; Phillips, 1996, 2000). Indeed, Hansen argues convincingly that that "at this particular postcolonial moment, masculinities continued to shape the process of state-building" (p. 330), while Morin et al. (2001) contend that mountaineering was "crucial in the creation of a gendered nationhood" (p. 121). It is this aspect we explore next.

## THE "KIWI BLOKE": ARTICULATING HILLARY TO REVERED FORMS OF MASCULINITY

Our analysis partly supports Kane's (2010) argument that, despite actual changes in New Zealand society, "the influence of the male-oriented pioneer mythology and its characteristics, although contested, remains prominent" (p. 32). The *Sunday Star Times* front page after his death made this aspect particularly clear in its headline that read (size approximates the original text):

To the world he was a

# HERO

To the Nepalese he was a

# GOD

To us he was the

# MAN

who embodied the spirit of New Zealand

The newspaper emphasized his gender via the oversized and capitalized "MAN," and then connected maleness to nationalism via the lowercase words "who embodied the spirit of New Zealand." A number of public postings also highlighted Hillary's gender, such as a comment that read: "The man was an inspiration to every New Zealander and someone we were all proud to call one of us. Rest in peace Sir Ed, you were quite simply 'The Man'" (Anon, 22 Jan, 12:30pm). Another wrote, "A true kiwi, a loss for all. One of those guys you're proud to claim as one of us" (Pauls, 11 Jan, 12:38pm). The colloquial term "bloke" was used in 22 public comments: "kiwi bloke," "good bloke," "great bloke," "real bloke," and "true bloke" appeared numerous times. The taken-for-granted nature of what constitutes manliness (or the national character) was evident in the high number of public comments that did not specifically identify the traits that Hillary embodied. For example: "Another kauri has fallen.[12] The last of the Great Blokes" (Anon, 12 Jan, 9:06am), and "A true legend, epitomised the kiwi spirit . . ." (Chris, 11 Jan, 12:12pm). Others, however, highlighted specific attributes, many of which articulate strongly to historic notions of Kiwi masculinity. For example: "What a wonderful man! To have touched the lives of people from the four corners of the globe let alone NZ. He was a 'true grass roots kiwi bloke' honourable, humble, a people's person and a man's man" (Tracey mt idea shea, 21 Jan, 11:12am). The intersection of masculinity and nationalism appears quite clearly in some posts: "A great man, a great New Zealander. Your motto was 'Be Determined.' You were. 'Aim high.' You did. A true blue Kiwi bloke, you did all Kiwis proud. Gods speed, arohanui"[13] (Karen, 12 Jan, 12:07pm). Several posts also used terms such "a good keen man" and "a good bastard," both of which carry similar cultural meanings to "good bloke." These arguably connect Hillary with a nostalgic vision of a rural past comprised of Pakeha men little concerned with social niceties, and more comfortable outdoors in the company of other tough, laconic men. For example: "Ed is what every New Zealander should try to be! Honest, reliable, hardworking and a good bastard to each other! Thanks for putting NZ on the map Ed. You're a true bloke!" (Chris h, 11 Jan, 12:47pm).

This strong sense of Kiwi masculinity pervaded much of the coverage, and very few of the adjectives used by letter writers or the media focused on Hillary's role as a family man or provided a voice to the women in his life. Coverage that did so was most often in the form of anecdotes, such as one used to illustrate Hillary's modesty and humor when he reportedly asked his wife, June, what he was called. "An icon," she replied, to which Hillary responded, "I'm certainly not an icon at home," and June agreed, "No man . . . is an icon to his wife" (Hubbard, 2008, p. C2). Here again the media coverage reinforced the notion of Hillary as refusing to buy into media and public adulation.

Much of the coverage and many public responses also highlighted Hillary's accessibility via stories of surprise that his telephone number was publicly listed, or about his willingness to help out or invite over for a cup of tea people who contacted him. The following post by an unnamed American was typical of this discourse:

> I'm an American who spent a year in New Zealand. During that time it was my goal to meet Sir Ed but had no idea how. It wasn't until my last week that I realised he was in the phone book! I simply called his wife and she invited me and a friend to come by the house to meet him. I'll never forget just sitting around his kitchen table chatting about Everest and life. It was so surreal. I still can't believe that such a giant would sit down with a nobody like me (in his own house!). (Anon, 12 Jan, 11:01am)

The sheer number of public posts that identified Hillary's generosity with his time and refusal to see himself as better than anyone else clearly articulated him to valued masculine and national characteristics related to modesty, humbleness, and egalitarianism. For example: "Goodbye Sir Ed! You were the first to reach the top of the world but it was your modesty, kindness and good nature that makes us all so proud to be New Zealanders" (Anon, 22 Jan, 10:14am).

## BEYOND HEGEMONIC MASCULINITY

However, while much of the coverage reinforced what Connell (1995) would call hegemonic masculinity, one central element of his popularity—Hillary's humanitarian work with the Sherpa people in Nepal—does not. Rather than revealing a desire to dominate or conquer (typically regarded as masculine), Hillary's work with the Sherpas reflected concern and caring for the wellbeing of others.[14] Importantly, our analysis revealed that much of Hillary's long-term appeal emerged from what he did after he climbed Everest. As one letter writer put it, "His continuous activity to help and improve life for Himalayan people makes him perhaps the last old style climber interested also in the mountain environment. A big difference from the modern Himalayan climbers who are only interested in their own professional interests" (Anon, 12 Jan, 11:12am). This statement clearly establishes an articulation with cosmopolitanism. This is much like New Zealander Sir Peter Blake, who was celebrated both as a national hero and as a cosmopolitan adventurer/environmentalist, and whose expeditions aimed to raise awareness and monitor the effects of global warming and pollution on the world's oceans (Bruce & Wheaton, 2009).

Hillary's use of his fame to raise money for projects to improve the lives of the Sherpa people played a key role in affirming his heroic status. Indeed, the majority of news coverage and public posts highlighted this aspect of his life, which, for many, was what made him a hero. Then-Prime Minister Helen Clark was not alone in linking Hillary's appeal to his later humanitarian work when she wrote, "Sir Ed described himself as an average New Zealander with modest ability. In reality he was a colossus. He was a heroic figure who not only 'knocked off' Everest but lived a life of determination, humility, and generosity" (Tribute to Sir Edmund," 2009, para. 3).

Wiles (2008) has argued that an important element of New Zealand identity involves a "custodial attitude" to "enjoying and protecting the physical environment" (p. 132). Thus, it is possible that Hillary's humanitarian work was articulated more directly to a *national* rather than a *masculine* identity, which, at the same time, expands the boundaries of traditional understandings of hegemonic masculinity. Indeed, the representation of his humanitarian work as reinforcing the egalitarian qualities believed to be quintessential New Zealand traits supports this interpretation (Phillips, 1996). For example, his work was widely represented in the media as being in *partnership* with the Sherpa people; in stark contrast to much international development work, Hillary's approach appeared to be to ask how he could help rather than to impose his ideas of what the Sherpas might need.

Overall, much of the coverage explicitly attributed to him specific characteristics linked to an archetypal or desirable New Zealand identity (rather than a caricature of what is typically known as hegemonic masculinity) that, among other elements, included an aspect of caring for others. While there appeared to be much taken for granted in terms of what this desirable New Zealand identity might entail, many writers were specific about the characteristics they felt Hillary embodied that made him not only a quintessential New Zealander but also someone to look up to and be inspired by. For example: "Ed was, and still is, the essence of being a great New Zealander. He encapsulated the adventure, the modesty, *the caring* [emphasis added], the drive, hard work and the integrity of what it is we all would like to be within ourselves" (Mark Thomas, 16 Jan, 1:06pm). Another wrote: "He proved anyone, including myself, can succeed regardless of class, education or wealth. Your humble role model and *selfless charity* [emphasis added] will live on unequalled" (Kiwipomm, 22 Jan, 10:11am).

An article in the *Dominion Post* asked the question "What are the qualities that make up reputation in a New Zealand context?" (Bishop, 2008, n.p.) Its answer perhaps best sums up the overall tenor of the coverage and public response, in the way that it highlights consensus about the characteristics that both the media and public presented as central to Sir Edmund Hillary's character:

> First, the person's achievements have to be significant in an activity of importance to New Zealanders . . . Secondly, they have to be decent people: that is proud but modest, and certainly not boastful or arrogant. They should not be too humble, because that can also be seen as false. In short, they should be "one of us," but better. And we have to feel that we are able to talk to them, not just about them. . . . Thirdly, "putting back," or contributing in some way after they have done the mighty deed is a big plus.

A second element of coverage that represented Hillary as performing a multidimensional version of masculinity was the recognition of his emotional vulnerability after his first wife and younger daughter were killed in an airplane crash in Kathmandu. Albeit briefly and overwhelmed by other elements, the *Herald* acknowledged the effect in both its daily and weekend editions. For example: "…it was a heart that was to suffer grievously . . . If that was the bleakest time of his life, Sir Edmund soldiered on, finding consolation in his work for the Sherpas" ("Editorial," 2008, p. A3). "The loss shattered Hillary. He sank into a deep gloom and later confided that he had more than once thought of taking his own life. The climb out of the depths of that despair was, in many ways, his most heroic ascent" (Calder, 2008a, p. C15). The *Waikato Times* briefly acknowledged that Hillary was "hit badly by the deaths" ("Tribute to Sir Edmund," 2008, p. 4). Media reports also argued that he had overcome a difficult childhood, with a domineering father and a sense of physical inferiority. Thus, the news media's representations of Hillary tell a story of a man who was brave, resilient, physically tough, and determined while simultaneously being personally vulnerable and demonstrating a cosmopolitan form of caring for others. We suggest that this more rounded representation, which partially challenges the hard man masculine performance that dominates representations of New Zealand masculinity, was a key element of Hillary's lasting public appeal. We note, however, that although many public comments addressed Hillary's humanitarian actions, none addressed the element that most challenges hegemonic masculinity: his emotional vulnerability.

## MOURNING THE PAST: CHANGING PERFORMANCES OF MASCULINITY/NATIONALISM

Throughout the coverage, there was acknowledgement that times have changed; numerous journalists and members of the public pointed out, often with sadness, that Hillary's (performance of) masculinity was something reflective of an era now gone. There was a strong recognition that the New Zealand of 2008 was significantly different from the past, as in the following four posts: "We certainly will not see his like again" (Anon, 11 Jan, 12:38pm); "Our last true great hero" (Anon, 11 Jan, 4:00pm); "Never will New Zealand ever have another person, who has commanded our attention so loudly, by being so quiet and humble. He was a man in a billion" (Rachel, 11 Jan, 1:59pm); and "Good bye to the last real Kiwi, humble, gracious, adventurous and generous. Our country will never be the same again" (Cookie, 11 Jan, 1:59pm). Both the media and letter writers used Hillary's death to reflect upon the changing nature of heroes in New Zealand, commenting in ways that clearly revealed their dissatisfaction with the behavior and attitudes of contemporary public figures. For example: "He has the old values that New Zealand was built on if [we] had more people like him this country would be a better place" (Colin, 11 Jan 2008, 12:12pm). The *Christchurch Press* suggested about Hillary:

> He insisted, not from false modesty but a genuine personal feeling, that he was an average New Zealander with moderate abilities. It was this, in part, which helped endear him so strongly to his fellow Kiwis. (Pause for a moment and compare this with the current crop of so-called celebrities who exude vacuous self-importance. They are as substantial as the polish on a pair of climbing boots.) ("The Values," 2008, p. 13)

Many who posted to the *New Zealand Herald* website agreed. For example, two commenters made similar arguments: "Most of today's so called NZ 'heroes, stars or celebrities' wouldn't be fit to lace his climbing boots" (Anon, 13 Jan, 7:26am); and "He makes today's 'heroes' look like so much kina (egg of the sea) washed up on the beach of non-heroisms" (Philster, 11 Jan, 2:49pm). A *Sunday Star Times* editorial reflected, "Compare the conqueror of Everest with today's concocted celebrities, the sporting figures on their surreal salaries, the shabby and ephemeral A-listers, the tawdry self-promoters of the media-made world, the politicians" ("Sir Ed," 2008, p. A11). In a similar vein, one person wrote: "In a world where children's role models are flawed and inappropriate Sir Edmund Hillary has given us a true picture of the very best in human nature" (M Denley, 22 Jan, 10:17am).

Elements of the discourses above represent a pattern previously identified by researchers in which New Zealanders tend to define themselves in terms of *what they are not* rather than *what they are* (see Wensing & Bruce, 2003). Historian Tony Simpson made this explicit in a *Herald on Sunday* column, proposing that "our true heroes are the ones who don't exhibit the character traits we don't like" (Simpson, 2008, p. 38).

However, others specifically contrasted positive qualities associated with Hillary (modesty, success, humanitarianism) against those they felt were the opposite of what Hillary embodied. For example: "He was strong and resolute, in mind and body, a gentleman from an age of gentlemen, humble and modest, grateful and generous, and amid the media and self promotion, the complaining and excuse making modern world, he was a pool of calm, reason and truth" (Anon, 12 Jan, 11:31am). Another claimed, "Our nation has lost its greatest New Zealander ever. He combined fearless determination with humility, a passion to help others, and a quiet gentleness. Strange bed fellows indeed. Not for him, [sic] was chasing corporates to sponser [sic] another, greater achievement" (Anon, 11 Jan, 5:50pm). The use of phrases such as "never replaced," "end of an era," "values that have been lost over the years," and "will not see the likes of you again" in public posts reinforces the concern that Hillary represented the kind of New Zealander who made the country great in the past, while lamenting the lack of such role models in this century. Numerous posts expressed a belief that it would be difficult if not impossible to replace what Hillary represented: "We know the world has lost one of its great humanitarians and one of our few remaining role models. . . . There will not be another Ed Hillary..." (Jeff, 11 Jan, 9:18pm).

## CONCLUSION

In drawing tentative conclusions from our analysis, we suggest that Hillary's iconic status stemmed initially from his "conquering" of Mount Everest in 1953. This achievement as an *Adventurer* occurred in a sociohistoric context of male dominance and relative national insecurity that allowed his physical feat to be read as a narrative of heroic masculinity. Moreover, this narrative provided a discursive resource that supported a developing form of New Zealand nationalism. As such, Hillary became a masculine icon of his nation. However, it was not simply his Everest conquest that allowed Hillary's heroic status to survive through to contemporary times. Indeed, we suggest that as the sociocultural context changed—from the patriarchy of the 1950s modernist era to the neoliberal postmodern pastiche of the 2000s—one reason that his popularity continued and strengthened was because he came to represent a more complex mix of masculine performances. On the one hand, he represented the *Kiwi Bloke* with his humbleness and rugged physicality; this representation has proved nostalgically popular in the contemporary era for many New Zealanders, particularly white males for whom the Kiwi bloke is associated with a romantic version of the past when life *seemed* more simple and secure (see Bell 2004; Cosgrove & Bruce, 2005). On the other hand, Hillary became increasingly renowned and respected for his *Humanitarian* work and care of others. His representation, as such, could no longer be simply read as an exemplar of a dominant form of masculinity (e.g., as a tough, quiet, strong risk-taker who conquered the land and did not give in to pain). Instead, his mediated representation proffered a rounder, perhaps softer, form of masculinity: He was undoubtedly masculine but was also portrayed as caring, helpful, and vulnerable.

We argue that this rounded representation of Hillary was an important factor in enabling his heroic image to survive over the last 30 years. This period of significant social change included growing critiques of the dominant forms of masculinity (e.g., Greg McGee's 1980 landmark play, *Foreskin's Lament*, provided a stinging critique of rugby masculinities), the growth in liberal feminism, multiculturalism, gay rights, and other political movements (e.g., the 1981 Springbok rugby tour protests). These significant social changes conspired to produce a shift in masculinities and gender relations from the 1980s onward (Phillips, 1987). Yet Hillary's iconic status remained intact, as the focus encompassed his humanitarianism, vulnerability, and cosmopolitan concern for others. We suggest that it was the media and public understanding of Hillary as a rounded human being that enabled him to be given an ongoing heroic masculine status and led to his being regarded as New Zealand's greatest hero.

## REFERENCES

Anderson, B. (1983). *Imagined communities: Reflections on the origin and spread of nationalism.* London, England: Verso.

Andrews, G. J., & Kingsbury, P. (2008). Geographical reflections on Sir Edmund Hillary (1919-2008). *New Zealand Geographer, 64,* 177–180.

Antarctic adventures [Editorial]. (2008, January 12). *Taranaki Daily News,* p. 9.

Tributes. (2008, January 12). *Dominion Post,* p. 3.

Bannister, M. (2005). Kiwi blokes: Recontextualising White New Zealand masculinities in a global setting. *Genders Online Journal, 42,* 1–24.

Belich, J. (2007). *Making peoples: A history of the New Zealanders from Polynesian settlement to the end of the nineteenth century.* Auckland, NZ: Penguin.

Bell, C. (2004). Kiwiana revisited. In C. Bell & S. Matthewman (Eds.), *Cultural studies in Aotearoa New Zealand: Identity, space and place* (pp. 175–187). South Melbourne, VIC: Oxford University Press.

Bell, M. (2003). "Another kind of life": Adventure racing and epic adventures. In R. Rinehart & S. Sydnor (Eds.), *To the extreme: Alternative sports, inside and out* (pp. 219–253). Albany, NY: State University of New York Press.

Bishop, J. (2008, January 25). Now Sir Ed has gone, who is our hero? *Dominion Post Online.*

Booth, P. (1993). *Edmund Hillary: The life of a legend.* Auckland, NZ: Moa Beckett.

Bruce, T., & Wheaton, B. (2011). Diaspora and global sports migration: A case study in the English and New Zealand contexts. In J. Maguire and M. Falcous (Eds.), *Sport and migration: Borders, boundaries and crossings* (pp. 189–199). London, England: Routledge.

Bruce, T., & Wheaton, B. (2009). Rethinking global sports migration and forms of transnational, cosmopolitan and diasporic belonging: A case study of international yachtsman Sir Peter Blake. *Social Identities, 15,* 585–608.

Butler, J. (1990). *Gender trouble: Feminism and the subversion of identity.* New York, NY: Routledge.

Calder, P. (2008a, January 12). Hillary's long life filled with the spirit of adventure. *New Zealand Herald,* pp. C14–15.

Calder, P. (2008b, January 12). Why he means so much to us. *Weekend Herald,* p. C20.

Connell, R. W. (1995). *Masculinities.* St Leonards, Australia: Allen & Unwin.

Connell, R. W. (2002). Masculinities and globalisation. In H. Worth, A. Paris, & L. Allen (Eds.), *The life of Brian: Masculinities, sexualities and health in New Zealand* (pp. 27–42). Dunedin, NZ: University of Otago Press.

Cosgrove, A., & Bruce, T. (2005). 'The way New Zealanders would like to see themselves': Reading white masculinity via media coverage of the death of Sir Peter Blake. *Sociology of Sport Journal, 22,* 336–355.

Denzin, N. K. (1996). More rare air: Michael Jordan on Michael Jordan. *Sociology of Sport Journal, 13,* 319–342.

Duley, B. (1997). *Authoring New Zealand: Media representations of national identity.* Unpublished master's thesis. University of Waikato, Hamilton, New Zealand.

Editorial. (2008, January 12). *Weekend Herald,* p. A3.

End of an era. (2008, January 26). Letter to the editor. *Nelson Mail,* p. 13.

Flood, M. 2002. Between men and masculinity: An assessment of the term "masculinity" in recent scholarship on men. In S. Pearce & V. Muller (Eds.), *Manning the next millennium: Studies in masculinities* (pp. 203–213). Perth, Australia: Black Swan.

Foucault, M. (1988). Truth, power, self. In L. H. Martin, H. Gutman, & P. H. Hutton (Eds.), *Technologies of the self: A seminar with Michel Foucault* (pp. 16–49). Amherst, MA: University of Massachusetts Press.

Foucault, M. (1978). *The history of sexuality, volume 1: An introduction* (R. Hurley, trans.). New York, NY: Random House. (Original work published 1976).

Giddens, A. (1991). *Modernity and self-identity: Self and society in the late modern age.* Stanford, CA: Stanford University Press.

Gilchrist, P. (2007). 'Motherhood, ambition and risk': Mediating the sporting hero/ine in Conservative Britain. *Media Culture Society, 29,* 395–414.

Grossberg, L. (1996). On postmodernism and articulation: An interview with Stuart Hall. In D. Morley & K-H. Chen (Eds.), *Stuart Hall: Critical dialogues in cultural studies* (pp. 131–150). London, England: Routledge.

Hall, S. (1984). The narrative construction of reality. *Southern Review, 17,* 2–17.

Hansen, P. H. (2000). Confetti of empire: The conquest of Everest in Nepal, India, Britain, and New Zealand. *Comparative Studies in Society and History, 42,* 307–332.

Hill, L. (2002). What it means to be a Lion Red man: Alcohol advertising and Kiwi masculinity. In J. Farnsworth & I. Hutchison (Eds.), *New Zealand television: A reader* (pp. 145–155). Palmerston North, NZ: Dunmore Press.

Hillary, E. (1999). *View from the summit.* London, England: Doubleday.

Hubbard, A. (2008, January 13). Sir Edmund Hillary: Kiwi legend: 1919-2008. *Sunday Star Times,* pp. C2–C3.

Kane, M. J. (2010). Adventure as a cultural foundation: Sport and tourism in New Zealand. *Journal of Sport & Tourism, 15,* 27–44.

Johnston, A. (2006). *Sir Edmund Hillary: An extraordinary life.* Auckland, NZ: Penguin.

Kite, R. (Producer/director). (2002). *Chinks, coconuts and currymunchers* [Television series]. Auckland, NZ: Kite Productions.

Laidlaw, C. (1999). *Rights of passage: Beyond the New Zealand identity crisis.* Auckland, NZ: Hodder Moa Beckett.

Law, R. (1997). Masculinity, place, and beer advertising in New Zealand: The southern man campaign. *New Zealand Geographer, 53,* 22–28.

Mac an Ghaill, M. (1996). Introduction. In M. Mac an Ghaill (Ed.), *Understanding masculinities: Social relations and cultural arenas* (pp. 1–13). Bristol, PA: Open University Press.

McKee, A. (2001). A beginner's guide to textual analysis. *Metro, 127/128,* 138–149.

McRobbie, A. (1997). The Es and the Anti-Es: New questions for feminism and cultural studies. In M. Ferguson & P. Golding (Eds.), *Cultural studies in question* (pp. 170–186). London, England: Sage.

Mills, S. (2003). *Michel Foucault.* London, England: Routledge.

Morin, K. M., Longhurst, R., & Johnston, L. (2001). (Troubling) spaces of mountains and men: New Zealand's Mount Cook and Hermitage Lodge. *Social & Cultural Geography, 2*(2), 117–139.

Obituary. (2008, January 13). *Sunday Star Times,* p. C8.

Pearson, D. (2006, July). *From empire to empire: Situating citizenship in British settler states.* Paper presented at the International Sociological Association World Congress, Durban, South Africa.

Phillips, J. (2000). Epilogue: Sport and future Australasian culture. In J. A. Mangan & J. Nauright (Eds.), *Sport in Australasian society: Past and present* (pp. 323–332). London, England: Frank Cass.

Phillips, J. (1987). *A man's country? The image of the Pakeha male: A history.* Auckland, NZ: Penguin Books.

Phillips, J. (1996). *A man's country? The image of the Pakeha male: A history* (2nd ed.). Auckland, NZ: Penguin Books.

Pickles, K. (2002). Kiwi icons and the re-settlement of New Zealand as colonial space. *New Zealand Geographer, 58,* 5–16.

Pringle, R., Kay, T., & Jenkins, J. (2011). Masculinities, gender relations and leisure studies: Are we there yet? *Annals of Leisure Research, 14,* 107–119.

Reader, B., Stempel, G. H., & Daniel, D. K. (2004). Age, wealth, education predict letters to editor. *Newspaper Research Journal, 25,* 55–66.

Rojek, C. (2001). *Celebrity.* London, England: Reaktion Books Ltd.

Simpson, T. (2008, January 13). A true hero, but still one of us. *Herald on Sunday,* p. 38.

Sinclair, K. (1986). *A destiny apart: New Zealand's search for national identity.* Wellington, NZ: Allen & Unwin.

Sir Ed: A rare creature of values and valour [Editorial]. (2008, January 13). *Sunday Star Times,* p. A11.

Spoonley, P. (1997, Spring). Images of Maori women in New Zealand postcards after 1900. *Women's Studies Journal, 13,* 7–24.

Spoonley, P., Bedford, R. D., & Macpherson, A. J. (2003). Divided loyalties and fractured sovereignty: Transnationalism and the nation-state in Aotearoa/New Zealand. *Journal of Ethnic and Migration Studies, 29,* 27–46.

Sport, trust and the feelgood factor [Editorial]. (2005, July 2). *The New Zealand Herald Online.* Retrieved from http://www.nzherald.co.nz/opinion/news/article.cfm?c_id=466&objectid=10333761

Maori and Kauri. (2011). *Te ara: The New Zealand encyclopedia.* Retrieved from http://www.teara.govt.nz/en/Kauri-forest/3

The values of Hillary are what NZ should aspire to. (2008, January 21). *The Press,* p. 13.

Tribute to Sir Edmund Hillary: Ever a New Zealand icon. (2008, January 23). *Waikato Times,* p. 4.

Tributes to Sir Edmund Hillary. (2009, January 1). *Stuff.co.nz.* Retrieved from http://www.stuff.co.nz

Turner, G. (1997). Media texts and messages. In S. Cunningham & G. Turner (Eds.) *The media in Australia: Industries, texts, audiences* (2nd ed.) (pp. 381–393). St Leonards, Australia: Allen & Unwin.

Turner, G. (1994). *Making it national: Nationalism and Australian popular culture.* St Leonards, Australia: Allen & Unwin.

Wahl-Jorgensen, K. (2002). The normative-economic justification for public discourse: Letters to the editor as a "wide open" forum. *Journalism and Mass Communication Quarterly, 79,* 121–133.

Wensing, E. H., & Bruce, T. (2003, Oct 30–Nov 1). *Sibling rivalry: Print media constructions of national identity*. Paper presented at the North American Society for the Sociology of Sport conference, Montreal, Canada.

Whannel, G. (1999). Sport stars, narrativization, and masculinities. *Leisure Studies, 18,* 249–265.

Who takes Sir Ed's title in Kiwi hearts? (2009, September 27). One News. Retrieved from http://tvnz.co.nz/national-news/takes-sir-ed-s-title-in-kiwi-hearts-3022401

Wiles, J. (2008). Sense of home in a transnational social space: New Zealanders in London. *Global Networks, 8,* 116–137.

## ENDNOTES

[1] These terms or their equivalents were the most commonly used in the 725 public posts to the *New Zealand Herald* website in the weeks after his death: inspiration (94), hero (77), icon (55), role model (36), and legend (31).

[2] Hillary was a very tall man, and his imposing stature (6'5" or 195cm) was mentioned in news coverage and public posts.

[3] The *kiwi* is a native, flightless bird typically regarded as New Zealand's national bird but it also serves as a colloquial term for New Zealanders. *Kiwi bloke* is, correspondingly, a colloquial phrase meaning the typical down-to-earth New Zealand male.

[4] The Order of the Garter is England's highest order of chivalry and is limited in number to 24 members (as well as the reigning sovereign and Prince of Wales).

[5] We note that the analysis of coverage in the Newztext database was limited to written texts because this database does not include images (although it does indicate via captions when images were included with stories).

[6] Compared with the online environment, letters published in print editions of metropolitan newspapers tend to reflect a narrower range of views, with somewhere between 5% and 50% of submitted letters being published (Wahl-Jorgensen, 2002). In addition, not only do print edition letter writers tend to be wealthier, older and better educated than the general population but the individual preferences of gatekeepers who select the limited number of letters and their views about what is appropriate play an important role in what appears in print (Reader, Stempel, & Daniel, 2004).

[7] We also note that even three years after his death, more than 10 Facebook pages devoted to Hillary remain (with members varying from 417 for the "Make a public holiday to honour Sir Ed" page to only three for "Ed Hillary—What a bloody legend!!!!!"). The majority of pages had fewer than 50 members, so we did not include them in the analysis.

[8] Laidlaw (1999) identifies amateur rugby as a key site at which ideologies of egalitarianism or classlessness were reinforced, as bankers and truck drivers, farm workers and lawyers played alongside each other.

[9] We note that India gained independence in 1947. Thus, both Tenzing Norgay (who was *appropriated* by India for its own purposes) and Edmund Hillary symbolized the coming to a close of the British Empire (see Hansen, 2000). Indeed, Hansen (2000) argues that Tenzing "had no conception of citizenship or national identity," saw himself "as neither Indian

nor Nepali," and was actually born in Tibet (p. 212). Hansen also points out that Tenzing's "predicament was typical for Sherpas, who often migrated between Nepal, India, and Tibet in search of seasonal labor" (p. 212).

[10] This was, however, only one interpretation. Others understood Hillary's success as representative of traditional loyalty to the motherland (Andrews & Kingsbury, 2008).

[11] Due to incomplete data for the *Waikato Times* and *Dominion Post*, it was not possible to calculate the percentage of photographs by category, but the trend was in the same direction.

[12] The *kauri* is a native tree. The statement represents a well-known Māori whakatauki (proverb)—Kua hinga te kauri o te wao nui a Tāne (the kauri has fallen in the sacred forest of Tāne)—that is often used when an important person dies (see "Māori and Kauri," 2011). In some public posts, another native tree, the totara, was used instead of kauri.

[13] As indicated in the footnote above, the use of Māori proverbs and language was not uncommon in the public postings, again indicating Hillary's popularity and perceived embeddedness in New Zealand culture.

[14] While caring for others is a gender performance more typically regarded as feminine, we would argue that Hillary's caring was on a global scale (rather than the more personal or intimate scale associated with female caring), thus taking it outside existing gender binaries.

# Manner(s) Maketh the Man: Embodied Masculinities in a Japanese University Rowing Club

Brent McDonald

## INTRODUCTION

Since the 1980s, there has been increased debate and theorization from Western research perspectives about gender (Connell & Messerschmidt, 2005; Kimmel, Hearn, & Connell, 2005). These conceptualizations of gender, and for the purposes of this chapter masculinity, recognize that one's gendered identity is not some form of "natural" expression of biology but is, rather, socially constructed and produced. Masculinity is not a "fixed entity embedded in the body or personality traits of individuals," rather masculinities should be considered "configurations of practice" expressed through social practice in specific social settings (Connell & Messerschmidt, 2005, p. 836). As such, masculinities are prone to challenge and change or reproduction and reification. Some forms of masculinity attain positions of dominance within a particular culture, whilst others may become marginalized or subordinated (Connell, 2005).

In the context of Japanese society, one of the common stereotypes of masculinity is the "salary man"—that is, the white-collar, devoted company employee (Roberson

& Suzuki, 2003). Salary man masculinity became a dominant form during the 1950s and has held its hegemonic position in Japan ever since (Taga, 2005). However, since the end of the bubble economy in the late 1980s to early 1990s, the idea of salary man masculinity has been increasingly challenged and even marginalized in some contexts (Dasgupta, 2003; Gill, 2003; Taga, 2003, 2005). The salary man may be a stereotype, but it is nonetheless a manifestation of a culturally privileged hegemonic masculinity. As Connell (2000) has suggested, the hegemonic form of masculinity is not necessarily the most common, "let alone the most comfortable" (p. 11). Indeed, it would be naive to suggest that the characteristics of the salary man today mirror those of the 1950s. Further, the construction of salary man masculinity does not begin in the workplace; rather, it must be understood as a broader cultural project, sustained by institutions (Connell, 2000). Education has been identified as a critical site for the shaping of ideas about gender (Connell, 2005) and is also a crucial form of cultural and symbolic capital in the trajectory to becoming the salary man (Sugimoto, 1998; van Wolferen, 1989). Similarly, sport can be seen as another institution where certain forms of masculine performance are lauded and encouraged. Sport in a multitude of contexts is often a place where reified characteristics are learned, embodied, and enacted. As with Connell's previous observation, these characteristics are not necessarily the most common and certainly not the most comfortable; however, they are readily identifiable in sport and inevitable to successful enactments of gender. Hence, behaviors such as violence, playing while injured, sacrifice, discipline, and following orders can become demonstrative of hegemonic masculine identity, which carries similar currency in cultural and symbolic capital (e.g., Connell, 2005; Messner, 1990).

This chapter investigates the ways in which Japanese masculinities are embodied and enacted through young men's involvement in an educational sports program, namely at the fictionalized Biwa University Rowing Club (BURC). The intersection of sport and education in Japanese universities provides an intriguing context in which to examine the individual negotiation of identity by members grounded in the broader hegemonic logic of masculinity. It is this logic that structures opportunities to successfully develop and maintain a particular social trajectory, which, amongst other things, may include belonging to social networks and gaining employment. As the university has been the production house of the salary man, the forms of masculinity that become embodied through membership of sport clubs have the potential to not only describe being a sportsman, but more significantly the changes, challenges, and shifts within the logic of masculinities.

In addition to Connell's (1987, 2000, 2005) work on masculinities, Bourdieu's (1977, 1984, 2001) theoretical tools of habitus, social field, and capital provide a complementary framework for understanding gender relations. Indeed, the concept of *habitus* is particularly useful in revealing how men negotiate masculinity. According to Bourdieu (1984), habitus is social norms and tendencies that seem so "natural," they fundamentally guide behavior and thinking. As Wacquant (2005, p. 316) has put it, habitus is "the way society becomes deposited in persons in the form of lasting dispositions, or trained capacities and structured propensities to think, feel and act in determinant ways, which then guide them" (Wacquant, 2005, p. 316). Looking specifically at manliness, Coles (2009) has suggested that men strategically perform masculinity without being consciously aware of it. This performance is enacted in the forms of movement, posture, gesture, and speech, which are practices that become naturalized to the body when repeated daily. The use of the body (habitus) in a gender-segregated sport such as rowing always involves more than merely pulling an oar handle; as a sport that relies on repetition (of movement, of training schedules, of technique, of preseason and competitive season), the negotiation of self within the group is through the gendered body, and it is a negotiation that relies on responses that are embodied.

Bourdieu's theoretical model aims to eschew the dualism of structure versus agency. Thus, the agent's embodied social history (habitus) operates within the structure of the social field that surrounds it. In utilizing a game metaphor, each player (agent) works within the constraints of the rules of the games (of course, some rules are more controlling than others, some are unwritten, some are conceptual, others are rigidly structural)—indeed, the rules of the field. One's ability to successfully play the game—that is, have the biggest impact, involvement, and enjoyment (agency)—is determined by one's skills, or embodied knowledge (habitus). Hence the best players are those who play the game as if they are always aware of the next move, next play, and next opportunity (automatically or seemingly below the level of consciousness). The primary requirement of being a good player is, therefore, that one must give oneself (mind, body and soul) to the game. The game worth playing is one that, having given oneself to it, one is no longer aware that they are playing it. As every (social) field contains many players, those who are the best are afforded greater opportunities, respect, and mobility, etc. In this way the ability to play the game in a certain way—that is, a way that is recognized by others as valuable—becomes a form of capital. As the best players may shape the rules of the game, their species of capital becomes desirable for all who play that game (Bourdieu, 1984). Whilst most players exist within multiple social fields at any given time, it is not a given that the capital valued within one field will hold its value in another. However, some species of capital (especially cultural and symbolic) do maintain their value in other social fields, therefore allowing the player (agent) to keep playing. As Bourdieu and Wacquant (1996, p. 76) have put it:

> The field of power is a field of forces defined by the structure of the existing balance of forces between forms of power, or between different species of capital. It is also simultaneously a field of struggles for power among the holders of different forms of power. It is a space of play and competition in which social agents and institutions which all possess the determinate quantity of specific capital (economic and cultural capital in particular) sufficient to occupy the dominant positions within their respective fields.

## SPORTING MASCULINITIES AND JAPANESE EDUCATION

Matsuda (2006) argues that sport delivered through the education system has had a major impact on the formation of the gendered body in modern Japan. A feature of the rapid modernization that Japan underwent after the Meiji Restoration (1868) was educational reform and the subsequent implementation of pedagogies based on Western models. Considering the central position of sport in Western education at the time, it is not surprising that Japanese bureaucrats and reformers, sent to study Western ways, returned home impressed with the potential value of sport in nation building (Kawai & McDonald, 2012). However, it is significant to note that from the very beginning, Western sports were assimilated to reflect Japanese sensibilities grounded in Confucianism and an ethos of muscular spirituality (Guttman & Thompson, 2001; Manzenreiter, 2001). Many of the young elites who first entered the high schools and, subsequently, universities, came from Samurai class background and, not surprisingly, the sports played became imbued with their own and their teachers' values (Kusaka, 2006). Further, as with the boys and young men of Eton, Rugby, Harvard, and Yale, these students were male. It is often overlooked that modern sports were designed for boys by men, and during the period of the mid to late 19th century, the explicit justification for sport in both Western and Japanese contexts was that it should be a vehicle for boys to develop into culturally appropriate men (muscularity), and more implicitly a place to become a disciplined servant of the nation (soldier and officer). It is evident, therefore, that sports are historically linked to patriarchy, and as such have represented and continue to represent men and boys above women and girls.

The significant observation from the initial uptake of sport in Japanese education is the level of importance it was afforded and the class values it represented. Despite the militarization of educational sport leading into Japanese involvement in the Second World War, the original ideas embedded in these activities focused on cultivating people of ability who could make a "contribution to modern society" (Inoue, 1998, p.84). This ideal returned post-war sport to what it had previously been: a site for moral and social education (Cave, 2004; McDonald, 2004).

Extracurricular sports clubs in Japanese education (*bukatsu*) are one of the major sites where aspects of masculinity are enacted and embodied (e.g., Cave, 2008; Chapman, 2010; Dalla Chiesa, 2002; Light, 2003, 2008; McDonald, 2009; Roberson, 2005). The bukatsu, as a "circuit of social practice," links individual bodily processes of young Japanese men with social structures such as discipline, hierarchy, and loyalty, through the embodied experience of being a member (Connell & Messerschmidt, 2005, p. 851). In the case of the rowing club BURC, the social world is created through the individual body-reflexive practices (training, racing, eating, drinking, partying, showering, suffering, etc.) of members. The successful negotiation of these practices (technically, aesthetically and culturally) is achieved when members demonstrate such embodied knowledge and mastery thereof. Embodied knowledge is demonstrated through the subconscious performance of masculinity during significant events, such as regattas, but more importantly in the most mundane of day-to-day actions at the club. Through examining the performances specific to being a BURC member, it is possible to uncover the deeper cultural and gendered discourses that are at play.

## I AM AN OARSMAN

For the young men at BURC, being a member is more than just a sporting pastime or physical activity; rather, it is a "total experience" that comes to define almost every aspect of their identity at university. The total experience is found in the commitment to training 6 days a week, 10 to 11 months of the year, over a period of 4 years, and to living in the boathouse. It should be noted that this experience is largely autonomous in that the club is student run and managed, and that the role of the university and coaches is very much on the periphery (McDonald & Hallinan, 2005; McDonald & Komuku, 2008). Being in situ adds to the concentrated effect of membership as it creates a definition of self—"I am an oarsman." This is captured concisely by one of the members:

> The main point, the foundation (*daikokubashira*) of my university life has been being a member of BURC. It is like a family (*kazōku*). We are a very close family here. It has been a very special place for me. (anonymous athlete, personal communication)

## CHAPTER 11

I have previously examined the relational nature of gendered identity, especially in regard to the vertical hierarchical relationships (*jōge kankei*) within BURC (see McDonald, 2009). Drawing on this, the social field of the men's club (and the gendered identities negotiated therein) is buttressed by the existence of other gendered social fields. These are the women's club, the OB's (alumni), and the *joshimane* (managers' club). Whilst the OB's provide the important function of becoming financial supporters and potential links to employment, they also serve to validate membership in demonstrating that they are men in society and that belonging to the club continues post-graduation. The women's club (although a separate entity) creates a heteronormative environment, especially as relationships often form between the men and the women of BURC. However, they also serve to reinforce the importance of the men's club. The women's club occupies considerably less physical space at BURC in terms of facilities and members (about one third to half the size of the men's club); it is also non-residential and (unlike at the men's club) no meals are served. All of this serves to inflate the scale and scope of the men's club by comparison.

The most important functionary group in relation to the construction of masculine identity at BURC is undoubtedly the *joshimane*. The *joshimane* function as what Blackwood (2010) would describe as "surrogate mothers" (p. 88). Female students from the university assume a role that is very much behind the scenes, especially in relation to cleaning, supporting and most importantly preparing meals for the male rowers. On any given day the *joshimane* will arrive in the mid-afternoon, carrying groceries, and proceed into the downstairs kitchen of the boathouse to begin making the evening meals for all members of the men's club. The meals are always ready for collection as rowers return to the boathouse after their evening training session, usually between 7 and 8 pm. Each meal, beautifully presented and resembling the pictures from the numerous cooking magazines that the *joshimane* use as a reference, is collected without much fuss by the male rowers, who, after a short Buddhist prayer, consume it with gusto and appreciative grunts. The *joshimane* watch on, without joining the meal, and at the same time busy themselves preparing the next day's breakfast (invariably fish and soup), which will sit on the stove in readiness for the completion of the morning's practice.

The presence of such a "domesticated" femininity serves to reproduce and naturalize the masculinist gender ideology at play in Japanese society. In some ways these other social fields prepare members for the highly gendered and demarcated nature of company employment in Japan (Ogasawara, 1998). Such companies, whilst employing men and women, rely on hierarchically homosocial workplace relationships in order to function. These are exclusively gendered vertical hierarchies that exist in many forms of employment. In this way, the important relationships in one's employment, and opportunities within that employment, exist strictly between men of higher and lower rank and between women of higher and lower rank. These hierarchies, grounded as they are by Confucian[1] influence, function most smoothly when all involved automatically perform the correct form of *reigi* (manners) required of one at a particular rank. Hence masculine manners (for example language usage, body language, the positioning of oneself in various spaces) correspond closely to the notion of habitus. The correct application of such masculine habitus is recognized as a form of cultural capital that enhances each agent's capacity within a variety of social fields, including some forms of employment. Indeed, the demonstration of such habitus serves not only to strengthen power relations within the field, it also reproduces and reinforces dominant notions of masculinity and femininity more broadly within Japanese society.

## SOCIAL TRAJECTORY

The strength of the sense of being a rower is reinforced by becoming a BURC member. This step is the achievement of a social trajectory whereby embodied capital is utilized to play the rowing game. For example, almost all the men at BURC had been rowers at high school. The high school rowing *bukatsu* operate similarly; that is, members' involvement is all-consuming, and these students have already demonstrated the necessary response to a variety of embodied moves required from the field. Their capital as high school rowers is recognized in a physical sense in that somewhere between a third and half of all members were at BURC because they had received *suisen* (special athletic entry) to BU. *Suisen* is the practice of directly recruiting students to the university, which subverts some of the academic requirements most students need to satisfy. As a result, physical capital is a project worth investing in. Achieving *suisen* also accrues in the bodies of rowers a particular form of symbolic capital. Being successful at high school is as much a demonstration and confirmation of having negotiated the social game of being a rower—the understanding of hierarchy, format, etc.—as it is about being able to pull the oar.

This social trajectory is as much about the building of self as it is about rowing in the boat. The university *bukatsu* is significant as a site where members not only develop an identity linked to sport, but also move from adolescence into adulthood. It is a crucial time within the context of maturation and various rites of passage that young Japanese men might experience during these years. The social trajectory continues once a member graduates; indeed, it is a trajectory that says, "This is the sort of man I am," as suggested by graduating captain Hiro:

> When I go for a job interview I will be able to respond to the questions, such as, 'Were you involved in clubs?' with confidence that I was the captain. That the team I belonged to was really traditional and strong. I will be very proud of my position in the rowing team. Even though it is a small club, the skills to lead the team are really important to lead in society. Because I was a leader once I know both sides [of hierarchy]. Once I work for the company, even if I am a lower employee I will know how the leader feels to the employees. Both sides: how leadership works and how other people work. I will understand how the boss feels or what the boss expects and I understand how to work as a team.

Entering the *bukatsu* at 18 and leaving at 22, members are initially *kohai* (junior) to all except their fellow freshmen. As their involvement develops, they move in their sophomore year to being both *kohai* and *sempai* (senior), and as their age increases so does their hierarchical position within the club. Coinciding with this, members will celebrate their 20th birthday, significant as the legal age for drinking and for voting, and as such they are no longer seen as minors. As each member reaches his final year he prepares to step out into the world and hopefully into employment. This process, if successfully completed, literally sees the transformation of the individual from *gakusei* (student) to *shakaijin* (person in society). In a way, the *raison d'etre* of members is best summed up in the following invitation put out to prospective freshman rowers from a famous Tokyo university:

> The value of spending four years
> I want to develop myself
> I want to make lifelong friends
> I want to be engaged with something with my whole energy
> I want to step forward into society with confidence
> It promises to make your university life one more than expected
> Your future will start here—H boat club

The expectation at the end of four years is that one literally enters the boat club a boy and comes out a man. The four-year commitment to being a member allows the confirmation of a particular masculine habitus, which does not stop on graduation from the club, but rather continues into the future.

## BEING A MAN IN THE BOATHOUSE

This chapter is generated out of a much larger ethnographic project inspired from my experiences of playing rugby in Japan from 1994–1996. The project was conducted

## "Manner(s) Maketh the Man": Embodied Masculinities in a Japanese University Rowing Club

at BURC from 2002–2006 and during several subsequent visits to the club over the last six years (2006–2012). The names that appear in the text are pseudonyms generated out of the process of creating fictionalized amalgams (Grenfell & Rinehart, 2003). The interpretation of masculinity results from the reflexive use of field notes, interview data, and (importantly) my own masculine identity within this group. It is important to position the "I" within this process of analysis. The observations of what it is to be "a man" within the context of the rowing club are reflexive of my own masculine identity and most noticeably the experiences and moments that created incongruities between gender and rowing. These moments represent events where the embodied responses of members were such as to create what Bourdieu has described as a habitus clivé (a divided habitus) (Bennett, 2007, p. 2); that is, my reflexive awareness was generated out of discrepancies from the field. These discrepancies occurred when social action by agents within the field disagreed to a significant extent. In doing so, they highlighted the importance of a particular moment, or more specifically the response to this moment, which therefore provided a reflexive opportunity to focus on the "common sense" of that action. In a way, therefore, these (often intense) reflexive moments pinpointed the most automatic forms of action as significant in making sense of the masculine habitus operating within the logic of the physical/social field of BURC.

My access to BURC was made possible because I possessed the relevant physical and symbolic capital to "make sense" in that space. I am referring to my being both male and a rower. At the time of the research I was a professional rowing coach and had been a competitive rower for almost fifteen years. Being able to occupy the same physical space and experience as well as the same physical pain and discomfort as the other members of the rowing fraternity was vital in establishing my "credentials" and gaining access. The discipline required to push through the pain barrier or to do the extra work is perceived as a major characteristic of those who succeed in sport, and Japanese rowing is no different. There is a certain solidarity that forms from the collective experience of suffering. The following is a field note that highlights both the logic of masculine performance demanded by the field and also my reflexive responses to this logic. Leading into a major regatta I found myself rowing in the boat due to the serious illness (food poisoning) of another member. Although only a few days away from competing, and against what might be considered fairly universal periodization,[2] we completed what can best be described as the "session from hell."

> It's about 6.15am when we push off the landing and head out for our session. It's going to be a fairly hard session though the workload was a

## CHAPTER 11

bit ambiguous so I'll just have to wait and see. We warm up for about 20 minutes and then do a couple of steady state pieces (heart rate about 160) for around 7 minutes each. The boat feels fresh, there's a fair bit of life in the movement, and the boat speed feels good. Taka turns around to me at the end of the second steady state and lets me know that we are about to begin sprint training; one minute of over-speed (maximum number of strokes per minute, maximum effort, heart rate at 200 plus) with thirty seconds' rest repeated 6 times. Yoshii, the coxswain, yells "*saiko*" and we begin the work.

The first minute is over before we know it but we hit about 46 strokes per minute and the lactic acid in my legs already tells me we are going to really hurt. "*Saiko*" and again we are into it. At some stage Hiro yells "faster legs" and is met with a raucous "*hai*" affirmation from one or two members in the boat. The rating goes higher and I can feel a burning sensation in my forearms as I start to lose my sense of grip on the handle. "*Lasuto*," (last stroke) yells Yoshii and we rest again; this time there are a couple of exasperated yells from other rowers that mean "my legs are on fire, my lungs are burning." "*Gambatte, fai-to*," (do your best, fight) yells Yoshii as we begin number three. This time Kobe yells something met with the appropriate reply. I can't make it out though. I can taste blood in my mouth and my hamstrings are burning from trying to pull myself up the slide to stay in time with the rest of the crew. The final ten seconds feel like an eternity and finally we make it and rest. The number of screams has increased from the last minute.

The coach in me thinks "we need more recovery time" but before I can engage the internal dialogue we are off again. Fatigue is starting to take its toll and the precision of the movement and power is starting to fall away. After about thirty seconds it becomes more noticeable and Hiro goes into another motivational rant "*fai-to*!!!!" "How the hell can he speak? I feel like I'm breathing through my ears." "*Lasuto*" and Taka slumps over his oar in obvious distress. I'm absolutely hurting but try not to allow it to show. We're on again and after about 30 seconds I go into survival mode, just hang on and get through. Kobe slumps instantly when the last stroke is completed as do a couple of other members. "Ok, this is it, one last minute." We're away and the intensity and precision has returned somewhat compared to the previous two. Everyone lifts for the final effort and

## "Manner(s) Maketh the Man": Embodied Masculinities in a Japanese University Rowing Club

in unison they respond to Hiro's urgings. "*Lasuto*" and it's over. I'm sitting in the bow so I can see all the crew. Instantaneously each member collapses either over his oar or lying backward. There are screams coming from almost everyone. I'm suffering too but can't scream or lie down. "My God that was hard!"

Done very publicly and just before the big regatta, the session described above achieves several goals and points to several key habitus of the BURC man. First, it is demonstrating in front of potential opposition that BURC has the right spirit and toughness. Rather than being seen as a weakness (as indeed it might in a different field) screaming out or collapsing at the end of each minute demonstrates the level of commitment and intensity the BURC members put toward their training. This very open display of pain reinforces how tough they are. Of course, I am unable to follow this lead because the habitus inscribed in me doesn't see this as a viable action; it is ironic that what would lose me capital in the Australian rowing field can actually gain capital in the Japanese rowing field. An action that would be construed as "soft" and place the exponent's masculine identity under suspicion in Australia can have the opposite effect in Japan, as it reaffirms the individual's willingness to suffer for the group and suggests that his spirit is strong as he is able to endure the pain and finish the job despite his suffering. The fact that the intensity and precision lifted for the last minute is an indication, however, that many rowers in the crew, myself included, opted to play it safe (while the rhetoric is to push through the pain barrier and give everything, the risk of giving everything is that one may not make the end, so it's about giving close to, but not, everything) as to guarantee that the session could be completed. This ability to read the "rules of the game," which is to ensure you can complete the session neither appearing to weaken nor failing to go on, is a delicate balance of self-management.

## PERFORMING MANNERS

Masculinity is negotiated through performativity and the successful linking of such performances to broader notions of cultural and symbolic capital. Being good or talented at rowing and the training that it entails at BURC is undoubtedly recognized as a form of masculine capital. If one is the strongest in the gym or fastest on the water, one is afforded greater power within the club; however, the value in performance is not so much how *well* one does it, but *how* one does it. Correct performance is displayed not in the results (victories, being the best, etc.) but in the process of performing. As with the responses of members to pain mentioned in the section above, the correct performance of suffering is more important than performance with the oar. Similarly, during the seasonal drinking parties that punctuate the year, those rowers who don't enjoy drinking manage their performance by appearing drunk. Such a response to the logic of the field is necessary in order to remain part of it. It also will become a useful strategy in the future, especially considering the role that drinking parties play within social and employment contexts (Ben Ari, 2002; Hendry, 1994). Another example of the performance of masculinity is the outpouring of tears that follows racing (both winning and losing) at a major regatta (see Light, 2001; McDonald, 2009). Within a cultural context where the display of emotion is not usually considered appropriate, crying post-race actually serves to enhance one's capital, as such a performance demonstrates that this was a particularly meaningful event to which one had committed much time and effort. Whether you had raced well or not is secondary to demonstrating how much the race had meant to you.

The importance of the process of performing is reinforced via the enormous commitment of time to training and the relatively few opportunities to actually race (most members will compete in only five or six regattas over the space of a year). As such, the performance is a demonstration of the habitus embodied by rowers, which is deployed consciously and subconsciously in a range of contexts, not the least of which is the mundane, day-to-day interactions within the club (in the context of repetitious and intense training, even pain becomes mundane). Further, this subjectification of masculine gender expresses itself most clearly during a sequence of significant events in the course of the season.

Perhaps the most significant learning at BURC is not how to row, but rather the development of the appropriate and necessary *reigi* (manners) required of men within the strictures of masculine relationships. The nuanced social skills to effectively maintain oneself within masculine social space are found by executing the correct etiquette in relation to one's hierarchical position in that space. This is demonstrated through the correct use of language (polite form when *kohai*, casual form when *sempai*), positioning in space (where to sit or stand, front/back space), and in the ancillary functions of membership (cleaning and washing equipment, preparing the boat). The symbolic capital afforded to manners cannot be underestimated, and its value is found not only in the execution of such politeness but also in receiving. Being able to give (manners) is only valued if they are received. As such, this interaction is grounded in the successful demonstration of a masculine habitus from all social players.

Correct *reigi* should not be limited to physical and verbal interaction; in fact manners are on display in the negotiation of time and space. The formulaic breakdown of time and space in any given training session is an example of the manners embedded in practice. The modulation (*merihari*) or use of time needs to fit within a framework determined from the field and enacted by its members. In breaking down any training session into the components of warm up on land, rowing time, discussion time in the boat, and warm down on land, it becomes clear that, regardless of the duration of the training session, the actual ratio of each component relative to the others remains constant. Whether training is scheduled for two hours or four hours, land-based warm up, warm down and debriefing takes up 55–60% of the total session time, with actual rowing time contributing to only 35% of any given practice. What this points to is the meaningful and somewhat ritualistic use of time which, rather than being regulated by a clock, is a member's internalized response to the field. For rowing to have meaning in a cultural sense, it needs to operate to a format or shape that represents two notions.

The first of these notions is that of self-cultivation, in which bodily practice seeks as its end "not power, but the recognition of mind-body integration" (Ozawa-De Silva, 2002, p. 36). Eschewing in this way the Western mind/body dichotomy, self-cultivation relies on *karada de oboeru,* which is learning through the body. One learns by dedicating oneself to a singular pursuit; self-cultivation is not found in being an "all rounder." Commitment of time validates that one is engaged in this process. Such "cultivation" extends not only to the boat but also to the social learning that is especially important in moments such as the warm up and warm down. These periods coincide with discussions about what is about to be or what has been done. The most important aspect of these periods is the consensus-based nature of decision making, which ties into the broader cultural sensitivity of harmony. The successful self-cultivation project tends to reiterate the largely unconscious nature of Bourdieu's habitus, the extension of which is its durability that "reinforces social order" and becomes the "ultimate source of social stability" (Brownell, 1995, pp. 12–13). Thus, self-cultivation in this way is indeed social cultivation as the body provides habituation of the permanency of social relations.

The second notion is the perception of difference, which is a type of moral and social superiority or distinction over other, nonrowing students. The recurring theme for BURC members was the notion of *merihari,* or proper use of time, and subsequent comparison with other students who are seen as idle and lazy. In some respects having idle time is perceived as a form of immorality. That is, an "empty space of time that is not spent in activity is not supposed to be" (Kato, 1984, cited in Manzenreiter, 1998, p. 366). Hence, organizing one's time and having discipline is a blueprint toward a moral life. Tana, who initially found the expectations of rowing life to be much more difficult than expected, expresses his appreciation for the value of being a member:

> The experience will be helpful to get a job. Not that I have graduated (from University), but that I have been a member of the rowing club. The experience of being a member of the rowing team. I learn about *merihari*, an everyday routine, I mean every day I get up and train and then go to class and then more training or work. A lot of university students don't know what to do every day. They sleep in, muck around, they don't have any daily routine, but at BURC we have a strong routine and schedule so we have a better lifestyle then other students. We learn these things from the many great *sempai* at BURC; students that don't belong to clubs don't have any of these things. I'm very proud of my time at BURC.

Tana indicates an experience that he perceives as more worthwhile than the choices of other students, not only in his belief that this experience will assist in gaining employment, but that his routine and schedule are important components of a moral lifestyle. Such adherence to routine is also in keeping with the expectations of future employment in company work (Dasgupta, 2003). As Brownell (1995, p. 12) has stressed, "practice makes permanent," and the embodied responses to probabilities in the game that were learned so effectively during membership at the rowing club are reflected in each graduate's habitus, the expression of which endures because it continues to develop capital in future fields of practice. The homogenization of bodies through and by training results in the development of a visible masculinity derived from a specific cultural language. It is therefore tied to other human attributes such as morality, character, and indeed spirit (McDonald & Hallinan, 2005).

## TOUGHNESS AND SOFTNESS

Ordinarily, due to the constant contact of hands on an oar, rowers will have either blistered or heavily calloused hands. This was the case for members of BURC; however, what was interesting was that many also had very well-manicured fingernails. Whilst this no doubt reflects the rowers' subtle negotiation of changes in male aesthetics, especially in the apparent revulsion of some aspects of the sporting body (e.g., roughness, hair, and sweat; see Miller, 2006), it also acts as a useful metaphor for the way that the dominant forms of masculinity are enacted within the club. The hand, being simultaneously soft and tough, reflects members' responses about being a man. For example, Musashi reminisces about his *sempai* when he was a freshman:

I had a *sempai*, Matsuda, who, when I was a freshman was very good to me. In the boat he trained so hard it was amazing and during parties and things like that Matsuda was a crazy man, you know, he would get very drunk and he was a lot of fun, but during private time he was very different. He was considerate and caring (*ki ga kiku*) to all *kōhai* (juniors). He made me feel very comfortable around him. He encouraged me to speak and express my opinion. His idea of *jōge kankei* (expectation of modesty by subordinates towards superiors) was very relaxed and he treated me like we were *dōkyōsei*. (classmates)

Being tough and soft, gentle and hard, points to an appreciation of masculinity that needs to be able to respond appropriately based on a variety of situational conditions. Similar to Champan's (2010) *judoka*, many members at BURC appreciated the lessons learned from being treated harshly and forced to endure. For example, after making a steering error that damaged one of the boats, the coxswain was held down and had his head shaved as punishment. On the other hand, they valued the relaxed *jōge kankei* that operated at the club. The Captain explains his approach, not only to leadership, but also to how to treat others (*ningen kankei*):

I have the final decision; it depends on the situation. I will ask for the others' opinion and if I am happy with that then that is the way we will go. However, if I disagree, I have the final decision so I will override the decision if I think it is necessary. Tonight in the boat I yelled at the crew. I was trying to re-invigorate them. The other members were not concentrating so I encouraged them to try hard and concentrate harder. Sometimes I have to get into the other members, other times I want them to feel comfortable and I stay quiet. How I act depends on what we need on the day.

This year is my final year at university; it's my last chance to win. But the other members, some of them are freshmen, second year [etc.] so they have the chance to win next year or in two years. But I want them to work harder to help achieve my goal. I don't want the other people to think that they have other years ahead to achieve these goals. However I don't want them to set the same goal as me. I hope that they will choose the same goal as me but if they don't there isn't much I can do about it and I must respect their choice.

CHAPTER 11

The Captain acknowledges the potential range of agency that members might have and respects this; at the same time, he is determined that things be done in agreement with his desires. The expression of masculinity is situational and also reciprocal. Similar to the giving and accepting central to the effective use of manners discussed earlier, the flowing field notes about freshman Taka and senior Hiro highlight the forms of reciprocal softness/toughness:

> At dinner Hiro grunts and pushes his cup forward for milk. Taka jumps into action, only the carton he goes for is empty. I have a carton near me and, [mistakenly] trying to help, fill Hiro's cup. Taka apologizes, first to Hiro and then to me, for not being prompter. He promises to be more attentive next time.
>
> At the back of the boathouse Hiro is again taking special interest in Taka and has rigged up an oar next to the ergo (rowing machine) to make it more realistic. As Taka is first year he is new to sweep[3] rowing and is having some trouble with the concepts. Hiro barely says a word to any of the other first years, but to Taka he is almost like a big brother or father figure. He stands next to Taka, physically modeling his movement, demonstrating and explaining in detail. Hiro is very positive and encouraging as Taka starts to make progress. Taka is at total attention and mimics the movements long after Hiro has gone.
>
> During meals, Taka organizes the food for Hiro even to the point at one stage of actually feeding Hiro with his own chopsticks.

The largely nonverbal interaction between these two men is demonstrative of the reciprocal masculine relationships at play within the boathouse. Similar to other giving and receiving of manners discussed previously, the relationship between Hiro and Taka relies on both to "play the game." The act of caring for the other, as Taka looks after Hiro's food and drink, is reciprocated by Hiro's attention to Taka's skill development. It is a relationship that is both public and intimate, and is demonstrated in differing degrees between other *kohai/sempai* relationships at the club.

## CONCLUSION

The university rowing club produces the structuring logic of gender in which masculinities are negotiated by the individual members. The near total experience of being a member and the supporting structural apparatus of the club, the boat, the river, the other clubs, the dorms, the kitchen, etc., produces the most meaningful experiences on bodies in this space. The centrality of the body in the individual's journey into and through university cannot be overestimated. Bodies have been invested in well before their arrival at BURC, and as such are a project of self-cultivation on a social trajectory to becoming a man in society. Hence the body expresses forms of masculinity through a range of performances that resonate within a specific cultural context and accrue their own currency in cultural and symbolic capital. This performance is not only in the boat but within the minutiae of detail in relationships between the men of the club. The homosocial nature of *jōge kankei* calls upon the development of a masculine sensibility in a variety of situational and reciprocal contexts. The strongest of these are in the performance of giving and receiving manners (or indeed, manner) that are embodied responses to the logic of the field occurring mostly at a subconscious level.

In other words, displays of appropriate behavior based on the particular situation (crying, suffering, caring, teaching, disciplining, feeding, drinking, etc.) are far more important and valued than performance with the oar. Of course, members express a desire to win (which is default rhetoric for many sports-people); however, the deeper meaning to membership is found in the actions whose cultural and symbolic capital is convertible in other social fields. After four years, few if any of the BURC members will ever hold an oar again. While this may also be true of women's sport, these are gendered performances as they only have relational meaning between men. The enduring nature of these practices is found in the usually singular nature of membership—that is, that members will often belong to very few alternative social fields. In this environment one is home, one belongs, and one doesn't need to worry about how to act or what to do.

It is clear that the idea of "being a man" is not a fixed, rigid form of identity but one rather of fluidity and multiplicity. If the valued forms of masculinity are currently still the domain of the university sports clubs in Japan, then the masculinities that are negotiated at BURC point to challenges, tensions, and perhaps shifts in what would be considered its hegemonic form. The BURC club members possessed a habitus that expressed the correct use of manners, time, and body, which may be derived from conservative forms of masculine capital. However, the elements of kindness and softness that seem to be equally valued by these young men suggest a negotiation of masculinity that requires more complex and deeply embodied responses to the social field of other men. In essence, the rowing club experience serves to inculcate and embody a range of masculine manner(s) that are employed or deployed in a variety of situational and relational contexts. In learning manner(s) the member transforms himself from a boy into a man. The bodily project of being a rower has at its end the creation of a man ready to be a productive member of society. In this case, manner truly does maketh the man.

## REFERENCES

Ben-Ari, E. (2002). At the interstices: Drinking, management, and temporary groups in a local Japanese organisation. In J. Hendry & M. Raveri (Eds.), *Japan at play: The ludic and logic of power* (pp. 129–151). London, England: Routledge.

Bennett, T. (2007). Habitus clivé: Aesthetics and politics in the work of Pierre Bourdieu. *New Literary History, 38*, 201–228. Project MUSE. Retrieved 5 Jul. 2014 from http://muse.jhu.edu/.

Blackwood, T. (2010). Playing baseball/playing 'house': The reproduction and naturalization of 'separate spheres' in Japanese high school baseball. *Sport, Education and Society, 15*, 83–101.

Bourdieu, P. (1977). *Outline of a theory of practice*. London, England: Cambridge.

Bourdieu, P. (1984). *Distinction: A social critique of the judgement of taste*. Cambridge, MA: Harvard University Press.

Bourdieu, P. (2001). *Masculine domination*. Cambridge, England: Polity Press.

Brown, D. (2006). Pierre Bourdieu's "Masculine Domination" thesis and the gendered body in sport and physical culture. *Sociology of Sport Journal, 23*, 162–188.

Brownell, S. (1995). *Training the body for China: Sports in the moral order of the People's Republic*. Chicago, IL: The University of Chicago Press.

Cave, P. (2004). Bukatsudo: The educational role of Japanese school sports clubs. *Journal of Japanese Studies, 30*, 383–415.

Chapman, K. (2010). Ossu! Sporting masculinities in a Japanese karate dojo. *Japan Forum, 16*, 315–335.

Coles, T. (2009). Negotiating the field of masculinity: The production and reproduction of multiple dominant masculinities. *Men and Masculinities, 12*, 30–44.

Connell, R. W. (1987). *Gender and power*. Sydney, AU: Allen and Unwin.

Connell, R. W. (2000). *The men and the boys*. Sydney, AU: Allen and Unwin.

Connell, R. W. (2005). *Masculinities*. (2nd ed.). Sydney, AU: Allen and Unwin.

Connell, R. W., & Messerschmidt, J. W. (2005). Hegemonic masculinity: Rethinking the concept. *Gender and Society, 19*, 829–859.

Dalla-Chiesa, S. (2002). When the goal is not a goal: Japanese school football players working hard at their game. In J. Hendry & M. Raveri (Eds.), *Japan at play: The ludic and logic of power* (pp. 186–198). London, England: Routledge.

Dasgupta, R. (2003). Creating corporate warriors: The 'salaryman' and masculinity in Japan. In K. Louie & M. Low (Eds.), *Asian masculinities: The meaning and practice of manhood in China and Japan* (pp. 118–135). London, England: Routledge Curzon.

Gill, T. (2003). When pillars evaporate: Structuring masculinity on the Japanese margins. In J. Roberson & N. Suzuki (Eds.), *Men and masculinities in contemporary Japan: Dislocating the salaryman doxa* (pp. 144–161). London, England: Routledge.

Grenfell, C., & Rinehart, R. (2003). Skating on thin ice: Human rights in youth figure skating. *International Review for the Sociology of Sport, 38*, 79–97.

Guttmann, A., & Thompson, L. (2001) *Japanese sport: A history.* Honolulu, HI: University of Hawaii Press.

Hendry, J. (1994). Drinking and gender in Japan. In M. McDonald (Ed.), *Gender, drinking and drugs* (pp. 175–190). Oxford, England: Berg.

Inoue, S. (1998). Budo: Invented tradition in the martial arts. In S. Linhart & S. Fruhstuck (Eds.), *The culture of Japan as seen through its leisure* (pp. 83–94). Albany, NY: State University of New York Press.

Kimmel, M., Hearn, J., & Connell, R. W. (2005). *Handbook of studies on men and masculinities.* London, England: Sage Publications.

Kusaka, Y. (2006). The emergence and development of Japanese school sport. In J. Maguire & M. Nakayama (Eds.), *Japan, sport and society: Tradition and change in a globalizing world* (pp. 19–34). London, England: Routledge.

Light, R. (2000). A centenary of rugby and masculinity in Japanese schools and universities: Continuity and change. *Sporting Traditions, 16*, 87–104.

Light, R. (2003). Sport and the construction of masculinity in the Japanese education system. In K. Louie & M. Low (Eds.), *Asian masculinities: The meaning and practice of manhood in China and Japan* (pp. 100–117). London, England: RoutledgeCurzon.

Light, R. (2008). Learning masculinities in a Japanese high school rugby club. Sport, *Education and Society, 13*, 163–179.

Manzenreiter, W. (1998). Time, space and money: Cultural dimensions of the 'Pachniko' game. In S. Linhart & S. Fruhstuck (Eds.), *The culture of Japan as seen through its leisure* (pp. 359–382). Albany, NY: SUNY Press.

Manzenreiter, W. (2001). Early sportscapes in late nation states: Modern bodies in the capital territory of Vienna and Tokyo. In E. Koh (Ed.), *Sociology of sport and the new global order: Bridging perspectives and crossing boundaries* (pp. 491–506). Proceedings from the 1st World Congress of Sociology of Sport.

Matsuda, K. (2006). Playfulness and gender in modern Japanese society. In J. Maguire & M. Nakayama (Eds.), *Japan, sport and society: Tradition and change in a globalizing world* (pp. 113–122). London, England: Routledge.

McDonald, B. (2004). The university rowing club as a site of moral and social education in Japan. *International Sports Studies, 26*, 15–28.

McDonald, B. (2009). Learning masculinity through Japanese university rowing: Joge kankei—hierarchical relationships. *Sociology of Sport Journal, 26*, 425–442.

McDonald, B., & Hallinan, C. (2005). Seishin habitus: Spiritual capital and Japanese rowing. *International Review for the Sociology of Sport, 40*, 187–200.

McDonald, B., & Komuku, H. (2008). Japanese educational sport and the reproduction of identity. In C. Hallinan & S. Jackson (Eds.), *Sport and cultural diversity in a globalized world* (pp. 97–110). Oxford, England: Emerald.

Mennesson, C. (2012). Gender regimes and habitus: An avenue for analyzing gender building in sports contexts. *Sociology of Sport Journal, 29*, 4–21.

Messner, M. (1990). Masculinities and the athletic careers: Bonding and the status of difference. In M. Messner & D. Sabo (Eds.), *Sport, men and the gender order: Critical feminist perspectives* (pp. 83–97). Champaign, IL: Human Kinetics Books.

Miller, L. (2006). *Beauty up: Exploring contemporary Japanese body aesthetics.* Berkeley, CA: University of California Press.

Ogasawara, Y. (1998). *Office ladies and salaried men: Power, gender, and work in Japanese companies.* Berkeley, CA: University of California Press.

Ozawa-de Silva, C. (2002). Beyond the body/mind? Japanese contemporary thinkers on alternative sociologies of the body. *Body and Society, 8,* 21–38.

Roberson, J. (2005). Fight!! Ippatsu!! "Genki" energy drinks and the marketing of masculine ideology in Japan. *Men and Masculinities, 7,* 365–384.

Roberson, J., & Suzuki, N. (2003). *Men and masculinities in contemporary Japan: Dislocating the salaryman doxa.* London, England: Routledge.

Sugimoto, Y. (1997). *An introduction to Japanese society.* Hong Kong, China: Cambridge University Press.

Taga. F. (2003). Rethinking male socialisation: Life histories of Japanese male youth. In K. Louie & M. Low (Eds.), *Asian masculinities: The meaning and practice of manhood in China and Japan* (pp. 137–154). London, England: Routledge.

Taga, F. (2005). East Asian masculinities. In M. Kimmel, J. Hearn, & R. W. Connell (Eds.), *Handbook of studies on men and masculinities* (pp.129–140). London, England: Sage Publications.

Van Wolferen, K. (1989). *The enigma of Japanese power: People and politics in a stateless nation.* London, England: MacMillan.

## ENDNOTES

[1] Whilst Confucian thought originally arrived from the Chinese mainland around 500 AD and was adapted to the indigenous Shinto philosophy, it was the Tokugawa Shogunate, who ruled Japan in isolation from 1600-1868, that pushed Confucianism in line with governance (see Van Wolferen, 1989, p. 203).

[2] Periodization refers to the planning-out of training over a prolonged period so as to achieve maximum performance on the day of the event. This session occurred inside the time frame of what would usually be considered a taper or lightening of intensity and workload, the intention being to freshen up for the event.

[3] There are two types of rowing: *sculling,* which involves the rower having two oars, one either side of the boat moving in symmetry; and *sweep rowing,* which involves each member having one oar and moving in an asymmetrical movement. The difference between the two is not necessarily great; however, the initial change from one to the other can be quite difficult.

# Index

## A

AAS . . . . . . . . . . 10, 11, 151-164, 169
acne . . . . . . . . . 10, 11, 153, 161-164
conglobata . . . . . . . . . . . . . . 161
fulminans . . . . . . . . . . . . . . 161
medicamentosa . . . . . . . . . . . . 161
American West . . . . . . . . . . . . . . 38
amplitude . . . . . . . . . . . . . . . . 17
anabolic androgenic
steroids (AASs) . . . . 10, 11, 151-164, 169
androcentric vision . . . . . . . . . . . 16
appearance and performance
enhancing drugs (APEDs) . . 152, 154, 162
Asa Branca . . . 9, 71, 73, 76-77, 81, 85, 86
Australian Rules football . . . . 10, 129-148
azoospermia . . . . . . . . . 153, 156, 158

## B

ballet . . 10, 84, 93, 102-103, 112, 116-122
belonging . . . . . . . 72, 112-116, 198, 202
bitch tits . . . . . . . . . . . . . . 158-164
body rhythm . . . . . . . . . . . . . 105-106
Brazilian cinema . . . . . . . . . . 9, 71-89
button soccer . . . . . . . . . . 95-96, 109

## C

capital, . . . . . . . . . . 2, 5, 11, 20, 101,
. . . . . . . . 162, 198,199, 200, 203-205,
. . . . . . . . . . . . . .207-208, 210, 213
symbolic . . . . . . . 101, 198, 205, 213
dance . . . 10, 91-93,-94, 102, 105, 111-126
education . . . . . . . . . . . . . 123, 125
in Cyprus . . . . . . . . . . . . . 114-115
in Greece . . . . . . . . . . . . . . . 116
in South Africa . . . . . . . . . . . . 113
in South Korea . . . . . . . . . . . . 114
in Turkey . . . . . . . . . . . . . 114-115
deactivation of thought . . . . . . . . . 105
discourse(s), . . 3, 16, 36, 41, 42, 44, 48, 73,
. . . . . . 98, 115, 176, 177, 180, 186, 190
class . . . . . . . . . . . . . . . . . . 41
colonial . . . . . . . . . . . . . . . . 115
comic . . . . . . . . . . . . . . . . . . 16
emotion(al) . . . . . . . . . . . 54, 57-68
feminine/masculine . . . . . . . . . . . 11
gender(ed) . . . . . . . . 41, 132, 177, 201
hegemonic . . . . . . . . . . . . . . 3, 73
heterodox . . . . . . . . . . . . . . . . 3
left-wing . . . . . . . . . . . . . . . . 73
masculinity . . . . . . . . . 91, 172, 176
media . . . . . . . . . . . . . 174-175, 181
of Empire . . . . . . . . . . . . . . . 181
orthodox . . . . . . . . . . . . . . . 3, 7
public . . . . . . . . . . . . . . . . . 171
sexist . . . . . . . . . . . . . . . . . 73
sexuality . . . . . . . . . . . . . . . . 41
subordinate . . . . . . . . . . . . . . . 3
television . . . . . . . . . . . . . . . 23

## D

dressage . . . . . . . . . . 9, 54-57, 60-64

# INDEX

**E**

emasculation . . . . . . . . . . . . . . . . .25
embodiment . . . . . . .3, 93, 104, 107, 151
equestrianism . . . . . . . . . .9, 53-67, 69
equestrianism, Uruguayan . . . . .9, 53-69

**F**

feminine . . . 20-21, 25, 29, 39, 47, 57, 82,
. . . . . 84, 93, 98, 118, 136, 145, 177, 179
femininity . . . 3, 5, 6, 18, 34, 36, 39, 40,
. . . 54, 57, 65, 73, 117, 120, 131, 202, 203
feminize . . . . . . . . . .16, 27, 42, 43, 45,
. . . . . . . . . . . . . . . 48, 57, 58, 97, 114
football, Australian Rules. . . . 10, 129-148

**G**

gay . . . . . . . . . . 6, 7, 34, 77, 81, 84, 93,
. . . . . . . . . . . . . . . .102, 117, 178, 191
gender
  ambiguity. . . . . . . . . . . . . . . 117
  heterodoxy . . . . . . . . . . . . . . . 7
  identity . . . . . . . . . . . . 1, 3, 57, 78
  politics . . . . . . . . . . . . . . .112, 114
  theorists. . . . . . . . . . . . . . . . . 117
gynecomastia. . . . . 10, 11, 152, 158-164

**H**

habitus . . . . . . . . . 6, 11, 94, 198-199,
. . . . . . . . . . . . 203-205, 207-210, 213
Harding, Tonya. . . . . . 16, 18-21, 24, 29,
. . . . . . . . . . . . . . . . . . . . . . 31, 33-34
hegemonic masculinity. . . 3, 5, 6, 38, 39,
. . . . . . . . . . . 47, 48, 60, 67, 73, 74, 75,
. . . . . .76, 80, 81, 84, 85, 86, 88, 93, 97,
. . . . . . 98, 102, 106, 107, 131-132, 145,
. . . . . . . . . . . . . .177, 186, 187, 190, 198
heterosexuality. . . . . . . .6, 74, 80, 106
Hillary, Sir Edmund . 11, 171-191, 195-196
homophobia . . . . . . . .6, 103, 116, 117

homosexual . . . . . . .72, 77, 79, 80-86,
. . . . . . . . . 99, 114-118, 121, 122, 131
human chorionic
gonadotropin (hCG) . . . . . . . 155, 157
hypermasculine . . . . . . . . . . . .2, 120
hypogonadism . . . . . . . . 152, 156-158

**I**

identity,. . . 6, 11, 40, 57, 93, 94, 124, 132,
. . . . . .146, 151, 177, 181, 201, 203, 213
  American . . . . . . . . . . . . . . . . .41
  collective (group) . . . . . . 38, 118, 125
  conflicts over . . . . . . . . . . . . . . .35
  construction of . . . . . . . . . . . . .82
  cultural . . . . . . . . . . . . . . . . . 182
  deep crisis of . . . . . . . . . . . . . 102
  formulation of. . . . . . . . . . . . . .36
  gender. . . . . . . . 1, 3, 57, 78, 197, 202
  group (collective) . . . . . 38, 118, 125
  hypermasculine. . . . . . . . . . . .2, 120
  male. . . . . . . . . . . . . . . . . . . . . 2
  masculine . . . 96-98, 134, 137-138, 145,
  . . . . . . . . 180, 187, 198, 202, 205, 207
  national . . . . . . . . 118, 119, 120, 172,
  . . . . . . . . . . . . 174, 179-180, 184, 195
  politics of . . . . . . . . . . . . . . . .31
  public. . . . . . . . . . . . . . . . . . .21
  sexual . . . . . . . . . . . . . . . . . . 117
  traditional. . . . . . . . . . . . . . . . .41
injury. . . . . . . . . 7, 10, 21, 130-133,
. . . . . . . . . . . . . . .138-144, 146-148
intimate self . . . . . . . . . . 10, 151-164

**K**

Kerrigan, Nancy . 16-21, 24, 28, 31, 33-34
kiwi. . . . . .11, 172, 175, 178-182, 184-186

**L**

lesbian . . . . . . . . . . . . . .20, 23, 34, 84
long-term health . . . . . 10, 130, 143-144,
. . . . . . . . . . . . . . . . . . . . . . 146, 169

## M

male body image . . . . . . . . 10, 151-164
male trait . . . . . . . . . . . . . . . 2, 60
man boobs . . . . . . . . . . . . . .158-164
masculine nationalism . . . . . . .119, 185
masculine territory . . . . . . . . 9, 71-86,
masculinity
(masculinities) . . . . . 2, 3, 60, 66, 83, 91,
. . . . . . . . . 94, 102, 103, 134-135, 177
  affirmation of . . . . . . . . . . . 57, 201
  aggressive . . . . . . . . . . . . . . . . . 8
  articulation . . . . . . . . . . . . . . . .73
  bisexual . . . . . . . . . . . . . . . . . . 9
  code of . . . . . . . . . . . . . . 10, 117
  concepts (definitions/notions
    /visions) of . . . . . . . . . 1, 36, 60, 103,
. . . . . . . . . . . . . . 144, 174, 176, 203
  construction of . . . 4, 112, 113, 131, 133
  dance and . . . . . . . . . . . . . 111-126
  discourse(s) . . . . . . . . . . . 91, 172, 176
  discussion of (discourse) . . . . . . 3, 72
  embodiment (expression/
    performance) of . . . . 74, 62, 104, 106,
. . . . . . . . . . . . . . . 107, 199, 208, 212
  forms of . . . . 4, 5, 73, 94, 102, 104, 123,
. . . . . . . . 131, 172, 177, 178, 179, 191,
. . . . . . . . . . . . . 197, 198, 210, 213
  gender and . . . . . . . . . . . . . . . 17
  hegemonic . . . .3, 5, 6, 36, 38, 39, 40, 47,
. . . . . . . . 48, 60, 67, 73, 74, 75, 76, 80,
. . . . . . . .81, 84, 85, 86, 88, 93, 97,
. . . . . . . . . 98, 102, 106, 107, 131-132,
. . . . . . . . 145, 177, 186, 187, 190, 198
  heteronormative . . . . . . . . . . . . . .83
  in Brazilian sport . . . . . . . . . . 92, 94
  inclusive . . . . . . . . . . . . . . . . . .74
  indigenous . . . . . . . . . . . . . . . .42
  logic of . . . . . . . . . . . . . . . . . 198
  marginalized . . . . . . . . . . . . . . 131
  media and . . . . . . . . . . . . . .136-137
  motor vehicles and . . . . . . . . . . .30
  new forms (models) of . . . . . . 3, 84, 86
  norms (practices) of . . . . . . . 4, 62, 74
  race and . . . . . . . . . . . . . . . . . .43
  reconfiguration of . . . . . . . . . . . . .76
  salary man . . . . . . . . . . . . . . . 198
  sport and . . . . . . . . . 4, 5, 6, 91, 136
  subversion of . . . . . . . . . . . . . . 3
  Uruguayan . . . . . . . . . . . . . .53, 67
  White . . . . . . . . . . . . 24, 36, 38, 41
myth of the Frontier . . . . . . . . . . .38

## N

neoconservative . . . . . . . . . . . 41, 43
New Wave . . . . . . . . . . . . . .9, 71-86

## P

pain . . . . . . . . . . . . 7, 10, 101, 103-104,
. . . . . . 106, 129-148, 191, 205, 207, 208
painkillers . . . . . . . . . . . . . .140-141
patriarchy/patriarchal society . . . .24, 97,
. . . . . . . . . . . . . . . . . 106, 191, 200
performed architecture . . . . . . . . . . 16
physical education . . . . . . . 10, 111-126
Pistorius, Oscar . . . . . . . . . . . 27-28
Poe, Richard . . . . . . . . . . . . . 42-43
polypharmacy . . . . . . . . . . . . . . 158
power . . . . . 2, 3, 6, 18, 24, 29, 31, 35, 39,
. . . . . . . . .40, 42, 44, 45, 54, 63, 67, 77,
. . . . . . . . 84, 85, 99, 101, 106, 115, 145,
. . . . . . . . . 146, 174, 176, 177, 178, 179,
. . . . . . . . . . . . .181, 200, 203, 207, 209
pseudogynecomastia . . . . . . . . .158-159

## Q

quality of life . . . . . . . . . . . . . . 144
queer studies . . . . . . . . . . . . . 17, 75

## S

scophilia . . . . . . . . . . . . . . . . .23
seagull . . . . . . . . . . . . . . . . .81, 84
selective estrogen receptor
  modulator (SERM) . . . . . . . . 155, 157
sensitivity . . . . . . . . . . 60, 106, 209

# INDEX

Shiflett, Dave . . . . . . . 36, 41, 42, 44, 48
show jumping . . . . . . . . . . 55-63, 69
sick humor/jokes . . . . . . . . 8, 15-31, 33
Simpson, Orenthal James (OJ) . . 16, 21-25,
. . . . . . . . . . . . . . . . .27-29, 31, 33-34
social construction . . . . . . . .4, 131-133
social
  field . . . . . . 11, 86, 198, 199, 202-203,
. . . . . . . . . . . . . . . . . . . . 205, 213
  order . . . . . . . . . . . 3, 16, 45, 209
sport,
  American Indian imagery in . . .8, 35-48
  Brazil(ian) . . . . . . . . . . . . . .91-107
  feminine . . . . . . . . . . . . . 136, 145
  Japan(ese) . . . . . . . . . . 116, 197-214
  masculine . . . . . . . . . . . . . . . 136
  New Zealand . . . . . . . . . 11, 171-191
steroid community . . . . . . 157, 158, 163
steroids . . . . . . . . . 10-11, 151-164, 169
support (while injured) . . . . . . . 141-142
surrogate mothers . . . . . . . . . . . 202

T
testicular atrophy . . . 10, 11, 152-155, 158
testosterone replacement
therapy (TRT) . . . . . . . . . . . . . 157

V
violence . . . . . . . . . . . 19, 22, 25, 27, 29,
. . . . . . . . 57, 74, 95, 115-116, 131,198
virtual ethnopharmacology . . . . . . 158

W
warrior . . . . . . . . . . . . . 8, 35-48, 114
Woods, Tiger . . . . . . . . . . . . . 29-31

Y
Yeagley, David . . . . . . . . 36, 41, 44-48

# About the Editors

**Jorge Knijnik,** PhD, has been with the School of Education and the Institute for Culture and Society at University of Western Sydney, Australia, since 2009. He was a recipient of the Building the Gender Equality Prize (2009) awarded by the Brazilian Research Council and United Nations Development Fund for Women. His research interests range from sport in society, culture, and history to gender and human rights in education, physical education pedagogies, drama studies, and fandom culture. His current research examines the socialization process within football fans in Greater Western Sydney and how football fandom has the potential to make a significant contribution to community cohesion and regeneration in the area. He is also involved in a number of projects examining the political and cultural contradictory legacies of sports mega events in Brazil. He is the author of *A Mulher Brasileira e o Esporte: seu Corpo, sua Historia* [Brazilian Woman and Sport—Body and History] (Sao Paulo, Mackenzie, 2003), *Genero e Esporte: Masculinidades e Feminilidades* [Gender and Sport—Masculinities and Femininities] (Rio de Janeiro, Apicuri, 2010), *Meninas e Meninos na Educacao Fisica: Genero e Corporeidade no seculo 21.* [Girls and Boys in Physical Education—Gender and Embodiment in the 21st Century] (Jundiai, Fontoura, 2010), and *Gender and Equestrian Sport—Riding around the World* (Springer, 2013 with Miriam Adelman).

**Daryl Adair,** PhD, is an associate professor in sport management in the UTS Business School, University of Technology, Sydney, Australia. A key focus of his research is the ways in which sport and culture interweave with indigeneity, race, ethnicity, and gender. He also evaluates policies related to both performance-enhancing drugs and illicit drugs in sport and physical activity settings.

# About the Authors

**Deborah Agnew,** PhD, is a lecturer in the School of Education at Flinders University, Australia.

**Rob Baum,** PhD, is head of The Gordon Institute for Performing and Creative Arts (GIPCA), faculty of humanities, at the University of Cape Town, South Africa.

**Toni Bruce,** PhD, is a research associate and professor in the Primary Health Care Directorate of the Faculty of Health Sciences at the University of Cape Town, South Africa. She is a feminist playwright, poet, and movement specialist who has performed in dance, movement improvisation, theatre, and circus across the world

**Murray Drummond,** PhD, is a professor and director of the SHAPE Research Centre (Sport, Health and Physical Education) in the School of Education at Flinders University, Australia.

**Michael Gard,** PhD, holds an adjunct position at University of Queensland, Australia.

**C. Richard King,** PhD, is a professor in the College of Arts & Sciences at Washington State University, USA.

**Brent McDonald,** PhD, is a lecturer in the School of Sport and Exercise Science at Victoria University, Australia.

**Victor Andrade de Melo,** PhD, is an associate professor in the Department of History at Universidade Federal do Rio de Janeiro, Brazil.

**Richard Pringle,** PhD, is an associate professor in the faculty of education at University of Auckland, New Zealand.

**Luiz Rojo,** PhD, is a senior lecturer in the department of anthropology at Universidade Federal Fluminense, Rio de Janeiro, Brazil.